The Unknown Tutankhamun

522 952 71 8

The Unknown Tutankhamun

Marianne Eaton-Krauss

Bloomsbury Academic
An imprint of Bloomsbury Publishing Plc

B L O O M S B U R Y
LONDON • NEW DELHI • NEW YORK • SYDNEY

Bloomsbury Academic

An imprint of Bloomsbury Publishing Plc

50 Bedford Square	1385 Broadway
London	New York
WC1B 3DP	NY 10018
UK	USA

www.bloomsbury.com

BLOOMSBURY and the Diana logo are trademarks of Bloomsbury Publishing Plc

First published 2016

© Marianne Eaton-Krauss, 2016

Marianne Eaton-Krauss has asserted her right under the Copyright, Designs and Patents Act, 1988, to be identified as Author of this work.

All rights reserved. No part of this publication may be reproduced or transmitted in any form or by any means, electronic or mechanical, including photocopying, recording, or any information storage or retrieval system, without prior permission in writing from the publishers.

No responsibility for loss caused to any individual or organization acting on or refraining from action as a result of the material in this publication can be accepted by Bloomsbury or the author.

British Library Cataloguing-in-Publication Data
A catalogue record for this book is available from the British Library.

ISBN: PB: 978-1-47257-561-6
ePDF: 978-1-47257-563-0
ePub: 978-1-47257-562-3

Library of Congress Cataloging-in-Publication Data
Eaton-Krauss, Marianne.
The unknown Tutankhamun / Marianne Eaton-Krauss.
pages cm.—(Bloomsbury Egyptology)
Includes bibliographical references and index.
ISBN 978-1-4725-7561-6 (pb)—ISBN 978-1-4725-7562-3 (epub)—ISBN 978-1-4725-7563-0 (epdf)
1. Tutankhamen, King of Egypt. 2. Pharaohs—Biography. 3. Egypt—History—Eighteenth dynasty, ca. 1570-1320 B.C. I. Title.
DT87.5.E283 2015
932'.014092—dc23
[B]
2015018901

Series: Bloomsbury Egyptology

Typeset by RefineCatch Limited, Bungay, Suffolk
Printed and bound in India

Contents

Preface

Who was Tutankhamun? Many if not most of those who come across this book in a bookshop or library, or who receive it as a gift, will have an answer to that question: 'why, he was the boy pharaoh who died young.' Or: 'he was the king whose tomb and treasure Howard Carter discovered in 1922.' My intention in writing this book is to demonstrate that there is a good deal more that can be said about Tutankhamun by studying the monuments – temples and other buildings, statuary and reliefs, jewelry and even the occasional seal impression – that bear his name or can be associated unquestionably with him.

Egyptologists have long devoted study to Akhenaten, the so-called heretic pharaoh, and his attempted 'revolution from above' which, given the inseparability of religion and state in ancient Egypt, cannot be adequately described as affecting simply religious belief and practice. But only since about 1970 have specialists turned their attention to the immediate aftermath of Akhenaten's reign, the post-Amarna Period. Egyptologists' theories about the succession and research into the restitution of the traditional cults and Akhenaten's legacy, not to mention the controversies surrounding those theories and the research underlying them, have not generally 'trickled down' into literature about ancient Egypt intended for interested laypersons and students, just as new insights about Akhenaten's own years on the throne have tended to be ignored in books for the general reader. Even some Egyptologists who specialize in earlier and later periods of Egyptian history are out of touch with recent developments in Amarna studies.

One significant factor contributing to this discrepancy between scholarship and its dissemination is that much consequential work on the Amarna Period and its aftermath has been (and continues to be) done by French and German scholars. Increasingly their work – along with that of others who do not publish in English – tends to be marginalized in Britain and North America. This results in significant contributions to research on Akhenaten and his reign's sequel remaining little known outside continental Europe.

Books on Tutankhamun in particular have often been published in connection with exhibitions – not just catalogues, but other books which take advantage of the interest generated by an exhibition. Such publications focus on the tomb, its discovery – how many times has the story been (re)told? – and the 'treasure' it held; the monuments of the reign outside the Valley of the Kings and what they may reveal about the years Tutankhamun occupied the throne are allotted little space. This book aims at redressing this neglect of building projects and other commissions which have their story to tell. Controversies among my colleagues and between them and myself are addressed; I do not shy away from expressing my own preferences for some ideas while rejecting though not ignoring others. However, I have found it necessary to admit more often than I would have liked that there is no definitive solution yet for some puzzles facing specialists.

Most professionals, including myself, have taken the easy way out, finding much to complain about in books about Egypt for students and the interested layperson, but being too lazy, incapable, or just possibly too timid to write for non-specialists, fearing colleagues' ridicule. After all, it is easy to criticize, but another matter altogether to compose a readable text while maintaining standards of scholarship. My intention in writing this book is to provide a challenging account, because decades of experience lecturing about Tutankhamun in North America and Europe have taught me that this is what audiences want and expect – not a 'dumbed-down' version like the scripts of televised docudramas regularly provide, featuring re-enactments which hardly qualify as entertainment, let alone as reliable reconstructions of events based on the data available.

At the beginning of this study I must express indebtedness to the German Research Foundation (Deutsche Forschungsgemeinschaft) for providing funding of the first two years I spent working on Tutankhamun, 1983–85. It is not only an obligation but also a pleasure to acknowledge here, as well as below in the text and endnotes, those colleagues and friends who – despite sometimes conflicting interpretations of data – have stood by me over the decades this book has been in preparation: W. Raymond ('Ray') Johnson first and foremost; Marc Gabolde, Rolf Krauss, Nozomu Kawai, and especially Nick Reeves who put me in touch with my publisher. I am also very appreciative of the weekends that Christian Bayer sacrificed to prepare many of the illustrations. And I am indebted to Dennis Forbes for the image of King Tutankhamun that graces the cover and especially to Patricia Spencer for reading the ms just before it was submitted. In addition to calling my attention to some references (and typographical errors), Patricia provided welcome encouragement.

This book is dedicated to Mohamed Saleh and to the memory of Mohammed el-Saghir. The unflagging interest of both in my work on Tutankhamun from its inception proved invaluable.

M. Eaton-Krauss
31 January 2015

Introduction

Egyptologists were familiar with Tutankhamun decades before Howard Carter discovered the king's tomb in 1922. Histories of ancient Egypt authored by German, French, and English specialists published around 1900 listed him among the successors of Amenhotep IV/Akhenaten, the 'heretic pharaoh'. That King Tutankhamun had at first been called Tutankhaten, a name incorporating the name of the solar god Aten worshipped by Akhenaten at Tell el-Amarna, was also common knowledge, and it was presumed, if not proven beyond a doubt, that his queen Ankhesenamun was Ankhesenpaaten, the third eldest daughter of Akhenaten and Nefertiti.

In the second volume of Henri Gauthier's monumental compendium of documents naming Egyptian kings, published in 1912, he placed Tutankhamun correctly toward the end of Dynasty XVIII as the successor of the enigmatic Smenkhkare and succeeded in turn by the God's Father Ay, with Horemhab bringing the epoch to a close.[1] But the relationships of these rulers to each other, and, perhaps more importantly, to Akhenaten were subject to conjecture. Gauthier sided with those who argued that the text on one of a pair of granite lions in the British Museum calling Tutankhamun a son of Amenhotep III need not be credited. And he theorized that Tutankhamun could have been an interloper who claimed the throne through his marriage to a daughter of Akhenaten and Nefertiti.

Independently of Gauthier, Gaston Maspero also concluded in 1912 that there was no unequivocal evidence in support of a blood relationship between Tutankhamun and the royal family of Amenhotep III and Akhenaten. Maspero expressed his opinion in a biographical essay about Tutankhamun included in a book publishing the results of excavations conducted in the Valley of the Kings under the sponsorship of the retired New York lawyer Theodore M. Davis.[2] Thirteen pages were adequate to present the meager documentation at that time available for an assessment of Tutankhamun's reign. Maspero's brief essay supplemented the description of some objects naming Tutankhamun that E. Harold Jones, an archaeologist in Davis's employ, had excavated a few years earlier from an undecorated one-chamber tomb in the Valley of the Kings known today as K(ings') V(alley) 58. In the publication, the find was tentatively identified as the remains of Tutankhamun's plundered burial. When the king's actual tomb (KV 62) was uncovered a decade later, it provided support for the filiation that Gauthier and Maspero had doubted.

Even today, with the centennial of Carter's discovery fast approaching, the find has lost none of its allure as one of the most sensational archaeological events of the past century. In the account of the initial season's work, Howard Carter and Arthur Mace expressed doubt that the tomb would furnish much information of historical significance for Tutankhamun's reign per se. But they did not neglect to mention the possible importance of the contents they found in the so-called painted box (Obj. No. 21 in Carter's card catalogue of the finds) which had been deposited in the Antechamber: 'With very few exceptions . . . the garments it contained were those of a child. . .' which suggested that Tutankhamun 'was quite a young boy when he succeeded to the throne'.[3]

The first scientific examination of the king's mummy, initiated towards the end of 1925, estimated the king's age at death at about eighteen, confirming the surmise of the excavators[4] – and giving birth to the saga of the 'boy-king'. Tutankhamun's youth and the 'remarkable similarity' of the mummy's physiognomy to the skull of the man (then believed to be Akhenaten) recovered earlier from another sepulcher in the Valley of the Kings (KV 55) led to reconsideration of Tutankhamun's claim to the throne. He must certainly have been born into the royal family.[5] Apart from this deduction and the evidence for the length of the reign provided by the year dates in the dockets on the wine amphoras stored in the so-called Annexe, KV 62 has contributed comparatively little to an understanding of the historical problems surrounding its owner, just as Carter and Mace had predicted.[6]

Over the intervening years, countless tourists entered Tutankhamun's modest tomb. The deterioration of the paintings in the Burial Chamber, resulting in part from the moisture brought into the tomb by these visitors, led to the decision to close the tomb temporarily in 2012. In cooperation with the University of Basel, the Zürich-based Society of Friends of the Royal Tombs of Egypt, and the Factum Foundation, Madrid, the Egyptian authorities responsible for antiquities planned to install an exact replica of the Burial Chamber near the house Howard Carter built for himself on the west bank at Luxor.[7] The facsimile, created by Factum Arte, was opened to tourism on 30 April 2014.[8] Other sites at ancient Thebes are accessible to anyone interested in visiting monuments commissioned in Tutankhamun's name, and objects from his tomb remain on exhibition in the Luxor Museum of Ancient Egyptian Art, and, at least for now, in Cairo's Egyptian Museum.[9]

Tutankhamun's nickname, 'King Tut', has attained the status of a household word which rivals pyramid and mummy in the popular imagination for conjuring up vivid images of ancient Egypt. The reaction of some professional Egyptologists is even nowadays rather different, bordering on disdain or even hostility. I well recall the response of a retired professor of Egyptology at a German university when I mentioned to him my intention to undertake a scholarly study on the reign of Tutankhamun; shaking his head he asked, 'Whatever for?'

Carter himself apparently lost interest in the king and his tomb; after the third volume of the popularizing account of the clearance came out in 1933, he does not seem to have published another word on the subject. Nor did Carter's erstwhile colleagues exhibit much enthusiasm for Tutankhamun and his treasure. Following Carter's death on 2 March 1939, events leading up to the Second World War will have also contributed to a lack of interest in the tomb. In the more recent past, the disinterest of Egyptologists has bordered on aversion, perhaps born of an impulse to distance themselves from the Indiana Jones image of archaeologists among the public and the fascination the glint of gold continues to exercise for non-specialists right down to the present.

Carter's niece Phyllis Walker presented his papers, including those relating to the clearance of KV 62, to the Griffith Institute, Oxford, in 1946, but several years would pass before Egyptologists showed any interest in them. In 1962 Alan Gardiner attempted to motivate scholars to study objects from the tomb when the painted box (Obj. No. 21, mentioned above) was published with Nina Davies's facsimiles of the decoration.[10] A year later, Tutankhamun's Tomb Series was initiated at the Griffith Institute with the expressed purpose of publishing monographs on groups of objects from the tomb. Under the editorship of John R. Harris, nine slim volumes saw the light of day before the series was discontinued in 1990. Carter's excavation diaries, the object cards, and Harry Burton's photographs, made during the tomb's clearance,[11] have been accessible to scholars of every nationality for some time, and nowadays anyone can consult them on the website of the Griffith Institute www.griffith.ox.ac.uk/discoveringTut/.

In 1963, Christiane Desroches-Noblecourt published the first popularizing account of Tutankhamun's reign to include a wealth of excellent, well-reproduced color photographs of objects from the tomb.[12] And she was the author of the catalogue and coordinator of the first blockbuster travelling exhibition of objects from the tomb on loan from Cairo which opened in Paris's Petit Palais on 17 February 1967.[13] That year her former colleague at the Louvre, Jacques Vandier, authored a lengthy scholarly article about Tutankhamun and his reign.[14] Vandier's study, the first for decades, retained authoritative status for several years. The second major exhibition of selected items from the treasure, which travelled from Cairo to London in 1972, did not inspire any major revision of Vandier's historical outline of the reign, nor did the third which began touring North America in 1976.[15] But when that same exhibition travelled on to Germany in 1980, new insights found their way into the historical outline of the period published in the exhibition catalogue.[16] From that time onward, specialists' interest in the historical Tutankhamun has accelerated, keeping pace with that of laypersons who continue to flock in record numbers to displays of replicas of the tomb and treasure, as well as to exhibitions of the genuine article on loan from Egypt.

The major advances of the past three decades in understanding the role of Tutankhamun's reign in the aftermath of the Amarna Period have not resulted from study of the tomb and the objects it contained, not least because only a comparatively small proportion of them have been subjected to scholarly scrutiny and publication. Despite claims that science and technology have made significant contributions, it is rather the application of traditional methodology to long-known but neglected evidence on the one hand and, on the other hand, the discovery and analysis of new data – in part, the result of continuing archaeological and conservation activity – which have proved crucial as set forth in the pages of this book that follow.

Bibliographical note

The notes (some extensive, for my colleagues' benefit) are relegated to pp. 129–60, following the Abbreviations. Articles and publications cited in two or more chapters are included in the Selected Bibliography, pp. 161–3.

Prince Tutankhaten

By the beginning of the twenty-first century, Egyptologists had come to share Howard Carter's opinion that Tutankhamun was related by blood to his immediate predecessors on the throne of Egypt, and therefore the last ruler of Dynasty XVIII who stood in the line of succession that began with Thutmose I. Until today no biological link has been found between that king and Ahmose, the founder of the New Kingdom whose defeat of Khamudi put an end to Dynasty XV, foreign rulers from the Levant who held sway over Egypt for about a century. But from *c.* 1480 BC, when Thutmose II succeeded Thutmose I, the kingship passed from father to son (or daughter, in the case of Queen Hatshepsut) down through the reign of Amenhotep IV, one of the children which Amenhotep III sired with Tiye, his principal queen. The familial relationships between Amenhotep IV, or Akhenaten, as he renamed himself to honor the solar god Aten, and his successors remains, however, a highly contentious issue which the recent study of a group of royal mummies, conducted by a team of natural scientists, radiologists, and pathologists, has not resolved. One faction supports Akhenaten's paternity of Prince Tutankhaten while the other favors Smenkhkare whose status, too, is open to doubt. Was he the son or the brother of Akhenaten, his co-regent and/or successor? Both camps are further divided on the identity of Tutankhaten's mother.[1]

The Hermopolis block

The so-called Hermopolis block has played a crucial role in discussions of Tutankhaten's parentage (Figure 1). Actually two adjoining fragments, decorated on both sides, it was recovered by a German expedition from Hildesheim during excavations at Ashmunein (ancient Hermopolis) in the 1930s; it is only one of several hundred blocks found there bearing figures and inscriptions in relief that once decorated the walls of Akhenaten's buildings at Tell el-Amarna, the capital city he founded across the Nile and somewhat upstream. During the reign of Horemhab, Tutankhamun's second successor, temples and palaces at Tell el-Amarna were dismantled and the blocks transported to Hermopolis for reuse. Some years later, after Ramesses II became Pharaoh, Horemhab's

Figure 1 The Hermopolis block.

a   Side A.
b   Side A, reconstruction.
c   Side B.

structures at Hermopolis suffered the same fate; they were torn down and the blocks reused a second time to construct a temple gateway.

The reliefs and associated texts on the blocks from Tell el-Amarna found at Hermopolis had been subjected to varying degrees of purposeful, as well as accidental damage at each stage of their history. By the time the German mission recovered the block with relevance for the filiation of Tutankhamun it had been broken in two and the halves separated. Specialists interested in Tutankhamun's family long overlooked the fact that the excavator had associated the two fragments in his publication. In 1997, Jacobus van Dijk reminded his colleagues, publishing his drawing of the text, and this was followed a few years later by Marc Gabolde's rendering.[2] Both Egyptologists based their drawings on photographs in the excavation report since the fragments themselves had gone astray. In 2008, Zahi Hawass, Chairman of the Supreme Council of Antiquities at that time, announced the re-discovery of the block in a storeroom at Ashmunein in his column 'Dig Days,' in *Al Ahram Weekly*.[3] And in 2013, he included a dramatic photograph of the side with the text in his seventh book on Tutankhamun.[4]

W. Raymond Johnson's reconstruction of the design on the other side of the block shows a column capital hung with a swag that includes ducks hanging by their feet (Figure 1b).[5] In the reliefs of non-royal tombs at Amarna, columns decorated like this support the roof of pavilions sheltering the royal family. But it is the other side of the block with six vertical columns of inscription that interests Egyptologists (Figure 1c). The texts are symmetrically arranged but not centered; more of the third column at the right is preserved than at the left. The right-hand text reads 'King's Son of [his] body whom he loves, Tutankhuaten'[6]; the partially preserved final hieroglyph which depicted a squatting man indicates that the person named is male. Until now, this is the only documentation of the name given the boy at birth, as either prince or king, with the unequivocal provenance of Tell el-Amarna. The text to the left begins in the same way – 'King's Daughter of his body' – and continues '[whom] he [loves], one greatly favored by the Lord of the Two Lands [i.e., the king]' but the girl's name is lost, save for the reed leaf of the word *aten* at the bottom of the last column at the left.

Van Dijk and Gabolde follow the lead of the German excavator who concluded that Ankhesenpaaten, the third eldest daughter of Akhenaten and Nefertiti, is the princess named here. But could the girl be instead one of the royal couple's three other daughters whose names also incorporate the name of the sun god Aten? In the name of the second oldest princess Maketaten, *aten* is written last in roughly one third of the examples known, but she had probably died before the text naming Prince Tutankhuaten was carved. Princess Neferneferuaten 'junior', fourth daughter of Akhenaten and Nefertiti, is not frequently documented, and in any case the writing of her name, like that of her oldest sister Meritaten, consistently begins with the *aten* element. The only daughter in whose name *aten* is regularly placed last is Ankhesenpaaten, so she should indeed be the princess named here.

Gabolde believes the text of the Hermopolis block proves that Prince Tutankhaten shared mother and father with at least one sister. He proposes identifying these parents as Akhenaten and Nefertiti, assuming that royal children born to different wives of the king are not depicted together on royal monuments. While this does indeed seem to be the case when the meager evidence from Tell el-Amarna is considered, Gabolde himself has argued in favor of an exception.[7] In the tomb there of Huya, the steward of the dowager queen mother Tiye, two scenes depict Akhenaten and Nefertiti with two daughters sitting opposite Tiye, who is accompanied by a princess named Baketaten. Some Egyptologists (including myself) accept the identification of this princess as the daughter of Amenhotep III and Queen Tiye and thus a sister of Akhenaten, as Norman de Garis Davies proposed when he published his facsimile of the scene more than a century ago. Gabolde, however, would identify her as the daughter of Kiya, Akhenaten's 'other wife' (see further, below). The existence of Kiya's daughter is documented by reliefs depicting her with her mother, but her name is not known. If Gabolde's interpretation of the scene in Huya's tomb is accepted, there is no reason to go along with his interpretation of the text on the Hermopolis block. Tutankhaten, too, might be Akhenaten's child by a consort other than Nefertiti. It follows from the traditional understanding of the scene in Huya's tomb that 'king' in Baketaten's title King's Daughter does not refer to the same person as 'king' in the label of princesses sitting with Akhenaten and Nefertiti, just as the king in Nefertiti's title King's Great Wife is not the ruler in the same title borne by Tiye in this scene.

The absence of Tutankhaten from the ubiquitous depictions of Akhenaten and Nefertiti with their children cannot be cited against the theory that the queen was his mother. As proponents of Nefertiti's claim justifiably point out, depictions of the royal family at Tell el-Amarna seem to conform to the well-documented tradition of omitting male offspring from such contexts, a tradition which obtained until the following Nineteenth Dynasty. But Gabolde argues that Tutankhaten is not entirely absent from such scenes since he identifies the infant depicted in the arms of a woman in the reliefs of Akhenaten's tomb in the Royal Wadi at Amarna as the prince.[8] The representations occur in scenes on the wall of chambers *alpha* and *gamma* in a three-room secondary tract opening off the stairwell that provides access to the tomb's pillared hall where Akhenaten himself was buried.[9] Three scenes all told (two in *alpha*) show Akhenaten and Nefertiti inside a room mourning the death of a woman; they stand at the bed on which the corpse lies. Two of these tableaux include the group of the woman and the baby, placed outside the room and facing away from it. In antiquity only the group in *gamma* was provided with a label. Nowadays even more of the text is lost than when a French Egyptologist copied it towards the end of the nineteenth century. Specialists disagree about the reference of the damaged text – did it name the woman or the baby? – and about the identities of both figures, as well as the sex of the infant.

The idea that the baby is Tutankhaten did not originate with Gabolde, but his predecessors had proposed Princess Maketaten (identified by label as the woman whose death Akhenaten and Nefertiti mourn in *gamma*) or Kiya (one proposal for the unlabeled deceased in *alpha*), rather than Nefertiti, as his mother. Van Dijk rejects these readings, suggesting instead that the infant in the nurse's arms is Maketaten, reborn in the Hereafter,[10] an idea that Geoffrey T. Martin has, in my view, successfully rebutted.[11]

Van Dijk also proposes that the juxtaposition of the texts naming the prince and princess on the Hermopolis block 'strongly suggests that these two royal children were actually married' when the inscriptions were carved. The princess's epithet, 'one greatly favored by the Lord of the Two Lands', provides support for the idea that she enjoyed a special status. The mention of this title on the Hermopolis block is unique. The only other Eighteenth-Dynasty women who bore a comparable epithet were Akhenaten's sister Satamun and Tiy, Nefertiti's wet-nurse and spouse of Tutankhamun's successor Ay. The former was 'favored [but not *greatly* favored] by the Lord of the Two Lands [i.e., her father, Amenhotep III]' while the latter was 'greatly favored by Waenre [Akhenaten]'. As King Tutankhaten's spouse, Ankhesenpaaten is 'great of favors',[12] and she retained the epithet (which her grandmother Tiye had borne as the principal wife of Amenhotep III) after the alteration of her name to Ankhesenamun. But when the princess became Tutankhaten's wife is anyone's guess; perhaps it was only at his accession, in order to safeguard the status of a daughter of Akhenaten and Nefertiti when the 'restoration' was in full swing, rather than to legitimize his claim to the throne, as often supposed.[13] In fact, very little is known about the marriages of royals in ancient Egypt, aside from the exchange of gifts in the context of diplomatic marriage. Among non-royalty, marriage apparently did not involve a specific ceremony or rite.[14] The title 'wife' before a woman's name described her marital status, but under what circumstances she acquired it is not known.

As for Prince Tutankhaten's parentage, van Dijk terms Akhenaten's own parents, Amenhotep III and Queen Tiye, whom some had proposed in the past, 'unlikely', and he excludes Nefertiti as his mother, because the monuments credit her with daughters only. Sometimes a daughter, but never a son, accompanies Kiya, the only other wife of Akhenaten named and depicted. Despite having used such evidence to deny Nefertiti's claim, van Dijk is reluctant to dismiss the possibility that Kiya also bore a son. And he conjectures that Kiya's disappearance from the record at the time he reckons Tutankhaten was born might have resulted from 'her producing an heir [who] posed a threat to the position of Nefertiti'.

Aidan Dodson, who thinks van Dijk's interpretation of the scene in the Royal Tomb is worthy of consideration, holds fast to his own conviction that Akhenaten and Nefertiti were Tutankhaten's parents.[15] Dodson explains the inscription on the Hermopolis block as captions identifying figures of Ankhesenpaaten and Tutankhaten in 'a double scene showing Akhenaten and Nefertiti worshipping the Aten with their children split between them'.[16]

In all likelihood, the names of the prince and princess did indeed label figures, but the orientation of the hieroglyphs in columns which face each other cannot be reconciled with Dodson's proposal. In scenes at Amarna of the royal couple worshipping the sun disk Akhenaten does not face Nefertiti as Dodson's description implies. When daughters accompany their parents in such contexts they follow their mother, who in turn follows Akhenaten.

James P. Allen's proposal for the original context of the Hermopolis block is equally vague.[17] He suggests that the prince and princess were part of a composition showing 'intimate interaction of some sort' between them, attesting 'the association of these two royal children, if not their marriage' before Tutankhaten's accession.

The existence of large-scale scenes depicting Akhenaten with his family in the relief decoration of temples (as well as in palace paintings) at Amarna is demonstrated by other blocks excavated at Hermopolis. Two of them – one in Brooklyn and another in Cairo – depict Nefertiti kissing a princess.[18] In such scenes on family stelas and in non-royal tombs at Amarna, the orientation of the children's bodies, rather than their heads, regularly determines the orientation of the labels identifying them. If that rule applies here, then the bodies of prince and princess faced each other, even if one or both turned his or her head back to look at a parent. The size of the hieroglyphs implies that the figures were comparatively large in scale. Numerous texts at Amarna naming daughters of Akhenaten and Nefertiti conclude 'born of the King's Great Wife Nefertiti, may she live forever'. If the texts on the Hermopolis block continued in the same fashion, it would have created a considerable distance between the figures, regardless of how they were associated in the scene. Perhaps the prince and princess were depicted with neither their parents nor siblings, facing each other, as is shown several times in the decoration of the small golden shrine from Tutankhamun's tomb, Obj. No. 108. However, it was made not only after Tutankhaten's accession but also after the names of both the king and his queen had been altered to cite Amun.

On balance then, the only certainty which the Hermopolis block provides is that the prince and princess were both children of a king, but not necessarily of the same king.

The DNA analyses

From September 2007 through October 2009, an Egyptian–German team, headed by Zahi Hawass, made CT scans of several mummies and extracted DNA from them for analysis.[19] One purpose of this project was to employ state-of-the-art technology in hope of clarifying familial relationships within Akhenaten's family. (The team was also interested in determining the cause of Tutankhamun's death, for which see Chapter 7.) The results of analyses of data obtained were announced in a press release of the Supreme Council of Antiquities on 17 February 2010 and simultaneously published in the *Journal of the American Medical Association*.[20] Critique was quick to follow.[21] The first doubts expressed by a non-medical source came from Dennis Forbes, editor of *Kmt: A Modern Journal of Ancient Egypt*; he pointed out the discrepancies between the press release and the *JAMA* article,[22] contrasting the certainties of the former with the cautious wording of the latter, even if both answered the question 'was Akhenaten Tutankhamun's father?' affirmatively.

Before embarking on discussion of the results trumpeted in the article, it should be noted that recent research has raised doubts about the uses and reliability of DNA testing in identifying individuals even in contemporary forensic medicine.[23] That said, the DNA analyses carried out by Hawass's team purportedly showed that Tutankhamun was the son of the man whose remains lay in the coffin excavated more than a century ago from the make-shift burial in KV 55, a simple one-chambered tomb not far from Tutankhamun's KV 62. Furthermore, this person was shown to be a son of the Elder Lady, a mummy identified as Queen Tiye (thanks to the fact that another tomb excavated early in the twentieth century – KV 46 – yielded the mummies of Tiye's parents) and the mummy labeled Amenhotep III. (In 1898, Victor Loret had discovered both the latter and the Elder Lady 'cached' in the tomb of Amenhotep II, KV 35.) But are the remains found in KV 55 really those of Akhenaten? What if Amenhotep III and Tiye had three sons – and Akhenaten, a younger as well as an older brother (the well-documented Thutmose[24])?

The ownership of the KV 55 coffin and the identity of the person whose remains were found in it are hotly debated among specialists on the Amarna Period. The anthropoid coffin (Plate I) depicts a person wearing the so-called Nubian, or pointed, wig composed of several overlapping layers of tiny, tight corkscrew curls. Whether the uraeus which asserts the regality of the owner and the plaited and curled (=god's) beard at the chin were part of the original design or secondary is disputed. The inlaid feathered pattern decorating the body of the coffin conforms to the royal standard of the New Kingdom, epitomized, for example, by the outer coffin of Queen Ahmose-Nefertari, the mother of Amenhotep I. The position of the arms, crossed over the chest, is documented for the coffins of both men and women. When KV 55 was discovered the objects once grasped in the hands were missing – a pharaoh's crook and flail, *ankh*-signs, or even papyrus-umbel scepters are possibilities, depending on the status and sex of the owner.

Nearly a decade and a half ago, Alfred Grimm argued that the coffin was originally made for Akhenaten early in his reign; having become obsolete, it was not used for his burial, and was thus available for his 'successor' Smenkhkare.[25] Before Grimm presented his analysis, the proposal for the coffin's ownership which satisfied specialists was that it had been commissioned, like the canopic jars from the same tomb, for Akhenaten's 'other wife' Kiya and subsequently altered for his own use.

In fact, Grimm's attempt to explain the design of the coffin as appropriate for Akhenaten is unconvincing. The coffin's Nubian wig – the coiffure also incorporated into the design of the lids for the canopic jars – is closely associated with only one person during the Amarna Period: Kiya.[26] There are a few instances of Akhenaten wearing the Nubian wig, but they are not comparable to a coffin prepared for a king's burial, nor do they date to the earlier part of Akhenaten's reign when Grimm supposes the coffin was made. Furthermore, Grimm has misunderstood the alterations to the inscriptions, which are reminiscent of those made to the small canopic coffinettes adapted for Tutankhamun's use from the burial equipment of the ruling queen (see Chapter 7, p. 106) whose reign preceded his. The strips of inlaid hieroglyphs down the front of the lid and around the upper edge of the coffin's basin named the original owner. These were completely replaced with strips naming Akhenaten while the text, executed in the technique called chasing in the gold sheeting under the foot of the coffin, was altered by patching. (These changes were probably made when a decision was taken to remove Akhenaten's body from the Royal Tomb at Amarna in preparation for reburial in the Valley of the Kings at Western Thebes – cf. Chapter 6, p. 91.) The obvious care with which the cartouches were then subsequently 'emptied' is evidence of intent to replace Akhenaten's name with another, not to deface the inscription. Since Akhenaten's epithets 'perfect little child of Aten' and 'great in his lifetime' were left standing, they must have been considered suitable for the new owner, just like the epithet 'perfect ruler' ⌐⌐ heading up the text down the lid of the coffin. (This title had been introduced by Akhenaten to replace the traditional king's title 'perfect god' ⌐⌐ around Year 12 of his reign;[27] it remained in use for a time after Tutankhaten's succession.)

But even if the dilemma of the coffin's ownership could be resolved one day to everyone's satisfaction, the identity of the person laid to rest in it would still be subject to doubt, since the texts were in the process of being altered to name a new owner. Before the Egyptian–German team published their conclusions, a few Egyptologists believed that those who deposited the coffin in KV 55 *thought* they were burying Akhenaten; other specialists were convinced that the remains were indeed those of Akhenaten while still others identified the deceased as Akhenaten's male successor (or co-regent?) Smenkhkare (his son or brother?). The results of the Egyptian–German team's examination of the remains from KV 55 have also proved equivocal, not only because of disagreements among the team members which surfaced when the televised documentary publicizing the project and its conclusions was aired.[28] Until now the evidence underpinning the team's assertion that the remains are those of a person

35–45 years of age at death remain unpublished. Instead the authors of the *JAMA* article simply assert: 'The mummy in KV 55 was previously thought to be in his 20s when he died. However, our new computed tomography investigation revealed that he lived to be much older.'[29]

The age span 35–45 would mean that Akhenaten was between 18 and 28 years old when he ascended the throne, which is reasonable, both as regards the events of his 17-year reign and the age he would have been when his children, including his putative son Tutankhaten, were born. But this estimate is higher than those made by experts in the past. The previous high of 30–35 was proposed in 1992, 'based on the re-evaluation of the biologic evidence by Professor James E. Harris and Professor Fawzia H. Hussein, Director of the Anthropological Laboratory, National Research Centre, Cairo'.[30] But the 'biologic' data to back it up, like the evidence that the authors of the *JAMA* article assert their examination revealed, have never been published and made accessible for peer scrutiny. Other specialists who have examined the remains from KV 55, beginning with G. Elliot Smith early in the twentieth century[31] and continuing down through 2000[32] propose 18–25 as the age-at-death – difficult if not impossible to reconcile with the innovations of the first five years of Akhenaten's reign, as has been noted in the past.[33]

Not long after the *JAMA* article appeared, Eugen Strouhal published the results of his examination of the remains from KV 55, undertaken in 1998.[34] He concludes that the age-at-death of this male individual is 'in the range of 19–22 years', which agrees with the results of R. G. Harrison's investigation, published nearly 45 years earlier.[35] The physical anthropologist Corinne Duhig supports Strouhal's age estimate in an article published alongside his.[36] She makes no claim to identify the body, but for Strouhal it is obvious that the remains are those of Tutankhamun's 'elder brother Smenkhkare'.

None of these experts confronts the intrinsic difficulty with aging corpses from earlier eras, namely the lack of well-dated contemporaneous remains for comparison. Dodson has called attention to this problem by noting the serious discrepancies between physical anthropologists' estimates of age-at-death for corpses from the eighteenth- and nineteenth-century AD crypts of Christ Church, Spitalfields, London, and the age-at-death recorded on their coffins.[37] He cites examples where the age-at-death of older persons was underestimated and, conversely, that of younger individuals overestimated.

According to the Egyptian–German team, the mummy known as the Younger Lady, cached along with those of Amenhotep III and the Elder Lady in the tomb of Amenhotep II long after the end of the Eighteenth Dynasty, was the mother of Prince Tutankhaten as well as the sister of the man laid to rest in KV 55. Since she was his sibling, according to the Egyptian–German team, she too must have been a child of Amenhotep III and Queen Tiye, but Hawass et al. decline to identify her with any of the daughters of the couple whose names are known.

Is Nefertiti, the current favorite of Dodson[38] as well as of Gabolde[39] to fill the role of Tutankhamun's mother, a feasible candidate for identification as the Younger Lady? The names of Nefertiti's sister and of her nurse are documented, not those of her father and mother. This silence in the record is in marked contrast to the repeated mention of Queen Tiye's parents – but it is her case which is exceptional, not Nefertiti's. What if one of the daughters of Amenhotep III changed her name to Nefertiti when she became Akhenaten's spouse? Still, if Nefertiti were indeed Amenhotep III's daughter and a sister of Akhenaten (and/or Smenkhkare?), the absence of the titles King's Daughter and King's Sister from her titulary would be remarkable, given the extensive documentation for her.

Alternative interpretations of the DNA data

Using the DNA markers reported by Hawass's team, first the Swiss Egyptologist Hermann Schlögl[40] and then Marc Gabolde[41] have proposed different reconstructions of Tutankhamun's family tree.

With the help of a specialist in genetics and a *Biotechniker*, Schlögl first identifies the mummy from Amenhotep II's tomb which an ancient Egyptian scribe labeled Amenhotep III when it was 'restored' about 1060 BC, as King Ay, Tutankhamun's successor. Schlögl follows Joann Fletcher's identification of the Younger Lady from the same 'cache' in KV 35 (now identified thanks to the DNA markers as the daughter of the man Schlögl thinks is Ay) as Nefertiti.[42] G. Elliot Smith – the first expert to comment on the Younger Lady's mummy, shortly after it was discovered – considered the damage to the face and chest to be post-mortem,[43] a judgment that held sway until the work of Hawass and his team. Schlögl accepts their assertion that the head injuries were 'lethal',[44] and he attributes them to a terrible chariot accident involving Nefertiti which occurred about Year 14 of Akhenaten's reign, plunging Egypt into a state of profound mourning. This idea ignores the evidence for Nefertiti's survival at least into Akhenaten's 16th regnal year.[45]

As for the mummy of the Elder Lady from KV 35, Schlögl rejects the identification of Hawass's team, proposing instead that she was a woman called Taemwadjsy whose name, accompanied by a single title, occurs in the inscription on an imitation stone vessel found in the tomb of Queen Tiye's parents.[46] According to Schlögl, she is another daughter of the couple and thus Tiye's sister. In order for the Elder Lady to be the wife of Ay (and mother of the Younger Lady, alias Nefertiti), she must have changed her name from Taemwadjsy to Tiy, because that is the name of Ay's wife as depicted in both his earlier, non-royal tomb at Amarna and in his tomb as king, KV 23, at Thebes. Since DNA analysis demonstrates that the mummy Schlögl identifies as King Ay and the Elder Lady, whom he says is Ay's wife, were the parents of the person buried in KV 55, the body cannot be Akhenaten (as the Egyptian–German team concluded) but rather

Ay's and Taemwadjsy's son Smenkhkare. Apparently his (childless) marriage to Meritaten (Akhenaten's eldest daughter) justified his claim to the kingship. For Schlögl, it seems the mummy of Akhenaten (the father of Tutankhaten in his scenario) has not been identified – or at least is not among those studied by Hawass's team. The genealogy proposed by Schlögl, like his reconstruction of the events in the later years of Akhenaten's reign, does not convince.

By contrast, the interpretation of the DNA markers proposed by Gabolde provides food for serious thought. He begins with persuasive arguments for accepting the identification of the king's mummy from KV 35 as Amenhotep III and in favor of the likelihood that the Elder Lady is indeed Queen Tiye. Pointing to the failure of Hawass's team to note the correspondences between the DNA of the king's mummy from KV 35 and of Yuya, Tiye's father, he suggests that Amenhotep III and his queen were cousins. For Gabolde, the archaeological evidence taken in conjunction with the DNA markers raises the possibility that a female mummy from KV 21 (KV 21A, identified tentatively by Hawass's team as Ankhesenamun) is rather Amenhotep III's mother Mutemwiya (a wife of Thutmose IV). He is also unpersuaded that the DNA analyses of Hawass et al. conclusively demonstrate that the Younger Lady is a full sister of Akhenaten (in Gabolde's scenario, the person whose remains were found in the KV 55 coffin); she might just as well be his cousin (and possibly Nefertiti), especially given the 'incestuous unions' in the royal family of the later Eighteenth Dynasty and the evidence for endogamy he adduces for the 'clan from Akhmim'. But once again the age at death of the person buried in KV 55 presents a problem: Gabolde thinks 27 to 30 is acceptable. Akhenaten would then have been about ten years old at his accession, which I find untenable.

In conclusion, a final word about Tutankhamun's mother may be added. Her absence from the record is noteworthy, especially in view of his tender age when he became king, and in marked contrast to other queen mothers of the later Eighteenth Dynasty who are conspicuous in the reigns of their sons – Tiaa under Thutmose IV; Mutemwiya under Amenhotep III; and Tiye under Akhenaten. No relief, statue, or inscription has yet come to light honoring the woman whose child was Tutankhaten; not a single object among the memorabilia in his tomb mentions her name. Whoever she may have been, it seems likely that she had died before his accession.

Tutankhaten's upbringing

That Tutankhaten was born at Tell el-Amarna and spent his infancy in the care of a wet-nurse and his childhood there with a tutor is plausible, but until now no data can be cited in support of this idea. The text naming him on the Hermopolis block is evidence that he was depicted in scenes of the royal family at Akhenaten's capital city. It should not come as a surprise then that Gabolde would identify the remains of a smaller-scaled male figure sitting on the lap of a second, larger, also apparently male, person as Tutankhaten.[47] The scene is partially preserved on another of the blocks from Tell el-Amarna reused at Hermopolis. More figural as well as inscriptional evidence for the prince may well eventually come to light, either through excavation or analysis of archival photographs. But until now, the claims made by others for additional documentation of the prince cannot be substantiated.

For example, an inscription on a relief fragment of unknown provenance now in a Swiss private collection supposedly mentions a 'sun shade' of Prince Tutankhaten.[48] Sun shades were shrines for worshipping the sun, set in a landscape of gardens and shallow pools within an enclosure. The precincts of this kind at Tell el-Amarna are associated exclusively with royal women.[49] Not only have the hieroglyphs on the relief fragment in private possession been incorrectly read;[50] doubts about the piece's authenticity are justified.[51]

Lyla Pinch Brock has identified Prince Tutankhaten as the smaller figure on a fragment of a painting from the King's House in the Central City (Figure 2).[52] But an iconographic feature precludes this idea.[53] The draftsman has drawn the feet of the smaller figure at the right, in attendance on a larger person with feet on a patterned cushion to the left, as convention dictated since the Old Kingdom: both the figure's feet are drawn as if seen from inside, without indication of the toes on the near foot. During the Amarna Period the feet of members of the royal family are consistently drawn to show the toes on the near foot,[54] as can be seen, for example, by comparing the feet of the larger figure at the left, and those of the king, queen, and princesses in other fragments of the same painting from the King's House now in the Ashmolean Museum. Since the figure in the painting does not have an 'Amarna foot', it cannot depict Tutankhaten but rather an official or retainer in attendance upon the royal family.[55]

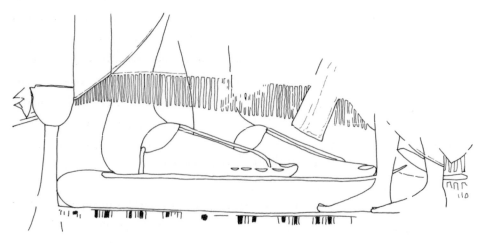

Figure 2 Painting fragment from the King's House at Tell el-Amarna. Egyptian Museum, Cairo, SR 111575/20647.

The posts of wet-nurse and tutor to the royal children were doubtless important throughout Egyptian history; in the Eighteenth Dynasty the persons who served in these capacities became prominent in the record. Senenmut is the most famous of the New-Kingdom tutors of royal children; several statues have survived which depict him with his charge, Queen Hatshepsut's daughter Neferure.[56] Other royal tutors are shown with the children in their care in the decoration of their own tombs, while wet-nurses are pictured in the sepulchers of their spouses or sons. The identity of Nefertiti's wet-nurse is well known; she was Tiy, the wife of Ay, Tutankhamun's successor on the throne of Egypt. Depictions of Tiy in the decoration of the tomb she shared with her husband at Amarna regularly mention her nurse's title in the associated labels.[57] During Akhenaten's reign royal wet-nurses were immortalized for the first time in royal relief. One example, excavated by the Egypt Exploration Society from the Great Palace at Amarna, preserves part of a scene which showed a princess suckling at the breast of a wet-nurse.[58] Two other reliefs featuring royal wet-nurses were among the blocks from Amarna reused at Hermopolis; the scene on one of them can be reconstructed to show a princess tying a special necklace – a token of royal favor – around her nurse's neck.[59]

Towards the end of 1996 a French expedition under the direction of Alain Zivie discovered the tomb of Tutankhamun's wet-nurse Maia in the Memphite necropolis of Saqqara.[60] It had been cut into a section of the escarpment where some years earlier the same mission had excavated the tomb of the vizier Aper-el/Aperia who had served under Amenhotep III and Akhenaten. Aperia counted tutor of the royal children among his titles, but the decoration of his tomb, unlike Maia's, does not include a depiction of him with any of his mentees. In the first chamber of her tomb Maia is shown with the king on her lap (Plate II). The Blue Crown he wears clearly designates him king while the inscriptions in the tomb name him Tutankh*amun*, not Tutankh*aten*, which dates the tomb not only after his accession, but also after his name was changed. The style of the relief further inside the tomb suggests that work continued for a time after Tutankhamun died. Indeed, Marc Gabolde has proposed that the scene depicting the king on Maia's lap was altered following Tutankhamun's death.[61] In the initial version, Maia held a blossom to the king's nose; subsequently, the hand was re-carved to show Maia raising it in a gesture of homage. But this proposal, like Gabolde's tentative suggestion that the wet-nurse depicted in the Royal Tomb at Amarna might possibly be Maia, is not compelling. The nurse's hand could have been altered immediately after the scene was carved, so that her attitude conformed to that of all the men in the sub-registers behind her who raise one hand in the same gesture of homage.

The woman in a sculpture depicting a nurse squatting on the ground and holding a male child on her lap (Plate III) has also been identified as Maia.[62] The statue came to light in a secondary context during EES excavations in the Sacred Animal Complex at North Saqqara. The boy's feet rest on a low footstool; its decoration of prostrate bound foreigners signals his regality, like the design of the pendant with a winged scarab he wears around his neck.[63] Much of the inscription carved on the sides of the base was obliterated when the sculpture was altered to fit into a second base, probably in the Late Period prior to its installation in the Sacred Animal Complex. Neither the name of the child nor of the nurse has survived, but her title can be read: she was not simply wet-nurse, but rather Great Wet-nurse of the King of Upper [and Lower Egypt], a rank not documented for Maia in the extensive texts inscribed in her tomb. The statue's inlaid eyes, now missing, attest the high status of the subject, but she cannot be confidently identified as Maia, nor does the child's physiognomy resemble Tutankhamun's as it is known from his many statues. Indeed, some iconographic features (such as the rosettes on the nurse's breasts) suggest to me a date prior to the Amarna Period.[64]

Zivie remarks on the significance of the fact that Maia possessed her own tomb; its size, exceeding that of the vizier Aperia's tomb, is also noteworthy. If Tutankhamun's mother had died when he was but a baby, his wet-nurse might well have exercised an influence on his upbringing, accounting in turn for her enhanced status when he eventually acceded to the kingship.

Another person whom Egyptologists have conjectured might have played a role in raising Prince Tutankhaten is a man whose titles included overseer of tutors. Like Maia, he is known only from his tomb. A team from the Australian Centre for Egyptology, Macquarie University, under the direction of Boyo Ockinga, discovered it at Akhmim, completing the excavation and recording in 1990.[65] The prominence of King Tutankhamun's cartouches (undamaged) in the decoration clearly dates the tomb to his reign. A chariot procession on the façade depicts a second person riding in the royal chariot with the king who himself holds the reins (Figure 3).

Ockinga notes that the depiction of anyone other than the queen in the royal chariot with the king is unique. Texts do attest that a driver accompanied Pharaoh in the cab of his chariot when he rode out to war or to hunt, but in relief and painting the fiction of his splendid isolation in such contexts was maintained with one possible exception: a small fragment of limestone relief from Amarna, now in the Brooklyn Museum. James F. Romano devoted two articles to this piece.[66] He interpreted the rounded shape in front of the youthful archer, whom he identified as Prince Tutankhaten, as the 'rump' of a driver bent low over the cab. The presence of a charioteer seems called for in any case, since there are no reins tied around the archer's waist, as in analogous scenes. But if the fillet the youth wears was once provided with a uraeus, as Romano reconstructed the scene, he should be a king, not a prince, because a uraeus was a prerogative of the king and queen during Akhenaten's reign. The small scale of the scene (the complete figure was about 5 cm tall) suggests that it once decorated a stela commissioned by a non-royal individual, not the wall in a temple or palace. Deities, rather than the king, figure on other such stelas from Amarna. Whether the youthful archer could be

Figure 3 Tutankhamun in his chariot; façade of the tutor's tomb at Akhmim.

King Tutankhaten/amun or, rather, a god named Shed, known from two other stelas excavated at Amarna, is moot.[67]

In the scene on the façade of the tomb at Akhmim the man who shares the chariot with the king does not drive it but rather serves as his fan-bearer. The king's cartouches are only partially preserved while the fan-bearer's name seems never to have been mentioned. Tutankhamun is the prime candidate for the pharaoh shown. Ockinga proposes that his companion was not the tomb owner, as might be presumed, but Ay, the husband of Nefertiti's wet-nurse, instead. Like Akhenaten's mother Queen Tiye, Ay hailed from Akhmim; a temple which he commissioned there after he succeeded Tutankhamun attests his ties to the town. Ockinga believes the idea that the tomb owner and Ay were members of the same family 'is *prima facie* very plausible' even if 'the exact nature of the relationship ... cannot be established with any certainty.'[68]

As already mentioned, Gabolde argues for a close connection of the royal family to a 'clan' from Akhmim. Be that as it may, there is no tangible evidence in support of the idea that Prince Tutankhaten spent some of his childhood at the town or in its immediate vicinity.

King Tutankhaten

The sequence of events which followed the death of Akhenaten is another hotly disputed issue among specialists.[1] Nowadays nearly all agree, however, that a woman occupied the throne for a time, however briefly, between Akhenaten's demise and the accession of Tutankhaten.[2] Thanks to Marc Gabolde, we know that this woman adopted the throne name 'Ankhetkheperure, beloved of Waenre [=Akhenaten]' and called herself 'Neferneferuaten, beneficial for her husband'.[3] But who was she and who was her husband?

According to the theory Aidan Dodson proposed in 2009 to replace his previous ideas about the later years of Akhenaten's reign and his demise, the woman was Nefertiti, who ruled as her husband's co-regent after his first (male) co-regent Smenkhkare died; and when Akhenaten himself died, she acted as regent for their son Tutankhaten.[4] Other Egyptologists are convinced that this ruling queen was Meritaten, eldest daughter/wife of Akhenaten, and/or sister/wife of Smenkhkare.[5] Allen, too, opts for a daughter of Akhenaten and Nefertiti, but he proposes the fourth-born Neferneferuaten-junior for the role and marries her to Smenkhkare, eventually succeeded by Tutankhaten.[6] To further complicate matters, some Egyptologists (I among them) and some specialists on the history of the Hittite empire are convinced that the queen who ruled Egypt before Prince Tutankhaten's accession was the widow known from later Hittite sources to have dispatched a letter to King Shuppiluliuma, asking him to send one of his sons to Egypt to rule as her spouse. Proponents of this scenario dispute the identity of the widow – was she Nefertiti or Meritaten? – as well as what happened when, following the Hittite ruler's assent to her request, his son was murdered – or died? – en route to, or after his arrival in Egypt. Members of yet another faction identify the widow as Ankhesenamun and date the episode about a decade later, after Tutankhamun's death.[7] It must be emphasized that **none** of the reconstructions of what happened, either immediately before Prince Tutankhaten's accession or after King Tutankhamun's death, can be reconciled with all the data currently available.[8] Since the choice of alternatives is a matter of conviction among Hittitologists as well as Egyptologists, with persuasive arguments on both sides, reviewing all the conflicting arguments here would serve little purpose.

The accession

There is no evidence that Tutankhaten was crowned at Thebes, as his second successor Horemhab claimed to have been about a decade and a half later.[9] Nor does another site suggest itself for the coronation of the prince. In general, Egyptian texts regularly refer simply to the appearance of a new king upon the throne. In depictions of kings' coronations on temple walls of later as well as earlier times, deities officiate at the ceremony, flanking the enthroned new pharaoh who wears the Double Crown of Upper and Lower Egypt. Presumably at this moment the king took possession of crook and flail, the insignia of kingship since the Old Kingdom. One of the two flails (Obj. No. 269f) and one of the three crooks (Obj. No. 44u) from Tutankhamun's tomb are child-sized.[10] The caps at both ends of the crook show the king's throne name (his *prenomen*) Nebkheperure, flanked by rearing cobras, while the single cap at the lower end of the flail displays his personal name (*nomen*) Tutankhaten, alongside the *prenomen*. The similarity in scale, design, materials, and technique suggests this crook and flail once formed a set, perhaps even made for the boy's accession.[11]

In 2001 Nozomu Kawai located the upper part of a limestone stela in the Egyptian Museum, Cairo, bearing reliefs that allude to the accession of a pharaoh (Figure 4).[12]

Figure 4 Lunette of a stela, provenance not known; Egyptian Museum, Cairo, JE 27076.

To the left below the winged sun disk spanning the top of the stela, Isis suckles a smaller-scaled king in the presence of an ithyphallic incarnation of Amun labeled Min-Amun-Re. Behind him, at the left-hand edge of the lunette there is a plot of 'lettuce', a typical attribute of Min. To the right, Amun and his consort Mut greet the king. She proffers him notched palm ribs to guarantee him an endless reign. The *hemhem*, a very elaborate crown replete with uraei worn by the king on the stela, is Tutankhamun's headgear in some reliefs of the Colonnade Hall at Luxor Temple and in the scene on the backrest of the gold throne from his tomb (Plate V).[13] The surface of the stela is not well preserved; the faces of all the figures are damaged, and no hieroglyphs in the cartouches labeling the king can be discerned. The style of the carving suggests it was made in the post-Amarna Period; Kawai proposes reading the winged sun disk with the traces he identified below it as Tutankhaten/amun's *prenomen* Nebkheperure. The lower part of the stela is lost and along with it the text naming the person who commissioned it, perhaps with his depiction as well. The piece was purchased in Luxor more than 125 years ago; while Karnak Temple is a likely provenance, other sites such as Min's cult center at Akhmim, or Coptos where the god was also at home, are possible, as Kawai has pointed out.

The reign of the boy-king begins

The first order of business for a new pharaoh from time immemorial was to bury his predecessor on the throne with all essential rituals. Given King Tutankhaten's youth, others will have assumed responsibility for these arrangements. All the items of funerary equipment commissioned for the ruling queen that have survived were recovered from Tutankhamun's own tomb, their inscriptions altered to replace her name with his (see further below, Chapter 7, p. 106). The logical deduction is that she was not afforded a pharaoh's burial.

Seal impressions bearing the throne name Nebkheperure were recovered from KV 55, the tomb in the Valley of the Kings which contained the burial of the man identified by Hawass et al. as Tutankhaten's father. In other words, the young king is associated with this interment. But do the seal impressions document at least his nominal responsibility for the funeral and burial at Western Thebes of this male individual who should then be his predecessor? Egyptologists have proposed other interpretations to account for them. For example, Dodson, who considers the remains those of Akhenaten's 'co-regent' Smenkhkare, believes that he was buried by the older king at Tell el-Amarna; the seal impressions would then attest the transfer of the body and equipment from a tomb there to the Valley of the Kings 'soon after Tutankhamun's change of name'.[14] Since the impressions do not bear the king's personal name, but his throne name Nebkheperure which he continued to use after *amun* replaced *aten* in the *nomen*, there is no way of dating the activity which they document in KV 55 within the reign as a whole.

Since (one of) Tutankhaten's immediate predecessor(s) had a funerary temple at Thebes,[15] it is more than likely that his/her original interment would have been planned for the Valley of the Kings, not the Royal Wadi at Amarna (cf. Chapter 6, p. 92). Regardless, Egyptologists who identify the ruling queen as Tutankhaten's immediate predecessor (though not necessarily Nefertiti) must nevertheless agree with Dodson that the man who ended up in KV 55 was first interred elsewhere and later, under Tutankhaten/amun, moved to his final resting place in KV 55, thereby accounting for the seal impression with the latter's *prenomen*. At present this seems to be the only logical explanation to account for them, with the identity of Tutankhaten's immediate predecessor left open.

There is considerable evidence that the return to orthodoxy was well underway when Tutankhaten became king. The funerary equipment which the ruling queen commissioned for herself and the foundation of a funerary temple by (one of) Akhenaten's immediate successor(s) at Thebes demonstrate that traditional funerary beliefs were once again respected and that the worship of Amun had been resumed with official sanction.

Akhenaten's new capital city in Middle Egypt functioned not only as the royal residence *par excellence*; it also displaced Thebes as the focal point of the royal family's religious life in the south. But Memphis, where there was a temple for the worship of Aten as practiced by Akhenaten,[16] retained an important role as an administrative center during the Amarna Period. Some publications still cite Tutankhamun's fourth regnal year as the probable date for the 'abandonment' of Tell el-Amarna, even though the city continued to be occupied, though not by the king and his entourage, down into the reign of Tutankhamun's second successor Horemhab. The general trend of the past few years has been to push back the date when the court departed Tell el-Amarna to the very beginning of Tutankhaten's reign. Indeed, like Gabolde,[17] I now think it likely that Tutankhaten never ruled there. Interestingly enough, it seems some doubt persisted as to whether the decision to leave, whenever it was made, would prove final. The pre-Second World War EES excavations found that the doorways of some official buildings and private houses, too, had been purposefully walled up, as if to secure them for future (re)occupation.[18]

Until now most of the numerous small finds from Tell el-Amarna that can be associated with Tutankhamun – faience ring bezels and molds for their manufacture – bear the king's throne name, Nebkheperure, not his personal name. Those few which use the *nomen* call him Tutankhamun; not a single scrap of evidence for King Tutankh*aten* has yet been found at Amarna.[19]

A stela fragment depicting King Tutankhaten before Amun and Mut

The only object with a cartouche reading Tutankhaten that does not come from KV 62, his tomb at Western Thebes, is the lunette from a small limestone stela which Ludwig Borchardt and Friedrich Wilhelm von Bissing gave to Berlin's Egyptian Museum at the end of the nineteenth century (Figure 5).[20] The left half of the lunette with the figures of Amun and his consort Mut is all that survived the Second World War. Their presence suggests Thebes, Amun's cult center, as a likely provenance for the stela, rather than Amarna,[21] but in fact the find spot is not known.

The king, identified as Nebkheperure Tutankhaten, wore a long, pleated robe with a sash and the Blue Crown with streamers. The enthroned gods labeled 'Amun-Re, King of the Gods', and 'Mut, Lady of Heaven, Mistress of the Gods' are the recipients of the floral offerings in his hands. When Adolf Erman published the piece at the beginning of the last century, he described the style as typical of the Amarna Period, and he noted that the man responsible for the design was apparently unacquainted with the traditional manner of depicting gods. Instead of showing them as the respected deities of earlier times, he had given them facial features suggesting they were amused. But the gravity that Erman missed in the gods' expressions is attributable rather to the sculptor's ineptitude, even if a detail of Mut's costume does suggest that he was unfamiliar with her standard iconography: here she wears a modius (a flat, platform-like crown) topped with double falcon plumes. Queens, not goddesses, are normally shown with this headgear, especially during the Amarna Period. In post-Amarna times Mut wears the Double Crown atop her wig with vulture headdress, as she seems to have worn prior to Akhenaten's reign.[22]

Figure 5 Lunette of a stela, provenance not known; Egyptian Museum, Berlin, ÄgM 14197.

Tutankhaten's thrones

Two thrones are the most significant objects that were made and inscribed for the king at the very beginning of his reign when he was still called Tutankhaten. Both survived down into modern times because they were deposited in his tomb, like other items he had used while alive.

Because the inlaid ebony throne (Obj. No. 351; Plate IV) reminded Howard Carter of the bishop's chair familiar to him from European cathedrals, he called it an 'ecclesiastical throne'.[23] The name has stuck, even though there is no reason to associate the throne with any sacerdotal role of the king. Unlike the gold throne (Obj. No. 91) and the scene of the royal couple on the front of its backrest (Plate V) which have been repeatedly illustrated and praised, the inlaid ebony throne has not attracted the attention it deserves nor inspired much positive comment. Its design and the many motifs used in its decoration are well within ancient Egyptian tradition and the excellent craftsmanship is exemplary.

The throne's design combines a curved and inclined backrest, supported by two stiles and a center brace – a well-known construction documented by preserved chairs since the Middle Kingdom – with an imitation folding stool. The use of imitation folding chairs like Tutankhaten's throne was not the prerogative of royalty. Officials are depicted in relief and painting sitting on such chairs, beginning in the reign of Amenhotep III and continuing down through Ramesside times. Some elements in the design of Obj. No. 351 (such as the goose-head legs) and its decoration (for example, the imitation cowhide 'draped' over the seat) were also accessible to non-royal persons. But the royal status of the owner is indicated by the frieze of cobras crowned with sun disks across the head-rail and the vulture with outspread wings below it (Plate IVb).

The backrest's decoration employs the architectural motif of niches, alternatively of ebony and ivory, and dispenses with figures altogether. This probably accounts for the absence from the design of the radiant sun disk, the icon Akhenaten introduced to depict his god Aten, which is so prominent on the backrest of the gold throne where it shines down on the royal couple. On the inlaid ebony throne, two little cartouches identify the simple disk in the center of the head-rail as Aten; they enclose the solar god's so-called didactic name in the form Akhenaten introduced in the later years of his reign.

The king's name is Tutankhaten in all the texts on the back of the backrest; on the front he is also called Tutankhaten in the cartouches crowned with sun disks below the head-rail and in the inscriptions on the vertical inset strips of ivory. But in the two horizontal strips which are made of ebony, he is the 'perfect god' Nebkheperure Tutankhamun. Noting these inconsistencies in the *nomen*, Carter concluded that 'the young king's return to the older faith of Thebes was gradual in transition and not spontaneous'.[24] Subsequent study has suggested that the horizontal ebony strips are secondary, replacing ones with texts naming Tutankhaten.

The feature of the texts providing evidence for dating the manufacture of the inlaid ebony throne before the gold throne is the use of the title 'perfect ruler' to introduce the inscriptions on three of the vertical strips made of ebony. As noted above, p. 8, in the discussion of the ownership of the coffin from KV 55, this title was introduced by Akhenaten to replace the traditional king's title 'perfect god'; the texts here show that it continued in use after Tutankhaten became king, if only briefly. By the time the gold throne was commissioned, however, the decision had been taken to reinstate the traditional title 'perfect god': the pristine texts on the back of the gold throne's backrest (Figure 6) still call the king Tutankhaten but employ the time-honored title 'perfect god' which is also used in the texts with the later *nomen* on the secondary strips of ebony on the front of the inlaid ebony throne's backrest.

Much has been written about the gold throne and photos of it have been reproduced in many books about ancient Egypt in general, as well as those focusing on the Amarna Period or Tutankhamun himself.[25] The initial publication of Carter and Mace did not fail to remark on the presence of both earlier and later forms of the king's *nomen* in the texts: Tutankhaten on the stiles and center brace supporting the backrest, as well as in the inlaid cartouche on the outside of the right armrest (Figure 7); Tutankhamun, executed in the goldsmith's technique known as 'chasing', in the gold foil of the cartouches on the inside of the left armrest and in the texts identifying the figures in the scene on the front of the backrest. As in the case of the inlaid ebony throne, these 'curiously mixed' cartouches were understood to illustrate 'the politico-religious vacillations of the reign'.[26]

In the mid-1970s Egyptologists began to take more interest in the gold throne and to express the first doubts that King Tutankhaten was its original owner. What looked like alterations in the decoration and the obvious changes in the cartouches aroused suspicion that it had been commissioned for a predecessor of his. Furthermore, even to the uninitiated eye it is obvious that the gold throne is scaled for an adult, not for a child.[27] The seat at about 52 cm (one ancient Egyptian cubit) above the floor is the highest of any chair preserved from pharaonic times. But surely its scale, like the decoration, is related to the exalted status of the owner – not his actual size – and the context in which it would be used. And in any case who knew at Tutankhaten's accession that he would not be using it for many years to come?

Specialists who argue against Tutankhaten's original ownership of the gold throne claim that the king and queen in the scene on the backrest do not 'look like' him and Ankhesenpaaten/amun. They believe that the king 'looks like' Akhenaten, but they do not agree on the identification of the queen in the tableau – was she originally Nefertiti or Kiya? Following up on this theory, Gabolde would interpret literally a passage in the

Figure 6 Back of the backrest of the gold throne from the tomb of Tutankhamun, Obj. No. 91; Egyptian Museum, Cairo, JE 62028.

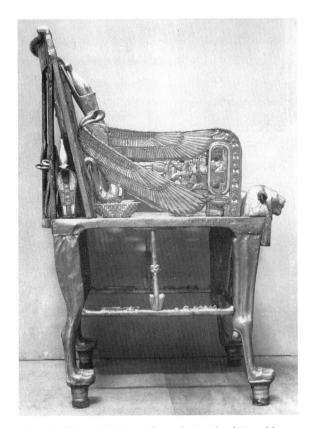

Figure 7 Proper right side of the gold throne from the tomb of Tutankhamun, Obj. No. 91; Egyptian Museum, Cairo, JE 62028.

text of Tutankhamun's so-called Restoration Stela (see Chapter 3, pp. 33–9) describing the king as appearing on the throne of his father to mean that the gold throne first belonged to Akhenaten.[28] However, the 'father' in question is not Akhenaten but Amun, repeatedly referred to on the Restoration Stela as the father who begat Tutankhamun and for whose cult the king provided benefactions.

On the one hand, as pointed out in my study, in the scene on the backrest the king's and queen's profiles, made of red glass, are virtual mirror images of each other. On the other hand, the few scenes depicting Tutankhamun together with his queen available for comparison (for example, in the vignettes of the small golden shrine, Obj. No. 108) show them with varying physiognomy; in one scene they resemble each other more than themselves in another. Furthermore, in ancient Egypt the initial likeness of a king at the outset of his reign customarily reproduced that of his predecessor (who in Tutankhaten's case was, after all, a close relative) until an individual portrait type was created especially for him. In other words, it would not be surprising if the king on the gold throne did 'look like' (his father/uncle?) Akhenaten.

The alteration of the names of the king and queen where they occur on the gold throne involved only the replacement of the hieroglyphs reading *aten* (or *pa aten*, in the queen's case) with those for writing *amun*. To accomplish the alteration expediently the hieroglyphs *aten/paaten* in the gold foil cartouches were smoothed down and re-chased. The procedure followed by the goldsmith is easily detected in the queen's cartouche because in the writing of Ankhesenpaaten, *pa aten* is regularly written last – in vertical cartouches, at the bottom, as can still be seen in her cartouche on the center brace at the back of the throne (Figure 6). The standard spelling of Ankhesenamun, however, gives precedence to the god's name; *amun* is written at the top of a vertically oriented cartouche. In the queen's label in the scene on the gold throne's backrest, *amun* is uniquely placed towards the bottom of the cartouche, followed by the hieroglyph of a squatting woman (to indicate that the person named is female), in order to fill the space originally occupied by *pa aten*. The couple's *aten* names on the stiles and center brace behind the backrest were probably left untouched because they would not normally have been 'on view'. The inlaid cartouche naming the king Tutankhaten on the outside of the right armrest was also left unaltered (Figure 7), perhaps because the artisans given the job of up-dating the cartouches decided not to bother cutting new inlays.

By contrast to the gold throne's altered cartouches, what may look like alterations to the figures and the scene on the backrest are explicable as ancient repairs to damage incurred during use. Signs of wear and tear are obvious; clearly the throne was not made for a single occasion such as the coronation. Eighteenth-Dynasty royal and non-royal reliefs and paintings document the pharaoh's ownership of at least two armchairs like the gold throne; in the depictions, they are shown on the deck of the royal barge or mounted on platforms as carrying chairs. But because the gold throne lacks the customary knee braces to reinforce the legs, it was not very sturdy and unsuitable for either purpose. Perhaps the most likely context for its use was at the feasts that were notable features of life at court. The scene on the backrest that seems to depict the queen offering her husband something to drink in a goblet may have made of the throne an effective substitute for the royal couple in their absence on such occasions.

Bows, harness ornaments, and scribal equipment

Other items from Tutankhamun's tomb inscribed with his original *nomen* include some ornamental gold appliqués, four bows, a scribe's palette, and two writing boards.[29]

The staff Obj. No. 227b has also been included in this list.[30] The *nomen* in both columns of text down the shaft now reads Tutankhamun. In Carter's hand-copy of these inscriptions he indicated that the later *nomen* replaced the earlier in one case and probably in the second as well. The association of this kind of staff with military activity is in perfect harmony with the epithets in the texts on it. They repeatedly praise the pharaoh's might and assert his prowess in subduing Egypt's enemies. Both columns of inscription start with the title 'perfect ruler,'[31] followed by the epithet describing the king as 'appearing in the White Crown', a usage typical for Akhenaten's texts. Another epithet compares the owner to Akhenaten's god, calling him 'Lord of Appearances like Aten'. The staff itself is similar in workmanship and material to the so-called bow of honor (Obj. No. 48h) from the tomb's Antechamber. Though not found together (the staff comes from the Treasury), the bow and the staff may have once formed a set. According to John R. Harris, the cartouche with the *prenomen* on the bow was altered not once but twice, first to read 'Ankhkheperure, beloved of Neferkheperure (=Akhenaten)' and then to Nebkheperure (Tutankhamun's *prenomen*). The staff, too, may well also have changed owners twice; the traces of *aten* in the cartouches with the altered *nomen* would then not have belonged to a writing of Tutankhaten at all.

Seventy-four embossed gold appliqués found with the chariots in the Antechamber of KV 62, just inside the entrance, were identified as having once decorated harness and other chariot equipment. Over half these ornaments bore the king's name. While some of these were inscribed with the *prenomen* alone, most showed a pair of cartouches; six of them (Obj. Nos 122xxx, -yyy, –zzz, -aaaa, -eeee, and –ffff) enclose the earlier *nomen*, Tutankhaten.

Nearly fifteen of more than 40 bows from the tomb are self-bows; the remainder are composite bows, made by layering wood, horn, and sinews. The four composite bows which bear cartouches naming Tutankhaten – Obj. Nos 48f, 48i (2), and 48j (1–2) – are not distinguished by size from the others – i.e., they are neither particularly small nor particularly suitable for a child's use. They were found in a bunch of 17 bows and 16 staves on a bed atop the lion-headed bier against the west wall of the Antechamber. Of the remaining 13 bows, five show Tutankhamun unaltered, while the inscription on one of them, the 'bow of honor' mentioned immediately above, apparently shows evidence of two alterations and thus two owners before it passed into Tutankhamun's hands.

The writing boards inscribed with the earlier *nomen* – both found among the objects on the floor of the Annexe – differ only minimally in size. Each is a piece of hard wood about 7 mm thick, covered with a layer of stucco over linen to provide a purchase for gilding – gold for Obj. No. 387 and silver for Obj. No. 398. Obviously a pair, they were probably intended for some ceremonial purpose. The same may be conjectured for the scribe's palette Obj. No. 271e (2), even if the pats of ink do show signs of use. It comes from a box in the Treasury which contained, among other things, a second palette, a holder for reed 'pens', and an instrument which has been described as a papyrus burnisher ever since Carter made that suggestion for its use. The inscription on the palette calls Tutankhaten 'beloved of Thoth [the god of writing], Lord of Sacred Writings'.[32] The text includes the king's Horus name alongside a pair of cartouches with the personal name Tutankhaten and the throne name (Figure 8). No example of a complete, five-part protocol has yet come to light in association with the original *nomen*, whereas there are many examples with the altered *nomen* Tutankhamun. It is possible,

Figure 8 Inscription on a gilded scribe's palette from the tomb of Tutankhamun, Obj. No. 271e (2); Egyptian Museum, Cairo, JE 62094.

though perhaps unlikely, that a complete protocol was formulated and proclaimed only with the change in the *nomen*.

The titulary

According to custom, a new king at his accession adopted a series of names, adding four elements to his personal name bestowed upon him at birth.[33] In general, the complete series of five names in a standardized sequence, each element introduced by a title, was not frequently employed in everyday contexts; the reigning king's *prenomen* alone was evidently considered adequate to identify him. Until now two of the standard elements of a royal titulary– the Nebty or Two-Ladies name and the Gold Horus name – are not found in association with the earlier *nomen* Tutankhaten.[34]

The standard translation of Tutankhaten – 'Living-image-of-Aten' – was suggested as long ago as 1877.[35] But this conventional rendering is not universally accepted by Egyptologists. Objections were raised, for example, in 1926 by Battiscombe Gunn, who argued that 'Living-image-of-Aten' did not accord with Akhenaten's theology. Gunn thought that calling the child 'the "living image" of the one Egyptian god who was studiously and completely shorn of any anthropomorphic associations . . . would have been utterly repugnant to Atenist ideas, as being not only blasphemous but ridiculous'.[36] Gunn proposed understanding *tut* not as a noun but as a verb with the meaning 'to be pleasing'; he then translated the name as a sentence: 'The-life-of-Aten-is-pleasing'.

The German Egyptologist Gerhard Fecht admitted that the standard translation 'Living-image-of-Aten' seems obvious, but he, too, thought it inappropriate to give a name to an infant that appeared to designate him king long before the fact. Furthermore, Fecht noted that texts of Akhenaten's reign use the noun *tit* for 'image', not *tut*. He, too, translated the name as a sentence, but with the verb *tut* meaning 'to be perfect/complete' and Aten as its subject: 'One-perfect-of-life-is-Aten'.[37] Fecht also remarked that the name's ambivalence, which must have been obvious to an educated ancient Egyptian (that is, one of the few who could read), was doubtless intentional. The unique writing of the *nomen* (Tut*ankhu*aten) on the Hermopolis block supports reading *ankh* as a verbal form and the conventional translation 'Living-image-of-Aten',[38] regardless of his parents' intention and what the populace at large may have made of the name.

A popular pastime among Egyptologists is interpreting a specific king's protocol – with the benefit of hindsight – as a program for his reign. However, our understanding of many terms employed is meager and the grammatical relationship between them problematic. This is nowhere more conspicuous than in the interpretation of throne names which in the New Kingdom regularly, though not exclusively, associated the king with the solar god Re. Like the *nomen*, the throne name was written in a cartouche. When the two names occur together, the *prenomen* takes precedence over the *nomen*. The title traditionally translated King of Upper and Lower Egypt introduces the *prenomen* whereas the *nomen* is preceded by the title Son of Re. Egyptologists cannot agree on whether a king's throne name refers to his relationship to the sun god or is a statement in sentence form about the sun god. Nor is there consensus concerning the meaning of the plural term *kheperu* which occurs not only in Tutankhaten's throne name Nebkheperure, but also in the throne names of several other Eighteenth-Dynasty rulers (Thutmose IV, Ay, and Horemhab among them). The simplest writing of the word *kheper* employs a single hieroglyph depicting a dung beetle, the insect intimately associated with ideas of regeneration and rebirth as expressed in Egyptian solar theology. The commonest translation proposed by specialists for the plural *kheperu* is 'manifestations', but this hardly brings us much closer to comprehending what it meant or implied for an Egyptian of Tutankhaten's era. The translation of Nebkheperure proposed by Ronald Leprohon as a partisan of the idea that the *prenomen* describes the king, not the sun god, is 'Possessor-of-the-manifestations-of-Re'.

Mesut is another word which Egyptologists translate as 'manifestations'; it occurs in Tutankhamun's Horus name, the initial element of the titulary.[39] Egypt's earliest kings are cited in contemporaneous documents only by their Horus names, associating them with the falcon god Horus. Until the introduction of a solar cult in the Second Dynasty, this stellar deity, manifest as a falcon soaring high above the earth, epitomized royal ideology. The Horus name is written inside a rectangle combining two views of a palace compound – the floor plan stood on end with the niched enclosure wall across the bottom (cf. Figure 8). A falcon wearing the Double Crown of Upper and Lower Egypt perches on top. Tutankhaten's Horus name *tut-mesut*, like the Horus names of other New Kingdom pharaohs, is prefaced by the epithet 'victorious bull'. Various translations of *tut-mesut* have been proposed. Despite the fact that *tut* is occasionally written in the king's Horus name simply with a hieroglyph depicting a statue, some grammarians translate it as a verbal form, rather than a noun. Suggestions as divergent as 'fitting-of-created-forms',[40] '(he) who unites the births',[41] and 'perfect of birth'[42] – to cite but a few – have been proposed; Carter and Mace used 'fair of births',[43] adopting Alan Gardiner's suggestion. But Leprohon proposes 'the (very) image of (re-)birth'.

As already noted, neither a Nebty name nor a Gold Horus name is associated with the king's *nomen* before it was altered to Tutankhamun. As a rule, both these elements are mentioned only in the context of the complete titulary, whether employed in a monumental inscription on a temple architrave or on a piece of furniture. The hieroglyphic group introducing a king's Nebty name depicts the tutelary goddesses of Upper and Lower Egypt as vulture and cobra; a falcon wearing the Double Crown and perching atop the sign for gold (a broad collar, its outer edge terminating in a row of teardrop-shaped beads) precedes the Gold Horus name. Far less common than the

Horus name, *nomen*, and *prenomen*, the Nebty and Gold Horus names show the most variation, and not only in Tutankhamun's case. In Leprohon's translation, the predominant version of the former describes Tutankhamun as 'Perfect-of-laws, who-has-quieted-the-Two-Lands [i.e. Egypt]' while the latter calls him 'Elevated-of-appearances, who-has-satisfied-the-gods'. Although neither is found with the earlier *nomen*, 'he who has satisfied the gods' does occur as an epithet describing Tutankhaten in the texts of the inlaid ebony throne. It is tempting to interpret the phrase as a reference to re-endowing the traditional cults, in the aftermath of Akhenaten's neglect, as recorded in the text of the Restoration Stela discussed in the following chapter.

When the decision was taken to sever the link between the new king and Akhenaten's god as expressed in the name Tutankhaten is not known. The lid of the cartouche-shaped box (Obj. No. 269) from the tomb with hieroglyphs made of painted ebony (Figure 9) shows a particularly attractive rendering of the altered *nomen* accompanied

Figure 9 Cartouche-shaped box from the tomb of Tutankhamun, Obj. No. 269; Egyptian Museum, Cairo, JE 61490.

by the king's standard epithet 'ruler of Upper Egyptian Heliopolis' (expressed by the three tall hieroglyphs grouped together at the bottom). This tag was introduced simultaneously with the change of name to honor the preeminent god of the traditional, pre-Amarna pantheon Amun. 'Upper Egyptian Heliopolis' refers to Amun's cult center at Thebes that bore the brunt of the iconoclastic phase of Akhenaten's reign. A few instances of the altered *nomen* without the epithet can be cited,[44] but until now there is not any certain example of it in a cartouche with Tutankhaten.[45]

The earliest precisely dated evidence for the altered *nomen* occurs in a graffito which an otherwise undocumented scribe named Tjai scribbled in ink on a wall when he visited the Step Pyramid complex of the Third Dynasty king Djoser at Saqqara, the necropolis of the old capital city Memphis.[46] Tjai left his mark on the second day of the fourth month of the summer season in the fourth year of Tutankhamun's reign. I suspect, however, that the name-change was effected much earlier, but for now this remains pure speculation.

Tutankhamun and the Restoration

The rehabilitation of the cult of Amun began before Tutankhaten came to the throne, as has been remarked in the earlier chapters of this book. But there is no denying that Tutankhamun's reign witnessed the completion of a multitude of projects that his predecessor(s) could not have hoped even to initiate, let alone realize, in the brief interval between Akhenaten's death and Tutankhaten's accession. For Tutankhamun's role in this process, Egyptologists regularly cite the inscription preserved on an impressive quartzite stela, 2.25 m tall, in the collection of the Egyptian Museum, Cairo (Figure 10). The text, which formally and irrevocably signaled the end of the Amarna Period, does not detail intentions but rather summarizes what had already been accomplished by the time it was formulated. In other words it does not announce the beginning of a program of restoration and renewal but rather states the claim for its successful completion.

The Restoration Stela

The stela[1] was discovered in the northeast corner of the Hypostyle Hall at Karnak Temple by the French archaeologist Georges Legrain in 1905. Two fragments of a second stela inscribed with the same text come from the Monthu Temple, located just outside Karnak's enclosure wall to the north. Legrain found one of them, shortly before he unearthed the complete stela;[2] the second fragment came from excavations conducted at the Monthu Temple in 1940.[3] It would not be at all surprising if additional stelas or fragments with essentially the same text were to surface one day elsewhere, such as in the environs of ancient Memphis.

On the virtually complete stela in Cairo, the text is written from left to right, reversing the normal orientation of Egyptian hieroglyphic inscriptions; this suggests that it represents one half of a pair. The text preserved on the fragments from the Monthu Temple is oriented from right to left, but nevertheless they are unlikely to derive from the presumed pendant of the complete stela, since the frieze of pinioned lapwings with human arms raised in adoration, below the bottom line of the text on the latter, does not occur on the fragments.

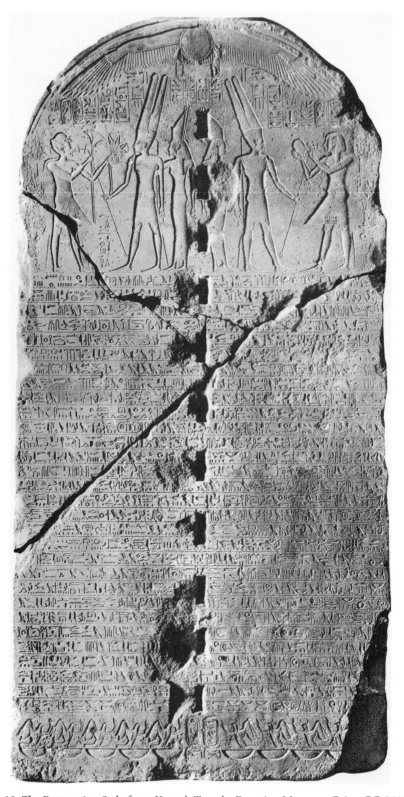

Figure 10 The Restoration Stela from Karnak Temple; Egyptian Museum, Cairo, CG 34183.

Friezes with the lapwing monogram were used as a dado ornament in those parts of New Kingdom temples to which access was not limited to a select few. While such friezes may be unusual in the design of stelas, one does occur on a stela of Amenhotep III[4] and on a stela set up by Horemhab as king in Amenhotep III's funerary temple on the west bank at Thebes[5] as well as on yet another large stela commissioned in Tutankhamun's name for Karnak but left unfinished at his death (see Chapter 5, pp. 74–5). Its use on these stelas suggests that access to them was comparatively unrestricted.[6] Those of Amenhotep III and Horemhab were discovered in secondary contexts, while the exact spot where Tutankhamun's unfinished stela stood at Karnak is not known. The complete Restoration Stela is quite likely to have been erected originally in front of Pylon III at Karnak Temple, nearby where it was discovered, accessible to passersby in Tutankhamun's day.

In the design of the Restoration Stela the lapwings pay homage to a pair of cartouches in the center of the frieze; originally, they enclosed Tutankhamun's throne and personal names. Like all the other cartouches on the stela, including those in the vertical column of text down both small sides, they were altered to name Horemhab, but the three remaining elements of Tutankhamun's complete titulary in the text were left untouched.

In the symmetrically organized composition of the lunette (Figure 11) Ankhesenamun stood behind Tutankhamun,[7] who presents offerings to Amun and Mut. All that is left today to document the queen's presence are the tips of the double plumes from her headdress at the left edge of the lunette, traces of her titles beginning 'Great Royal Wife, Mistress [of the Two Lands]', and the very bottom of the cartouche (without any

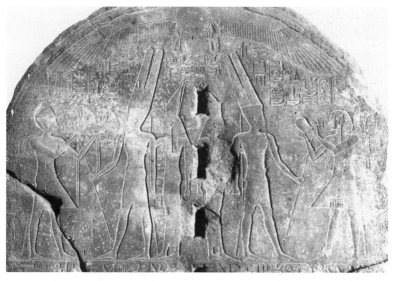

Figure 11 Lunette of the Restoration Stela from Karnak Temple; Egyptian Museum, Cairo, CG 34183.

hieroglyphs) which once identified her, located to the left of the Blue Crown's streamers lying over Tutankhamun's shoulder (Plate VI). Perhaps Ankhesenamun once assisted her spouse by shaking a sistrum, like Queen Tiye in the company of Amenhotep III.[8] A traditional prophylactic inscription, intended to protect the king from harm approaching him from behind, was cut into a layer of plaster applied over the pitted surface where the queen once stood. The standard formula probably replaced the queen's figure at the same time the text below was usurped in Horemhab's favor.

Both depictions in the lunette of Amun-Re, King of the Gods, and Mut, Mistress of Isheru, as the labels style the couple, are conventional; he wears his characteristic crown with double plumes and a long, stiff, pendant streamer hanging down his back; she, the Double Crown with uraeus atop a tripartite wig. Mut embraces Amun with one arm, and in the other hand she holds the sign of life (*ankh*). Amun, too, grasps an *ankh*; another is attached to the end of a long *was*-scepter that he extends to Tutankhamun's nose, just as he had to other kings as early as the Middle Kingdom. In contrast to the figures of the gods, those of the king are not identical. To the left he wears the Blue Crown while proffering bouquets and to the right, the royal *nemes* head-cloth, as he elevates a libation vessel.

Marc Gabolde's proposal that two different sculptors were responsible for carving the figural decoration of the lunette is persuasive. The right-hand half was never given the finishing touches evident at the left.[9] The proportions of the figures have nothing in common with the art of the Amarna Period, unlike those in the lunette of the small stela in Berlin (cf. Figure 5); rather, the style is typical for the reign of Tutankhamun as epitomized in the reliefs of the Colonnade Hall of Luxor Temple (cf. Plate XVII) which cannot have been carved early in the reign.

All that remains of the date that introduced the text is 'fourth month of the inundation season, day 19'; the regnal year is lost. In the usurped cartouches that now read 'Horemhab, beloved of Amun', the god's name was taken over from the writing of Tutankhamun. In other words, the stela was carved after the name change from Tutankhaten to Tutanhamun,[10] but whenever that may have been before his fourth regnal year is not known. To a certain extent, the date mentioned on the stela is irrelevant, since it may well have been retrospective.

In the introductory lines of the text, Tutankhamun's complete titulary is augmented by a variety of epithets associating him with a number of traditional deities. Commenting on gender aspects of the text, John Baines terms the mention of goddesses alongside gods a 'crucial feature' of the inscription.[11] In this context, a reference to a passage in the text of Akhenaten's 'Earlier Proclamation', recorded on boundary stelas at Tell el-Amarna, would have been relevant: in it Akhenaten claims that the site he chose for founding a new capital in Middle Egypt 'did not belong to a god or a goddess ... to a male ruler or to a female ruler'.[12]

The Restoration Stela inscription properly speaking begins with a characterization of the state of the country at Tutankhamun's accession:

> . . . the temples and cities of the gods and goddesses, starting from Elephantine [as far] as the Delta marshes . . . were fallen into decay and their shrines were fallen into ruin, having become mere mounds overgrown with grass. Their sanctuaries were like something that had not come into being and the buildings were a footpath – for the land was in rack and ruin. The gods were ignoring this land; if an army [was] sent to Djahy to broaden the boundaries of Egypt, no success of theirs came to pass; if one prayed to a god, to ask something from him, he did not come at all; and if one beseeched any goddess in the same way, she did not come at all. Their hearts were weak because of their bodies, and they destroyed what was made.[13]

Legrain presumed this portion of the text made specific reference to the effects of Akhenaten's 'revolution' on the cults of the traditional gods, an interpretation which has held down to the present. In the mid-nineteenth century the Prussian expedition to Egypt and Nubia under the direction of Carl Richard Lepsius copied another post-Amarna Period text with a similar passage. Carved on the wall of a rock-cut temple at Akhmim, it credits Tutankhamun's successor King Ay with the intent to restore a temple of the local god Min which had fallen into ruin.[14] Horemhab, too, claimed in his coronation inscription to commission new statues and renew 'wrecked' sanctuaries.[15] Skepticism is not out of place, when it comes to understanding these texts to refer specifically to the consequences of Akhenaten's policies, since throughout Egyptian history a new king was customarily credited with reestablishing order as it had obtained in earlier times. Detlef Franke traced this genre back many generations to before the foundation of the Middle Kingdom.[16]

Even if the mention of neglect leading to 'decay' and 'ruin' be understood as an allusion to the years Akhenaten occupied the throne, an interpretation of the last sentence cited above as a reference to the images of the gods, 'defiled during the Heresy'[17] goes too far. Certainly revenues were diverted from the income of the temples of other gods to Aten's cult,[18] but, as has been clear for some time, Akhenaten did not order the closure of the temples of all traditional deities nor were representations of them along with their names attacked throughout Egypt.[19] Outside the Theban region, active persecution was directed almost exclusively towards specifically Theban gods – Amun and Mut above all, but Monthu as well, if less consistently.[20] At Thebes other gods suffered because their cults were practiced there in conjunction with the worship of Amun. The policy of restoration, as far as it can be traced outside Thebes, amounted essentially to re-carving Amun's name where it had been hacked out under Akhenaten, often in the personal names of earlier kings, and restoring the god's desecrated figure. That the text of the Restoration Stela affords Amun pride of place reflects the necessity to restore him to the preeminent position he had enjoyed prior to Akhenaten's reign precisely because attacks had centered on his cult.

The only other god specifically mentioned by name in the body of the text on the Restoration Stela as a beneficiary of the king's largesse is Ptah, the creator god and patron of artisans. Both epithets applied to him – South-of-his-wall and Lord of Ankhtawi – refer to Memphis where his cult was centered. Ptah's presence, in contrast to any other god besides Amun, is explained by another passage: when Tutankhamun determined to effect 'benefactions for his father Amun', he was residing in a palace founded by Thutmose I at Memphis. It was only natural then, that the chief god of Memphis should be cited alongside Amun as a recipient of the king's favor,[21] even if the benefactions allotted him were not so grand as those for the King of the Gods – Ptah's new processional bark would have only eleven carrying poles, by contrast to thirteen for Amun's.

According to the text of the stela, electrum, embellished with lapis lazuli, turquoise, and 'every [other] precious stone', was used to fashion images of Amun and Ptah, as well as those of other, unspecified gods. Sanctuaries were built anew and endowed to guarantee the supply of offerings for the daily ritual, activities which were typically mentioned in this genre.[22] The king also asserted that he ensured the smooth functioning of the cult by appointing priests, by sending 'maidservants of the palace' to be temple singers and dancers, and by providing slaves 'from the tribute of His Person's capturing'[23] for the workshops attached to the temple. These last have been called 'prisoners of war' resulting from 'Tutankhamun's military activities or at least those of his chief generals'.[24] It is not necessary, however, to interpret this passage literally. Amenhotep III, whose reign is known to have witnessed only a single military campaign (in Nubia), made the similar claim of assigning 'children of the chiefs of every foreign country out of plunder of His Majesty' to work in his funerary temple.[25] It would seem that such wording is another stock phrase.

The text of Tutankhamun's Restoration Stela does not specifically mention restoring monuments as expressed by the special term *semawy-menu*. There are not many inscriptions naming him which employ this phrase; in fact, it became common only in the reign of Seti I, the second pharaoh of Dynasty XIX. No evidence has yet come to light for re-carving figures or inscriptions damaged during Akhenaten's reign dating before the alteration of the *nomen* to Tutankhamun. The subject of the remainder of this chapter is such restoration work properly speaking which can be confidently attributed to Tutankhamun's reign.

All but one of the comparatively few inscriptions employing the phrase *semawy-menu* which ascribe such activity to Tutankhamun's order are found in Theban temples. Other restoration work has been associated with the king on the basis of style, but Egyptologists are often unwilling to accept attributions based on stylistic criteria. Reliefs commissioned by Ay, and by Horemhab during the earlier years of his reign, can indeed sometimes be difficult to distinguish stylistically from work produced in the mature style of Tutankhamun's later years, just as it is not possible in many cases to separate statues of Amun made under Tutankhamun from those commissioned by his immediate successors. There are, however, a number of restored relief representations of Amun attributed in inscriptions alongside them to Horemhab or Seti I, which reveal modifications of an *earlier* phase of restoration (cf. Plate VIII). Examples are not rare, but only recently have they attracted the attention of Egyptologists. Peter J. Brand has studied this phenomenon for which he employs the term secondary restoration.[26] Brand has convincingly argued that Tutankhamun must be the king responsible for the initial work of restoration which was subjected to alteration mandated by Horemhab or Seti I. Gabolde suggests that alterations of this kind commissioned by Horemhab could have been intended to justify his usurpation of the texts naming Tutankhamun.[27] As for Seti I, Brand theorizes in his study that the king had the faces of human-headed deities in particular re-cut, so that they no longer reproduced the official likeness of Tutankhamun.

There is only one inscription from outside the Theban area which specifically attributes restorations to Tutankhamun by name. It shows that such work of restoration during the king's reign extended far to the south, beyond the southern border of pharaonic Egypt.

Restoration at Jebel Barkal?

During the later Eighteenth Dynasty, Egypt's hegemony over the Upper Nile Valley was extensive. The viceroy charged with administering this vast territory bore the title King's Son of Kush, although he was not related by blood to Pharaoh. The viceroy's remit stretched from the Fourth Cataract and the site of Jebel Barkal, which Egyptians had occupied since the time of Thutmose III at the latest, downriver to Hierakonpolis, well inside the traditional southern border at Aswan, probably so as to include the gold mines of Upper Egypt along with those in Nubia.[28] Tutankhamun's Nubian viceroy Huy is well known, thanks above all to his tomb at Western Thebes with its colorful paintings (see Chapter 5, p. 72). Personnel involved with the administration of Nubia at the time – Egyptianized Nubians as well as Egyptians – are depicted and named in those paintings.[29]

At Jebel Barkal the Amarna Period per se is evidenced by attacks on the name of Amun in earlier Eighteenth-Dynasty texts and by a considerable number of so-called *talatat* – small blocks approximately 52 cm long, 26 cm wide, and 23 cm thick – found reused in later structures. (*Talatat* are diagnostic of Akhenaten's building projects at Thebes and Tell el-Amarna. The format was introduced in the interest of expediting Akhenaten's ambitious construction program; a single workman could handle such a small, comparatively lightweight block alone.) Possibly restoration work was begun under Tutankhamun, since towards the end of 2013, some decorated *talatat* came to light that had been reused to build a small chapel erected by Huy at Jebel Barkal.[30]

The Soleb lions

One of a pair of lions discovered at Jebel Barkal bears Tutankhamun's name, but another inscription on it and on its mate make it clear that they arrived at the site only centuries after the king's death. The two statues depicting somewhat over life-sized recumbent lions were transported to Jebel Barkal by a third-century BC ruler of the Kingdom of Napata – whether from Amenhotep III's temple at Soleb further north below the Third Cataract, where they stood originally, or from some intermediary location is not known. In the nineteenth century, the lions ended their peregrinations in London, when Lord Prudhoe, Fourth Duke of Northumberland, presented them to the British Museum in 1835.[31]

In conception, scale, style, and workmanship, they resemble each other so closely that there can be no doubt that they were commissioned simultaneously. An inscription carved on the chest of one lion claims that a king whose name was read initially as Ay, Tutankhamun's successor, arranged for its transport and installation at Soleb. (The other had apparently reached its intended destination during Amenhotep III's lifetime.) But according to Marc Gabolde's reading of the cartouche it seems that it was not King Ay after all but rather Akhenaten, when he was still called Amenhotep, who claimed responsibility in the inscription for the lion's transport to Soleb.[32] It has long been clear that Akhenaten worked in the temple of his father at Soleb, inserting himself into the decoration, but William J. Murnane, just before his untimely death in 1999, submitted an article providing evidence for dating the heretic pharaoh's initial activity at Soleb to the very beginning of his reign, as Amenhotep IV.[33] Subsequently the cartouches with the personal name Amenhotep were altered to read Akhenaten; after his death they were altered yet again, back to Amenhotep.

One of the rare *semawy-menu* inscriptions naming Tutankhamun is cut on the base of the same lion. (The text was often cited in the past, because it calls Amenhotep III Tutankhamun's father.) In the inscription, the lion is described as 'made' by Tutankhamun for Amun-Re, Lord of the Thrones of the Two Lands; Atum, Lord of Heliopolis; and Iah, the moon god incarnate in the lion, with whom Amenhotep III was identified at Soleb.[34] Given this *semawy-menu* text with its explicit attribution of restoration work to Tutankhamun and his well-documented interest in associating himself with his illustrious ancestor, it is certainly within the realm of probability that the restorations of Amun's figures in the reliefs and the re-carving of the texts in evidence at Soleb were done at his command. This work included the restoration of Amenhotep III's personal name in the cartouches which Akhenaten had ordered re-cut to duplicate the inoffensive (in his view) throne name of his father (Nebmaatre).

Amada

About 120 km downstream from Egypt's contemporary southern border with Sudan lies the site of Amada. In a temple erected there by Thutmose III and Amenhotep II, Amun-Re was worshipped alongside the solar deity Re-Horakhty. In the reliefs of the temple this god is depicted as a falcon-headed man; in the early years of Akhenaten's reign, he revered the god in this guise. Brand suggests that Tutankhamun could have ordered restoration work on the figures of Amun here,[35] but no text exists to substantiate this idea, nor does the style of the poorly preserved reliefs support attribution to the immediate post-Amarna Period. In fact, the authors of the facsimile edition of the decoration remarked upon the striking resemblance of the restored figures of Amun 'à celles de d'epoque éthiopienne' while noting that this dating is, of course, impossible.[36]

Elephantine

In the Temples of Khnum and Satet on Elephantine Island at Aswan, Egypt's southern border in antiquity, all the texts labeling restored figures of Amun attribute the work to Seti I.[37] The style of the restorations does not suggest they were carried out during Tutankhamun's reign.[38] In lieu of documentation for more than a passing interest on Tutankhamun's part in associating himself with the pharaohs who built and decorated these temples (Hatshepsut and Thutmose III), it remains doubtful that he would have felt compelled to commission restoration of the reliefs. Given the efforts made to emphasize Tutankhamun's association with Amenhotep III, a more likely remit for sculptors he might have sent to Elephantine would have been to repair damage to the decoration of a small temple Amenhotep III erected there to serve as a way station where the bark transporting the divine image might 'rest' in the course of religious processions. But the only records of the reliefs and inscriptions of this structure were made long ago, before its destruction in 1822, and they are totally inadequate to determine even the extent of damage Akhenaten's agents had inflicted, let alone to recognize restoration work. One of the early nineteenth-century copies of the decoration includes the cartouche of Seti I, but whether he was the originator of the restorations or simply staked a claim to the work of Tutankhamun is moot.[39]

Restoration of reliefs and inscriptions on the Nile's eastern bank at Thebes

Since monuments on both sides of the Nile at Thebes, in the city and in the necropoleis on the west bank, were those most closely associated in all of Egypt with the worship of Amun and so bore the brunt of Akhenaten's vendetta against the god, it is here that evidence for restoration should be most conspicuous. Royal sculpture and paintings were not the only targets. Statuary set up by private individuals in temples and the decoration of their tombs were also attacked. Tutankhamun's program of restoration focused on fulfilling his obligations to his heavenly father which were many, given the desecrations mandated by Akhenaten in several temples associated with the worship of Amun at Thebes. But re-carving Amun's name in inscriptions on officials' statues, like re-carving and repainting his images and name in non-royal tombs, was left up to the private initiative of the families involved.[40]

Karnak Temple

Damaged scenes and texts located along the routes which processions would take through Karnak Temple, rather than those in less accessible areas, were obviously a priority when the crews charged with repairing damage perpetrated by Akhenaten's agents started to work.

At Tutankhamun's accession, the gateway now numbered Pylon III provided the main entrance on the east–west axis to the Karnak precinct from the Nile. More than thirty years ago Bill Murnane identified Tutankhamun as the king who had inserted small-scaled figures of himself into the scene on the east face of the Third Pylon's north wing (Plate VII).[41] The complete relief shows a monumental divine bark; symmetrical scenes depict Amenhotep III on deck presenting offerings to Amun inside his shrine. Tutankhamun added small-scaled figures of himself behind Amenhotep III, assisting him at the ceremonies. Murnane convincingly argued that Horemhab was responsible for the subsequent erasure of the little pharaohs. Tutankhamun's hand, or rather those of sculptors dispatched in his name, has been recognized in the series of vignettes depicting Amenhotep III worshipping Amun which decorate the hull of the god's boat. Brand suggests that each tableau is entirely new, carved to replace wholesale a damaged scene.[42] This, too, will have been at Tutankhamun's initiative. The figures of Amun, but not those of Amenhotep III, have been subjected to secondary restoration, with King Horemhab again the likely culprit. (Tutankhamun's own project here, by contrast to restoration work carried out in his name, is discussed in Chapter 5, pp. 75–6.)

Three of the few *semawy-menu* inscriptions naming Tutankhamun accompany depictions of Thutmose III before Amun and Mut on the eastern face of the pylon counted today as the sixth.[43] In Tutankhamun's time this pylon was the fourth gateway on the east–west axis of the temple through which processions approached the sanctuary, the Holy-of-Holies, beyond. The reliefs flanking the doorway through the pylon show Amun holding Thutmose's hand while proffering an *ankh*-sign to his nose (Plate VIII). Here the figure of the god hacked out by Akhenaten's agents was initially re-carved, as in several other scenes both at Karnak and elsewhere at Thebes, somewhat smaller than the king shown opposite him in the scene. Shortly after the work was completed, most probably at the same time the texts naming Tutankhamun were altered to credit Horemhab with the restorations, the figures of Amun were slightly enlarged.

Brand has identified a number of other secondary restorations along the east–west processional axis of the temple, including perhaps even the restoration of figures of deities in the decoration of Hatshepsut's obelisks which inscriptions claim for Seti I.[44]

At Tutankhamun's accession, the entrance to Karnak from the south was a construction site where the pylon that Amenhotep III had begun to build had reached only eight courses when his death halted the work.[45] Processions approaching the temple from the precinct of the goddess Mut to the south would have entered Karnak through the gateway known today as Pylon VIII. We are again indebted to Bill Murnane for pointing out the presence of Tutankhamun's throne name among the restorations of the decoration of Amun's bark here.[46] First Horemhab, then Seti I reworked the scenes, each replacing Tutankhamun's name with his own.

An inscription on two blocks from the doorway of a granary styled 'Amun-rich-in-provisions' also names Tutankhamun as the king responsible for restoring it.[47] The structure had been erected by Amenhotep III, but exactly where within the Karnak precinct it originally stood is not known, because it was dismantled and the blocks were used during Horemhab's reign to rebuild a chapel of Amenhotep II between Pylons IX and X, in proximity to the Sacred Lake. This was the sector of the precinct where offerings were prepared and consecrated; Tutankhamun himself commissioned reliefs honoring deities associated with provisioning on a wall in the same general area (see Chapter 5, p. 74).

When Horemhab became king, he devoted attention to this part of the temple, erecting the Ninth Pylon and decorating the Tenth, along with the interior surface of the east wall between them where he relocated Amenhotep II's structure.[48] Horemhab will have been responsible for tearing down Amenhotep III's granary. Tutankhamun's inscription claiming responsibility for the restoration preserves evidence that Horemhab's original intention was not to demolish the structure but simply to alter the texts so that he might take credit for the work: the cartouche that once encircled Tutankhamun's throne name Nebkheperure was smoothed down, preparing the surface for re-inscribing. But before this was done, the decision was taken to dismantle the building instead.[49]

Another storage facility for grain erected by Amenhotep III apparently stood outside the temple precinct. The plan of the mud-brick structure included three monumental sandstone gateways decorated with painted reliefs. Many of them ended up in the Second Pylon, commissioned by King Horemhab. Suzanne Bickel has recorded more than fifty blocks from the gateways so far; doubtless others remain lodged inside the pylon.[50] Although the function as well as the scale and location of this granary differed from 'Amun-rich-in-provisions', contemporaneous texts suggest that the administration of institutions like these was closely related.

The reliefs of the three gateways exemplify the 'baroque' style of Amenhotep III's reign. The decorative program included standard scenes depicting the king before Amun; kneeling fecundity figures proffering trays of provisions filled the dado. During the iconoclastic phase of Akhenaten's reign, his workmen attacked not only the representations of Amun but fecundity figures as well, possibly, as Bickel has suggested to me, to deprive Amun's cult of the abundant provisions which the images were intended to ensure in perpetuity.[51] In the aftermath of Akhenaten's reign they, too, were restored. It is easy to distinguish the restorations ordered by Tutankhamun from the bold relief employed for the original decoration by Amenhotep III's sculptors (Figure 12). Because the work of repair was executed in the fine low relief distinctive of Tutankhamun's reign, they can be confidently assigned to his initiative, even if no *semawy-menu* text naming him has yet come to light on them.

Figure 12 Amenhotep III (right) worshipping Amun (restored, at the left); relief from a granary at Karnak Temple.

One more monument bearing Tutankhamun's name must be briefly considered before moving on to the evidence of 'renewals' during his reign at Luxor Temple. The upper part of a stela found at Karnak shows Tutankhamun presenting a tall sheaf of flowers and papyrus stalks to Amun, Mut, and Senwosret I, second king of Dynasty XII.[52] The building activity of this Middle Kingdom ruler at Karnak Temple is amply documented. On the stela, he is depicted as a New Kingdom pharaoh; neither the Blue Crown Senwosret I wears, nor the stylishly pleated kilt, draped to mid-calf at the back, was known in his day. Very little remains of the text once inscribed below the lunette with the figures, but enough of the first line is preserved to show that it began with Tutankhamun's Horus name. When Otto Schaden commented on the piece he noted that the text 'makes reference to "renewals"'.[53] In the interim Nozomu Kawai has studied the stela; he intends to publish a facsimile drawing and a translation of the inscription with commentary.

Luxor Temple

Secondary restorations are also in evidence at Luxor Temple, where Amenhotep III's reign had witnessed construction extending over several years. The initial restoration work of the post-Amarna Period was commissioned by Tutankhamun,[54] perhaps at the same time his sculptors began carving reliefs in the monumental Colonnade Hall left undecorated at Amenhotep III's death (see Chapter 5, pp. 78–9), in yet another effort to associate himself with that king. In the so-called Solar Court of Luxor Temple and in the hypostyle beyond, Tutankhamun's restorations were 'revised' by Seti I, who added his own *semawy-menu* texts.[55]

On the west bank at Thebes, Tutankhamun's restoration work could be expected not only at the funerary temple of Amenhotep III, but at Deir el-Bahri and Medinet Habu, two sites intimately associated with processions mounted on the occasion of popular festivals when Amun paid an annual visit to the Theban necropolis.

The funerary temple of Amenhotep III

The only *semawy-menu* texts naming Tutankhamun recorded so far at Western Thebes are found on reliefs from the funerary temple of Amenhotep III. This immense complex stood on the flood plain at the foot of the western mountains. Nowadays the imposing Colossi of Memnon depicting the enthroned pharaoh which fronted the temple in antiquity are the most conspicuous colossal statues on the west bank at Thebes. Scientific exploration of the site now known as Kom el-Heitan, above all by the mission under the direction of Hourig Sourouzian, continues to produce discoveries of major significance for the history of Amenhotep III's reign.

At some point, perhaps not long after Akhenaten had begun to reside at Tell el-Amarna, he transferred the mortuary cult of his deceased father to the new capital; offering rituals to insure Amenhotep III's continued existence in the Hereafter were presumably suspended in the temple that he had built for the purpose at Western Thebes. The artisans sent to obliterate the name and figure of Amun entered it and proceeded to do their work; evidence for their thoroughness is preserved, even in the label identifying the king's mother in the composition of the Colossi of Memnon where a small-scaled figure of her stood beside his left calf. Mut, the name of Amun's consort, was one element of the queen's name Mutemwiya. The hieroglyphs spelling Mut in Mutemwiya were hacked out during Akhenaten's reign – and subsequently restored in the post-Amarna Period.[56]

In view of Tutankhamun's solicitous attention to the monuments of Amenhotep III on the east bank of the Nile at Karnak and Luxor Temples, it was to be expected that he ordered restorations in Amenhotep III's funerary temple, given its essential role in providing for his forbearer's continued existence in the afterlife. A hint in this direction is provided by the fragment of a small stela in New York.[57] The titles of Userhat, the stela's owner who is depicted on the stela kneeling with his wife in prayer, link the mortuary cult of Amenhotep III with Tutankhamun's. Would it not be natural to suppose that Tutankhamun ordered restoration of the reliefs in the temple to provide an appropriate setting for the rituals on Amenhotep III's behalf?

Excavations by the Swiss Institute at the nearby funerary temple of King Merenptah, son and successor of Ramesses the Great, brought many blocks to light which came originally from the north entrance to the precinct of Amenhotep III's temple. They had been appropriated for reuse in the foundations of Merenptah's structure less than 150 years after Amenhotep III's death.[58] The reliefs on them show reinstated figures of Amun and re-carved inscriptions naming him. Here, too, 'secondary restorers' were also at work, altering the proportions of the figures; the *semawy-menu* texts now cite Seti I as the king who commissioned the initial restorations, but the traces of Tutankhamun's name preserved in the cartouches assert his claim to them.[59]

Deir el-Bahri

The Deir el-Bahri bay was the principal goal of the procession when Amun left Karnak, crossing the Nile to visit the Theban necropolis for the annual Beautiful Festival of the Valley. As long ago as the beginning of the last century it could have been suspected that Tutankhamun's reign witnessed activity here, for it was in the temple of the

Eleventh Dynasty king Nebhepetre-Mentuhotep at Deir el-Bahri that Edouard Naville discovered the fragment of Userhat's stela mentioned immediately above that links the funerary cults of Amenhotep III and Tutankhamun. *Semawy-menu* texts in the Dynasty XI temple and in the adjacent temple of Queen Hatshepsut name Horemhab and Ramesses II.[60]

Despite the absence of any inscriptional evidence for Tutankhamun at Deir el-Bahri, it is likely that he was the first pharaoh to commission restoration work there. The cartouches incorporated in the decoration of Amun's boat in the main sanctuary of Hatshepsut's temple now cite King Horemhab, but just as in the depiction of the god's boat on the Eighth Pylon at Karnak Temple, it is clear that his name replaces another. Tutankhamun is Horemhab's far more likely predecessor here than Ay.[61] Similarly the fragmentary reliefs recovered from Thutmose III's temple at Deir el-Bahri also feature Horemhab's cartouches in the decoration of Amun's boat; these too may well prove to be secondary, especially since traces of restorations earlier than those of Horemhab have been identified by the painstaking research of the Polish archaeologists who are preparing the reliefs for publication.[62]

Medinet Habu

The last site on the west bank where Tutankhamun is likely to have commissioned restorations is the Eighteenth-Dynasty temple at Medinet Habu. Construction and decoration of this structure, which was second in importance only to Deir el-Bahri when it came to Amun's cult on the west bank at Thebes, is associated with both Hatshepsut and Thutmose III. The work at the temple by the team of epigraphers and draftsmen from the Epigraphic Survey of the University of Chicago's Oriental Institute has not yet found evidence of secondary restorations, nor any trace of Tutankhamun's name in the *semawy-menu* texts. The cartouche in the restoration text on the façade was re-carved, apparently in the Late Period, to enclose Thutmose III's throne name, leaving no trace of the original hieroglyphs. The only late Eighteenth-Dynasty *semawy-menu* inscription in the temple names King Horemhab. If Tutankhamun's name was replaced here, then its erasure was done very carefully indeed.[63]

Restoration work in the north

No inscription claiming that Tutankhamun was the ruler responsible for restoration work has been found north of the Thebaid. At Hermopolis, Amenhotep III had erected colossal statues of baboons, incarnations of Thoth, god of writing and patron of scribes, who was at home there. Under Akhenaten, Amun's name in the cartouches of his father was attacked. Inscriptions preserved on the bases of two of these colossi name Ay as the pharaoh who restored them.[64] Beginning in the reign of Horemhab at the latest, blocks from Akhenaten's temples and palaces at Tell el-Amarna were transported the short distance to Hermopolis for reuse in construction work at Thoth's temple. (The historical importance of some of these reused blocks was considered in Chapter 1, pp. 1–5, 12–13.)

Further north, Seti I is known to have restored reliefs and inscriptions on architectural elements and stelas, but such monuments are scarce.[65] No unequivocal evidence suggests that this work is secondary nor that an earlier ruler was responsible for any initial restoration of Amarna-Period desecration.

The ancient city of Memphis is another place where restoration work by Tutankhamun could be expected, and not just because he was residing there when the text of the Restoration Stela was promulgated. Amenhotep III is known to have undertaken significant construction at Memphis.[66] 'Neb-maat-Re[Amenhotep III's praenomen]-united-with-Ptah', the temple he built at Memphis for Ptah, must have been very impressive indeed, judging by the quantity of preserved inscriptional evidence relating to the precinct and its administration.[67] Thanks, however, to the construction activity of later kings (Ramesses II in particular), few blocks from Amenhotep III's structures have been recovered at Memphis. Colossal statues of Ptah, which now stand in the foyer of Cairo's Egyptian Museum, belonged to the original sculptural program of the temple; these were reworked by Ramesses II.[68] Crisply carved reliefs on quartzite blocks depict Amenhotep III worshipping Ptah and his consort, the lion-headed goddess Sakhmet. The only purposeful damage to the reliefs that can be attributed to Akhenaten is the erasure of the hieroglyphs reading Amun from the cartouche with his father's personal name. Ray Johnson is preparing a study of the fragments which can still be found in the vicinity of the Ptah Temple, along with blocks which were removed long ago from the site.[69] No inscription has yet been found identifying the king among Akhenaten's successors who was responsible for restoring Amenhotep III's cartouche. While Tutankhamun seems likely, evidence in support of this supposition has not surfaced yet.

Some relief-decorated blocks from Heliopolis, just to the north of modern Cairo, present a conundrum. Since time immemorial, Heliopolis was the center of Egypt's solar religion. Early on, Egyptologists sought the source of Akhenaten's theology in Heliopolis, even going so far as to suggest that he was 'educated' by priests of Re and Atum, the solar deities worshipped there. But this idea is nowadays discounted.[70] According to the text on the boundary stelas of Tell el-Amarna proclaiming its foundation, Akhenaten intended to provide a tomb at his new capital city for the sacred Mnevis bull, an animal closely associated with the solar cult at Heliopolis.[71] At Heliopolis blocks inscribed for Tutankhamun were discovered reused in a tomb which was commissioned by Ramesses II for the burial of one such sacred bull. Today they are kept in storage at the Egyptian Museum in Cairo. Up until the present, they have not been illustrated; discussion of them has been based entirely on the descriptions included in Georges Daressy's initial publication of nearly a century ago.[72]

The decoration of the blocks included at least two registers of enthroned gods and larger-scaled fecundity figures bearing offerings. According to Daressy, a depiction of Amun and one of Khonsu, son of Amun and Mut, were attacked. His commentary on the inscriptions describes Horemhab's usurpation of Tutankhamun's cartouches; the presence of the latter's Horus name in pristine condition is not inconsistent with Horemhab's treatment of Tutankhamun's monuments elsewhere. Ay's name as king is supposedly also present on the blocks. This meager information has been tentatively interpreted as evidence for restoration work carried out during Tutankhamun's reign on a monument damaged by Akhenaten's agents,[73] even though Daressy makes no mention of any attempt to restore the figures. (Nor do the minimal remains of the texts cited in Daressy's account include any traces which might be restored to include the phrase *semawy-menu*.) Nozomu Kawai has located these blocks and examined them in detail.[74] He concludes that the decoration and texts do not provide evidence of restoration but document instead independent building activity at Heliopolis during Tutankhamun's reign, continued by Ay, and subsequently usurped by Horemhab.

Until now, the farthest to the north that restoration work of Tutankhamun's reign has been postulated is Tell el-Daba in the eastern Nile delta – the site of the capital of the Dynasty XV Hyksos pharaohs. A lintel found in the presumed precinct of the god Seth, 'great of strength', at Tell el-Daba bears a text with the cartouches of Horemhab. But his *nomen* and *prenomen* are palimpsest, leading Manfred Bietak to suggest they replaced Tutankhamun's names to document the latter's role in restoring Seth's temple after depredations of the Amarna Period.[75] Since, however, evidence is lacking for attacks on Seth and his cult during the Amarna Period, it is more probable that the lintel comes from new construction work at Tell el-Daba assignable to Tutankhamun's initiative.

Patricia Spencer has drawn my attention to Balamun, a site with a temple that might well have been in need of post-Amarna restorations. In later times it was of considerable importance for Amun's cult, but as at other sites in the delta, Late Period construction at Balamun obliterated all but minimal traces of earlier temples. Inscriptional evidence does survive, however, to document Amun's worship at Balamun in pre-Amarna New Kingdom times, and a statue of unknown provenance, depicting Neb-wa, first prophet of Amun 'residing in Balamun', is dated by Horemhab's *prenomen* on the standard the priest carries.[76] Furthermore, according to the text of a stela in Liverpool, Tutankhamun's treasurer Maya was ordered to (re)establish offerings for the gods from Elephantine in the south to Balamun in the Delta.[77]

Sculpture in the round restored during Tutankhamun's reign

Not a single statue depicting Amun, nor of his consorts Mut and Amunet, created before Akhenaten assumed the throne, survived his reign intact. All that remain are fragments, and only two of them preserve the god's physiognomy – both reflecting the official portrait of Amenhotep III.[78] A formidable task facing Tutankhamun was to replace the destroyed images that had once served as foci of the orthodox cult so that Amun with his consorts at his side might reclaim his rightful place as King of the Gods.

A few statues which depicted Amun with one of Akhenaten's predecessors could be repaired. One of them was an under life-sized triad carved from Egyptian alabaster showing Amun enthroned between a king and a queen whom the inscription on the base identify as Thutmose I and his wife Ahmose (Figure 13).[79] At the beginning of

Figure 13 Restored triad from the Karnak cachette depicting Amun seated between Thutmose I and Queen Ahmose; Egyptian Museum, Cairo, CG 42052.

the last century, the group was recovered from the so-called Karnak cachette, a pit in the floor of the courtyard between the wall enclosing the central structures of the temple on the east–west axis of the precinct, and Pylon VII. It contained some 700 stone statues in a variety of sizes, many in a deplorable condition, along with about 16,000 statuettes and other objects made of bronze. The pit was probably dug in the second half of the first century BC and filled with statuary cleared out of the crowded temple by the priesthood.[80]

The style of the torsos and heads of all three figures comprising this group of Amun, Thutmose I, and Queen Ahmose do not have anything in common with sculptures carved in the early Eighteenth Dynasty when Thutmose I ruled. In particular, the modeling of the eyes and mouths are closely paralleled by sculptures datable to Tutankhamun's reign, as Matthias Seidel pointed out. The god's head is noticeably larger than those of either the king or queen and his face is more carefully modeled. Clearly Amun was more important here than the royal couple. In fact, the torsos and heads of all three were carved in one piece with a tall back slab to replace this part of the group which had fallen victim to Akhenaten's iconoclasm. The veining of the stone of Amun's legs is different from the rest of the lower part of the group, showing that they, too, had to be replaced. The new elements were skillfully worked to fit the breaks, and plaster was used to camouflage the joins. But comparatively seldom did it prove possible to effect repairs of statues attacked at Akhenaten's orders; his minions were generally all too thorough, which made the commissioning of a wealth of new images mandatory.

4

Statues for Amun

During the post-Amarna Period, efforts to redress damage inflicted under Akhenaten included not only the restoration of reliefs and inscriptions but also the creation of new statues of Amun and his consorts to replace those destroyed. Well over fifty sculptures of Amun, some depicting him alone as a single figure and others showing him in the company of other deities and/or the king, are dated by an inscription, or datable on the basis of stylistic and/or iconographic criteria, to the post-Amarna Period.[1] At the conclusion of the last chapter, a triad which belongs to the latter genre was introduced as a comparatively rare example of a damaged sculpture which could be repaired. The youthful face of Amun in the center of the group and stylistic details, such as the so-called *sfumato* carving of the eyes, so typical of the Amarna Period, suggest that the restoration was commissioned earlier rather than later during Tutankhamun's reign.

The quartzite colossi of Amun and Amunet

A much more impressive triad which was attacked at Akhenaten's orders showed Thutmose III standing between Amun and his female counterpart Amunet, each embracing the king with one arm. Visitors to Karnak Temple can still see this monumental quartzite group, re-erected in the so-called Festival Hall of Thutmose III, beyond the central sanctuary. It was for this structure that Thutmose III initially commissioned the sculpture. The appallingly damaged condition of the gods' figures at either side of the king probably does not much differ from the appearance of the group in Tutankhamun's day. Restoration was clearly not feasible, although the god's name was re-inscribed in the epithet 'beloved of Amun-Re' on the king's belt buckle – remarkable in itself, given the sorry state of the group as a whole. New colossal sculptures had to be commissioned to replace the figures flanking Thutmose III.[2] These statues of Amun and Amunet (Plate IX) have also been re-erected at Karnak where visitors passing through the Sixth Pylon cannot miss them: they stand at the left in the vestibule in front of the significantly later granite sanctuary.

The inscription on the back pillar of the Amunet colossus describes the goddess as 'residing in Akhmenu', the name Thutmose III gave his Festival Hall at Karnak. This text makes it clear that the intended original destination of the statue was his building whereas the text on Amun's back pillar describes the god as residing less specifically in Karnak (*Ipet-sut*).

There can be no doubt that the statue of Amun was ordered and finished during Tutankhamun's reign because the first element of the king's titulary, his Horus name *tut-mesut*, is still in pristine condition at the very top of the back pillar. The names in the cartouches further down in the text on the back pillar have, however, been altered; they now name Horemhab the pharaoh 'beloved of Amun'. Enough traces of the original hieroglyphs, however, remain to show that they once spelled Tutankhamun's personal and throne names. It comes as no surprise that Amun's face (Figure 14a) resembles the official portrait of Tutankhamun, familiar from many other images of him. Unlike the god of the Old Testament who made man in his image, the Egyptians made their gods in the image of one particular man, viz. the ruling king.

Horemhab's name in the cartouche preserved in the inscription down the back pillar of the Amunet statue is also secondary. The traces of hieroglyphs beneath the palimpsest signs reading Horemhab have been interpreted to document not one but two successive usurpations. According to this theory, the initial usurper was Ay, who stood accused of replacing Tutankhamun's name with his own, before Horemhab had the cartouche altered in his own favor. But the traces in the cartouche once identified as belonging to hieroglyphs in Tutankhamun's name are illusory; the only name inscribed prior to usurpation by Horemhab was Ay's. Nor is there unequivocal evidence that Ay usurped monuments from Tutankhamun. Quite the contrary – Ay was interested in associating himself with his predecessor and was at pains to continue projects initiated by Tutankhamun.

Tutankhamun may well have commissioned the Amunet colossus simultaneously with that of Amun, to replace her figure along with Amun's in the triad made for Thutmose III's Festival Hall. But if so, only the Amun was finished when Tutankhamun's death intervened, leaving the responsibility for finishing the statue of the goddess to his successor. Or it may have been Ay himself who issued the order to create the Amunet colossus to complete the project. Regardless, the differences in the physiognomy and style of Amunet's face in comparison to Amun's are attributable to Ay's initiative (cf. Figure 14a–c). The goddess's face is rounder, and her eyes are further apart; her eyebrows were probably painted onto the brow bone whereas Amun's are 'plastic' – i.e. rendered in relief – and his eyes are emphasized with cosmetic strips, also in relief, which are absent from Amunet's face.

Most of the Red Crown of Lower Egypt, the single distinctive element of Amunet's iconography, is preserved in her colossus. Only the narrow vertical element which once projected upwards at the back of the Red Crown is lost, along with the top of the back pillar. The Red Crown distinguished her, as well as a few goddesses with a well-documented connection to Lower Egypt, from others who were consistently depicted with long tripartite wigs. The use of the Red Crown in Amunet's iconography may have

Figure 14 a – b   Head of the quartzite colossus of Amun, Karnak Temple.

c   Face of the quartzite colossus of Amunet, Karnak Temple.

resulted from its resemblance to Amun's special crown (see further, below), rather than on account of any association of her with Lower Egypt for which there is no evidence.

Amun with child-like physiognomy

The child-like physiognomy of four post-Amarna sculptures of Amun suggests that they were made during the earlier part of Tutankhamun's reign. Two are isolated heads that derive from statues depicting the god as a single figure, enthroned or striding, while the other two come from groups. The best known among the latter is a masterpiece – a small head of Tutankhamun made of fine-grained crystalline limestone which the

MMA acquired in 1950 (Plate X).[3] A nearly life-sized right hand preserved on the back of the crown worn by the king belongs to the figure of the god who completed the group.

The identification of the king as Tutankhamun has never been challenged since Ambrose Lansing first published the head, in 1951. Recently, the lower part of the group was located in a storage area at Karnak, providing confirmation of the previously presumed Karnak provenance of the sculpture.[4] The join of the head to the knees of the larger fragment from a seated male figure is minimal, but nevertheless conclusive: the composition once depicted the diminutive king standing in front of the larger figure.[5] The interpretation of such compositions is ambiguous; some Egyptologists describe the god as crowning the king, but the gesture could also be understood as simply expressing the idea that the sovereign is under the god's protection.

Owing to the destruction of Amun's statues under Akhenaten it is difficult to generalize about how popular compositions like this had been in earlier times. But there are representations of statues in relief and painting, as well as a few fragments from actual sculptures, which document the existence of groups made before the Amarna Period depicting Pharaoh before a god.[6] The king may kneel or stand, with his back to the god or facing him. In both the representations and the fragmentary surviving statues, the god is most often Amun, but Atum, the creator god of great antiquity at home in the north at Heliopolis, is also documented. Because a few statues of Atum were erected at Karnak, it is not absolutely certain, in the absence of an inscription, that the god with his hand on Tutankhamun's crown in the MMA sculpture was Amun, although he is certainly the more likely candidate.[7]

There can be no doubt that Amun is the god in the second group which was also made early in Tutankhamun's reign (Figure 15). It is a triad, and like the triad discussed at the conclusion of the last chapter, it was found in the Karnak 'cachette'.[8] But here the king, not the god, occupies the center of the group, with Amun to his left and a goddess at his right.

The sculpture fared better than many others removed from the 'cachette'; the upper part with the torsos and heads of the figures is comparatively well preserved, even if the goddess has lost her face. She cannot be Amunet, because the tripartite wig she wears does not belong to Amunet's iconography; the goddess must be Mut, Amun's better-known consort.

The iconography of Mut and Amun

The earliest statue of Mut which has come to light so far dates to the time just before the beginning of Dynasty XVIII. It showed her seated beside a king whose personal name (Sobekemsaef) was borne by more than one ruler, making it impossible to date the group precisely within the Second Intermediate Period. Only the lower half of the dyad with its inscribed base is preserved.

Figure 15 Triad from the Karnak cachette depicting Amun, Mut, and Tutankhamun enthroned; Egyptian Museum, Cairo, CG 42097.

Nor did many representations of Mut in relief survive Akhenaten's reign intact.[9] One of them shows her wearing the Double Crown, her standard headdress in post-Amarna times.[10] Perhaps the Double Crown was introduced into Mut's iconography to enhance her status in comparison to Amunet, who wears only the Red Crown of Lower Egypt.

Mut's attributes also include the venerable vulture headdress (absent from the figure in this triad from the 'cachette'), worn over a tripartite wig, and a uraeus. Here a sun disk nestled between cow horns sits atop her head. By the New Kingdom, the combination of cow horns and sun disk was generic headgear for goddesses in statuary as well as in relief. When an inscription is lacking, it can prove difficult if not impossible to identify a goddess depicted wearing this 'Hathor headdress'. A later statue, nowadays in Turin, which shows Mut wearing closely comparable headgear, depicts Ramesses II occupying the king's place between Amun and the goddess.[11] The only difference between the goddesses' attributes in the two sculptures is the presence in the Turin statue of a modius, interposed between the wig and the cow horns with sun disk.

Amun's headgear in the Tutankhamun triad belongs to the god's standard iconography: a crown topped by a pair of tall falcon feathers. The crown, like the White and Red Crowns of Upper and Lower Egypt worn by the pharaoh, fits snuggly across Amun's forehead and the nape of his neck, leaving the ears uncovered. It is shaped rather like an inverted truncated cone, with the circumference increasing and flaring a bit towards the top – which is not flat but ever so slightly domed. This crown is Amun's own, unlike the corselet he also wears here. In reliefs Amun shares this garment, which can be detailed with an imbricated pattern as in the triad, with a number of other male divinities, but few gods other than Amun are depicted wearing it in statuary. There is a stylized knot in the widely spaced straps on top of Amun's shoulders; such knots are frequently included in relief representations of the corselet, but in statuary this detail seems to be diagnostic for statues made in the post-Amarna Period.

Maya Müller suggests that representations of the corselet worn by Amun have influenced the way Mut's halter dress is rendered in statuary: the upper edge of the garment terminates just below her breasts, and the spacing of the straps leaves her nipples exposed.[12] The halter dress depicted like this is rarely attested in statuary for any goddess except Mut.

The king at the triad's center wears the royal *nemes* head-cloth with uraeus, surmounted by ram horns, sun disk, and a pair of ostrich feathers, flanked by rearing uraei. He is a bit shorter than Mut, who is herself slightly shorter than her spouse. These proportions reflect the natural difference in size between adult men and women on the one hand, and, on the other, a younger contemporary. It seems likely that Tutankhamun assumes here the role of the lunar god Khonsu, the divine couple's son, but it has also been suggested that the embrace exchanged between the king and the gods might express the reciprocity between cult and state, instead of a familial relationship.[13]

Typical of Egyptian art in general is the version of the king's physiognomy recognizable in the facial features of the god, even if Amun's face is more idealized and not as child-like as Tutankhamun's here (cf. the detail of the king's face in the group illustrated on the cover of this book). The statue, like the stela discussed in Chapter 2 (Figure 5) showing King Tutankh*aten* offering to Amun and Mut, was probably made early on, at a time when there may have been some uncertainty about Mut's iconography. The triad was carved from a reused block which had originally been decorated with fecundity figures in relief. Could it have been a 'rush' job, commissioned at the beginning of the reign in connection with the rehabilitation of Amun's cult at Karnak, perhaps even while the king was still known as Tutankhaten?

The only statue associating Tutankhamun with Amun which comes from outside the Theben region is also a triad. Hardly more than a large fragment, it comes from Faras. Presumably it once stood in the temple built by Tutankhamun there, far to the south in Nubia (see Chapter 5, p. 71), where it was excavated early in the twentieth century by an expedition from Oxford University.[14] The composition showed three approximately three-quarters life-sized enthroned figures with the king occupying the center. Tutankhamun's figure is the best preserved, but even that is little more than a faceless torso. Probably the *nemes* he wears was once surmounted by some additional headgear – for example, a pair of feathers or the Double Crown – to balance the tall double plumes of the god. By contrast to the triad from Karnak, the king here does not return the embrace of the deities who flank him. Rather, he holds a flail (which is nearly obliterated) and a crook in his right hand against his chest while the left rested on his lap. Even less remains of Amun to Tutankhamun's left, and only a hand on his left shoulder attests the original presence of a deity at his right. The lengthy text on the back slab alludes to the restoration, calling Tutankhamun beloved of 'Amun, Lord of the Thrones of the Two Lands, foremost [god] of Karnak, and of Mut, the Great, Mistress of Isheru', making it likely that she was depicted in the figure to the king's right.[15]

Exceptional statues depicting Amun

Two isolated heads depicting Amun are datable on account of their child-like physiognomy early in Tutankhamun's reign. One of them, now in the Luxor Museum (Figure 16), is only about half life-size and made of the same crystalline limestone as the head of Tutankhamun in New York.[16] It was excavated from the Temple of Monthu to the north of Karnak's enclosure wall. The provenance of the other head of Amun is not known; today it is in the collection of the Ny Carlsberg Glyptothek, Copenhagen.[17] Life-sized and carved from granodiorite, it is the only statue of Amun from the post-Amarna Period that had inlaid eyes. During the Eighteenth Dynasty, the use of inlaid eyes in sculpture seems to have been limited to statues of royalty and gods. The appreciation of the fine sculpture in Copenhagen is impaired by their loss at the hands of thieves in antiquity who pried them out of the sockets for the material of which they and their settings were made.

Amun as depicted in another sculpture commissioned by Tutankhamun has matured into a handsome teenager (Plate XI). Since the recovery of the large fragments of the statue from the Karnak 'cachette', it has been restored more than once. The restored section of the torso with arms is too long, as the back view of the sculpture clearly reveals (Plate XIb), and the paint applied to the plaster restorations makes it difficult to distinguish the modern additions with the naked eye. Nowadays the somewhat under life-sized limestone figure welcomes visitors to the Luxor Museum.[18] The sculpture exemplifies the striding pose which became standard for statues of men in

Figure 16 Head from a statue of Amun, excavated in the Monthu Temple; Luxor Museum of Egyptian Art, J. 67.

wood and metal as well as stone about thirteen centuries before Tutankhamun was born. The hands at Amun's sides grasp knot amulets. He wears his personal headgear and the corselet with knotted straps. In this statue the special kilt worn only by gods is at least partially preserved, its pleated sections overlapping in front. A bull's tail is rendered in relief on the 'negative space' between the legs of the striding figure. Since the Middle Kingdom, sculptors included a bull's tail in the composition of statues of the king enthroned, showing it in relief on the front of the seat between the lower legs of the figure. During the reign of Amenhotep III, the bull's tail was introduced into the composition of striding statues, where it remained uncommon until after the post-Amarna Period. An even more unusual feature of this statue is the preservation in pristine condition of Tutankhamun's cartouches in the inscription down the back pillar. The text styles him 'beloved of Amun-Re, foremost [god] of Karnak'.

There are a comparatively large number of heads from post-Amarna statues of Amun with no secure provenance. Most were acquired decades ago, but new pieces keep turning up on the art market – some of truly amazing quality but often in such a fragmentary condition that it is well-nigh impossible to venture a guess about the type of composition from which they derived. Judging by sculptures both with and without provenance preserving some of the body, statues depicting Amun alone, either seated or striding, were common among the sculptures commissioned during the post-Amarna Period. Equally popular were compositions showing the enthroned or striding god with the king, who might be depicted on the same scale or smaller. Less frequently, Mut accompanied her spouse. And until now, only a single post-Amarna group has turned up in which the couple is joined by their son, the moon god Khonsu.[19]

Khonsu

The work of the University of Chicago's Oriental Institute Epigraphic Survey under the direction of Ray Johnson has confirmed the supposition that Khonsu's cult was well established at Karnak before the Amarna Period at or near the site of the Ramesside Khonsu Temple, in the southwest corner of the Karnak enclosure.[20] The post-Amarna group depicting the Theban triad of Amun, Mut, and Khonsu stands nowadays in the hypostyle hall of the later structure. A somewhat over life-sized figure of Amun enthroned occupies the center of the battered sculpture. Precious little remains of the smaller-scaled standing figures of Mut, at his right, and Khonsu, to his left. The heads of Khonsu and Amun are both lost while the face of the goddess[21] has suffered damage. Nor are there any inscriptions, so that it is not possible to attribute the group with certainty to Tutankhamun's, rather than Ay's or even Horemhab's initiative. Khonsu could be depicted as a falcon-headed man; in this group he assumed his more characteristic guise – a purely anthropomorphic figure, completely enveloped except for head and hands. The preserved right hand grasps a crook against his right shoulder.

A colossal granite statue of Khonsu found at the end of the nineteenth century beneath the pavement of the Khonsu Temple provides an idea of the pristine appearance of his figure in the group (Figure 17).[22] In his hands he grasps a long staff as well as the crook and flail. The lower end of the staff rests on the statue's base while the upper end combines three potent amuletic devices depicted in the hieroglyphs for life (*ankh*), 'dominion' (*was*), and stability (*djed*). The creator god Ptah of Memphis carries the same staff, but the crook and flail do not belong to his iconography, and his beard has a blunt, horizontal lower end while the plaited beard with a curled tip at Khonsu's chin is an iconographic feature he shares with other gods. Neither Ptah nor Khonsu wears a wig or crown, and the bodies of both are 'enshrouded', making it rather difficult to tell them apart when a depiction is only partially preserved.[23]

Figure 17 Colossal statue of Khonsu from the Khonsu Temple at Karnak; Egyptian Museum, Cairo, CG 38488.

In the composition of Cairo's colossal statue, Khonsu's natural hairline is indicated in relief across his forehead, at the temples, and in front of his ears (Figure 18a–b). The plaited side-lock on the right side of his head characterizes him as a youth. A diadem

Figure 18 a – b   Head of the Khonsu colossus from the Khonsu Temple at Karnak.

securing the uraeus at his brow is tied around his head and over the side-lock. One item
of Khonsu's iconography was never included in this sculpture: the disk of the full moon
nestling in the crescent atop his head. Since the Middle Kingdom, Khonsu was associated
with the moon; his youth is suggestive of regeneration embodied in the lunar cycle.[24]
The striking resemblance of the god's face in the colossus to likenesses of Tutankhamun
was noted long ago.[25] Given the king's youth at his accession and his repeated claim
to be the son of Amun, it is perhaps remarkable that there is so little evidence for efforts
to identify him with Khonsu.

In the statue Khonsu wears a special necklace (Egyptian: *menat*) which was used like
a rattle in the cult. The counterpoise – an obligatory part of the *menat* – is depicted in
relief on both sides of the back pillar behind the god's head. The inscription on it reads
'Khonsu in Thebes, Lord of Joy'. In the stone sculpture of the post-Amarna Period, there
is usually a recessed surface between the subject and the back pillar, especially behind
the head of the figure. Here the 'negative space' behind Khonsu's head is not recessed
and so provides an appropriate surface for depicting the *menat*'s counterpoise.

The broad, lobe-like protuberances at the sides of Khonsu's head, his hooded eyes,
and the contour of his lips are very similar to those same features of the heads produced
in the atelier of the sculptor Thutmose at Amarna to complete composite statues of
Akhenaten and Nefertiti's daughters,[26] even if the god's skull is not as exaggeratedly
elongated as those of the princesses.

Statues of the Theban 'ennead'

The gods of the so-called Theban ennead numbered many more than nine, among
them Amun, Monthu, Khonsu, Osiris, Set, Nut, Tefnut, Atum, Shu, Geb, Horus, Sobek,
Isis, Nephthys, Hathor, and Tanenet. Two granodiorite sculptures found in Karnak
which were made during the post-Amarna Period may have belonged to a series of
statues depicting these gods enthroned.

One of them is composed of two long-separated fragments that Ray Johnson
recognized as belonging to one and the same sculpture. The female torso, purchased in
Egypt by Sir Charles Nicholson, has been in Sydney, Australia, since about 1860; the
head, which is in the Egyptian Museum, Cairo, came to light in 1900 during excavations
in the Ptah Temple within the Karnak enclosure.[27] In 1998 a cast of the head could be
joined to the bust in Sydney (Plate XII) and a cast of the bust with the head in Cairo.

A flat circlet supporting a sun disk nestled between cow horns forms the headgear
the goddess wears atop her tripartite wig. Her halter dress has knotted straps. The
figure's swelling abdomen and the small, sagging breasts with their pronounced nipples
are reminiscent of a limestone statue depicting Nefertiti from Tell el-Amarna.[28] The

small, slanting, and hooded eyes, the straight nose, and the horizontal mouth are features found in sculptures depicting Tutankhamun. The identity of the goddess depicted in the sculpture remains elusive, since, as noted above, the headdress of cow horns and sun disk is not distinctive – Isis as well as Hathor and Mut, too, wear it. The stylistic affinities to works of the Amarna Period suggest that the sculpture was made early in the post-Amarna Period.

The exact provenance at Karnak of the second statue that I would attribute to a series depicting the gods of the Theban ennead was not recorded before it was deposited in a storage facility at the site. The upper torso with the head is lost, but the inscription on the front of the seat identifies the male deity as the earth god Geb, making the sculpture one of the rare stone statues of him known. The text also mentions Tutankhamun, even if the cartouche with his *prenomen* Nebkheperure was subsequently usurped by Horemhab.[29]

A granodiorite statue in the Louvre without provenance probably belongs to the same series.[30] Like the two sculptures from Karnak, it is about two-thirds life-size. The base with the lower legs of the now headless male figure is not preserved. The cursorily carved inscription on the front of the seat to the proper right gives only the name of the god: Horus. He wears a corselet with knotted straps. The lappets of a striated wig on the chest of the figure show that a tripartite wig camouflaged the juncture of a falcon's head with the torso. This was the standard solution Egyptian sculptors devised for combining a human body with the head of an animal.

The proposed series of statues depicting various members of the Theban 'ennead' may well have been among the furnishings of the 'Mansion of Nebkheperure [Tutankhamun]' (see Chapter 6, pp. 95–8 below), complementing the deities' representations in relief on the piers in the ambulatory.

Tutankhamun at prayer

There are five relatively well-preserved statues depicting Tutankhamun himself as a participant in the cult. Two of them were recovered from the Karnak 'cachette'.[31] Both of these slightly under life-sized sculptures depict Tutankhamun striding, his hands open and resting, palm downwards, on the front of his kilt; one of them is illustrated here in Figure 19a as originally restored. This type of statue, which Egyptologists have traditionally understood to show the pharaoh at prayer, was first created towards the end of the Middle Kingdom (cf. Figure 19b). The posture assumed by the king is one of the attitudes intended to express humility in the presence of a divinity. Even if Tutankhamun's statues of this type from the 'cachette' were without provenance, there could be no doubt about the identity of the god to whom the king pays homage. The

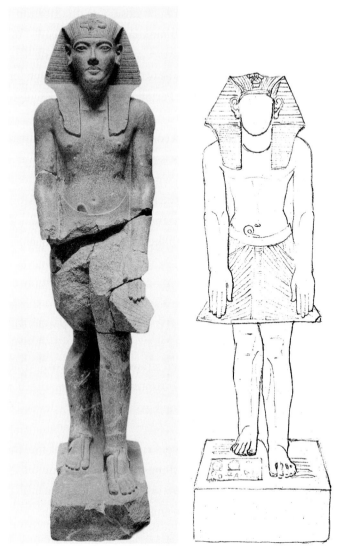

Figure 19 a   Statue of Tutankhamun praying as initially restored; Egyptian Museum, Cairo, CG 42091.
b   Statue of Amenemhet III praying; Egyptian Museum, Cairo, CG 42014.

inscriptions on the belt buckle of the royal kilt, on top of the base, and down the back
pillar all style the king 'beloved of Amun-Re'.

In both statues, Tutankhamun wears a king's *nemes* head-cloth. Like the *nemes*, the
sandals on Tutankhamun's feet distinguish the king from the gods; traditionally, in
relief and painting as well as statuary, deities did not wear sandals.[32] The elaborately
pleated kilt with a triangular-shaped projecting panel is first documented towards the
end of Dynasty XII in the royal wardrobe in association with the posture depicted in
these sculptures. These items of costume – *nemes*, sandals, and special kilt – may well
have been deliberately chosen for this sculptural genre to underscore a king's status as
a mortal in the presence of the god.

For all intents and purposes, the two statues from the 'cachette' are identical. It would seem logical to suppose that the figures were intended to be set up together, perhaps to flank a doorway in the temple. It is all the more curious, therefore, that during Horemhab's reign the texts on them were treated differently.

When Horemhab became king, he ordered the replacement of Tutankhamun's names with his own in the cartouches where they occurred on the monuments. The normal procedure was to erase all but the sun disk (**re**) in the *prenomen* (Nebkheperu**re**) and **Amun** in the *nomen* (Tutankh**amun**). The sun disk was then incorporated into the writing of Horemhab's *prenomen* (Djeserkheperu**re**), while Amun became part of the epithet 'beloved of **Amun**' which was added to his personal name (Figure 20). Other

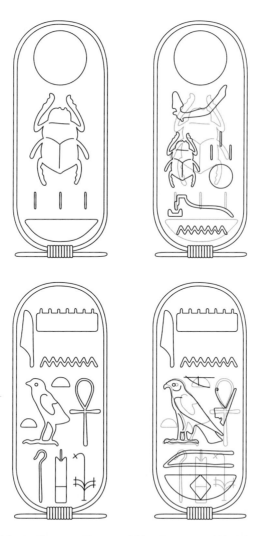

Figure 20 Tutankhamun's cartouches – Nebkheperure Tutankhamun, Ruler of Upper Egyptian Heliopolis – altered to read Djserkheperure, whom Re chose, Horemhab, beloved of Amun.

elements of Tutankhamun's five-part titulary were left untouched – as, for example, in the text of the Restoration Stela and on the back pillar of the quartzite Amun-colossus discussed at the beginning of this chapter. Sometimes even Tutankhamun's personal and/or throne names were simply overlooked when they were inscribed in an inconspicuous location, such as both cartouches incised on the so-called astronomer's kit hanging from the king's waist in a frequently illustrated statue of the king in the Louvre which depicts him standing in front of Amun.[33] Although the cartouches on the back pillar of the same statue were prepared for usurpation, they were never re-inscribed.

The inscription down the back pillar of one of the two statues from the 'cachette' showing Tutankhamun praying is another example of usurpation which was not carried to completion. But in the case of its mate the workmen responsible for the usurpation did not bother at all with the text down the back pillar – Tutankhamun's cartouches remained untouched; only the inscriptions on top of the base and on the belt buckle were altered to name Horemhab. These were the texts to which anyone approaching the statue would have had immediate access, but the back pillar may well have been right up against a wall or doorjamb. Apparently the crew assigned the job of altering the names on this particular statue decided to skip the inconspicuous inscription down the back.

Tutankhamun as a standard bearer

Fragments from three statues are preserved which once depicted Tutankhamun bearing a standard of the kind that is carried by priests in temple reliefs when they are depicted participating in processions. An approximately life-sized head from one of them, carved of granodiorite, was uncovered at Karnak and is now in the collection of Cairo's Egyptian Museum; the top of the standard which terminates in the head of a ram, Amun's sacred animal, is preserved.[34] The king wears the Double Crown above the *nemes* with uraeus. There are no legible inscriptions, but the physiognomy is Tutankhamun's,[35] and the hard-edged style is entirely in keeping with the sculptures of his reign carved in granodiorite.

The inscription on the belt buckle of another standard-bearing figure, which the British Museum received as a gift in 1903, calls the king 'beloved of Amun-Re', suggesting that it, too, comes from Karnak.[36] The sculpture, which is missing its head as well as the lower legs and base, is only about one-third life-size and carved from schist. Tutankhamun's Horus name at the top of the standard is only partially preserved but the damage seems accidental rather than an attempt at purposeful erasure, by contrast to the cartouche further down. The king's *prenomen* Nebkheperure on the belt buckle is intact. The single cartouche preserved in the inscription down the back pillar has been

Figure 21 Standard-bearing statue of Tutankhamun, provenance not known; British Museum, London EA 37639.

prepared for usurpation but then only partially – and ineptly – re-inscribed for Horemhab.[37] Viewed in profile (Figure 21), the figure, with its slack, protruding belly accommodated by a low-slung belt, could be mistaken for Akhenaten.

The belt and belly of the torso from a third standard-bearing statue are similar; the flattened navel, however, distinguishes it from the torso in London, while providing yet another link to the sculptures of Akhenaten's reign.[38] Like one of the triads of Tutankhamun discussed above, the statue was found at Faras, where building activity during the king's reign is documented.[39] This provenance, along with the features of the physique, is circumstantial evidence that Tutankhamun is the subject.[40]

The earliest standard-bearing statue known was created for a pharaoh towards the end of the Middle Kingdom.[41] The next examples were made only a few generations before Akhenaten became king.[42] He did not order any; divine standards, like gods' barks, had no place in the worship of Aten. Tutankhamun reintroduced the genre when the first non-royal standard-bearing statues were also carved. Probably the earliest, and one of the finest among them, comes from the Karnak 'cachette'.[43] Appropriated in the Twenty-second Dynasty, its texts were recut to replace the name of the original owner who has been tentatively identified as Tutankhamun's treasurer Maya.[44] His tomb at Saqqara was re-discovered by an Anglo-Dutch team at the end of the last century. The inscriptions there and on other monuments of his include titles and epithets relating not only to his role in religious festivals but also alluding to his responsibilities in the work of restoration.

Tutankhamun presenting offerings

The fifth sculpture depicting Tutankhamun as an acolyte (Figure 22) entered the Egyptian collection of the British Museum before 1879.[45] Its provenance is not known, and the base with the lower legs was then missing, along with the lower arms, which were extended as if to steady the chest-high 'pillar' in front of the figure. The reliefs covering the surfaces of this 'pillar', which tapers towards the bottom, depict viands – grapes, pomegranates, and grain – as well as bagged ducks, suspended by their feet. Papyrus and lotus 'grow' from the base while lotus blossoms and buds hang down from the top. In 1977 Labib Habachi made a sketch of a chunk of the statue which he recognized in a storage area of the Egyptian Museum in Cairo; it preserves the king's left knee with part of the kilt above and a segment of the back pillar with most of Horemhab's name in a cartouche. Working in the Egyptian Museum years later, Nozomu Kawai relocated the fragment and another showing the king's left foot wearing a sandal.[46]

This type of royal statue, like those depicting the king praying and as a standard bearer, was created towards the end of the Middle Kingdom.[47] The earliest statue of its kind known from the New Kingdom was commissioned by Thutmose III; remarkably, the type survived to be reproduced in miniature during Imperial Roman times.[48] The inscription down the back pillar of the British Museum statue describes the king depicted in it as doing 'what is beneficial for his father Amun-Re';

Figure 22 Tutankhamun as an offering bearer, provenance not known; British Museum, London, EA 75.

the cartouches, which reveal no trace of usurpation, do not name Tutankhamun but Horemhab instead. This has led to the attribution of the statue to Horemhab's own initiative, but the physiognomy is unquestionably Tutankhamun's. Either an inscription naming Tutankhamun was completely removed from the back pillar, which was then re-inscribed for Horemhab, or no inscription was carved down the back pillar while Tutankhamun was alive so that Horemhab could add his text when he became pharaoh.

Tutankhamun's concern to provide provisions for the cult is documented not only by this statue but also by reliefs in the Karnak precinct. They are among the many projects undertaken during the reign; some were new, initiated in Tutankhamun's name, while others, dating back to the time of Amenhotep III, were taken up again from the point where Akhenaten's reign had caused work to cease. Both types of project are covered in the following chapter.

Plate I Lid of the coffin from KV 55; Egyptian Museum, Cairo, JE 39627.

Plate II Tutankhamun on the lap of his wet-nurse Maia as depicted in her tomb at Saqqara.

Plate III

a   Statue of a wet-nurse holding a royal child on her lap, from the Sacred Animal Complex at
    Saqqara; Egyptian Museum, Cairo, JE 91301.

b   Detail; the boy's face and the scarab pendant on his chest.

c   Detail; the boy's feet resting on a footstool decorated with figures of prostrate captives.

a

b

Plate IV
a   Inlaid ebony throne from the tomb of Tutankhamun, Obj. No. 351; Egyptian Museum,
    Cairo, JE 62030.
b   Front of the backrest of the inlaid ebony throne.

Plate V Scene on the front of the backrest of the gold throne from Tutankhamun's tomb, Obj. No. 91; Egyptian Museum, Cairo, JE 62028.

Plate VI Detail, left side of the lunette of the Restoration Stela from Karnak Temple; Egyptian Museum, Cairo, CG 34183.

Plate VII Detail, relief on the east face of the north wing of Pylon III at Karnak Temple showing (above) the faint outline of the erased figure of Tutankhamun behind Amenhotep III and (below) five of the restored panels with Amenhotep III worshipping Amun.

Plate VIII Restored figure of Amun (in the center) holding Thutmose III by the hand with Tutankhamun's restoration inscription (usurped by Horemhab) behind the god.

Plate IX Re-erected quartzite colossi of Amun and Amunet in the alcove behind the Sixth Pylon, Karnak Temple.

Plate X Head of Tutankhamun from a limestone group depicting him standing in front of a life-sized seated male deity from Karnak Temple; Metropolitan Museum of Art, Acc. No. 50.6, Rogers Fund 1950.

a

b

c

Plate XI

a   Slightly under life-sized limestone statue of Amun with Tutankhamun's physiognomy from
    the Karnak cachette; Luxor Museum of Ancient Egyptian Art, J. 198.
b   Back pillar of the statue.
c   Head of the statue.

Plate XII The bust in Sydney (Nicholson Museum R40) joined to a cast of the head in Cairo, Egyptian Museum, CG 38888, with Mohamed Saleh.

Plate XIII (inset) Gold ring with Tutankhamun's *prenomen*; excavated at Tell el-Ajjul, Gaza; Jerusalem, Rockefeller Archaeological Museum, Inv. No. 33.708.

Plate XIV Tutankhamun (usurped by Horemhab) presenting offerings to the Theban triad; relief on the outer face, east wall of Court I between the main temple and Pylon VII, Karnak Temple.

Plate XV Tenth Pylon, Karnak Temple with the avenue of sphinxes flanking the processional avenue southwards to the Mut Precinct.

Plate XVI Colonnade Hall of Luxor Temple from the south.

Plate XVII Tutankhamun censing and pouring a libation. Detail of the scene at the entrance to the Colonnade Hall, Luxor Temple.

Plate XVIII The sarcophagus (Obj. No. 240) in the Burial Chamber of Tutankhamun's tomb.

Plate XIX Nephthys at the southwest corner of the sarcophagus (Obj. No. 240) in the Burial Chamber of Tutankhamun's tomb.

Plate XX Relief block from a scene of 'driving the calves'. Karnak Temple, south blockyard.

Plate XXI Detail of a hunting scene showing a wild steer beneath the hooves of the horses pulling the king's chariot.

Plate XXII Five of the gilded statuettes-in-shrines; figure of Sakhmet (Obj. No. 300a) in the foreground. Egyptian Museum, Cairo, JE 62704.

Plate XXIII Two of Tutankhamun's larger gilded shabtis, Obj. Nos 330g (left) and 110 (right), with two smaller shabtis, now in the Luxor Museum of Ancient Egyptian Art.

Plate XXIV Scene of towing the coffin on the east wall of KV 62's Burial Chamber.

Tutankhamun's Building Projects

Discoveries of seal impressions, scarabs, and the like bearing Tutankhamun's name, and/or that of his queen Ankhesenamun, have been reported from far and wide.[1] In and of themselves, such items can hardly provide information about the importance of the site where they were excavated during the reign of the king whose name they bear, let alone evidence for his presence. Furthermore, they can furnish only a *terminus a quo* – the earliest possible date – for the context in which they were found, since they could be heirlooms. One such heirloom is a gold signet ring bearing Tutankhamun's *prenomen* Nebkheperure (Plate XIII). It was excavated in 1933, together with a scarab of Ramesses II, by Finders Petrie from a family tomb at Tell el-Ajjul in Gaza.[2] Petrie was of the opinion that it was the official seal of a governor who administered the region which lay within the Egyptian sphere of influence in Ramesside times. The idea that it had been fashioned by a local goldsmith is supported not so much by what Petrie considered the clumsy rendering of the hieroglyphs, but rather by the weight of the gold used in its manufacture, which conforms to the Babylonian standard of a double shekel.

In Tutankhamun's case in particular, it is unlikely that scarabs and other small finds bearing his name remained in circulation for any great length of time after his death since his reign was effectively purged from the record (see the Epilogue). Faience ring bezels inscribed with his *prenomen* Nebkheperure have been found at various sites – such as at the mining settlement of Gebel el-Zeit on the Red Sea[3] – where they occupy their proper place in the sequence of comparable objects dating from before the Amarna Period down through the beginning of Dynasty XIX.[4] For this reason they simply furnish evidence for some activity while Tutankhamun was on the throne of Egypt. Seal impressions incorporating a pharaoh's cartouche document the arrival of official correspondence or, like those on the handles of amphoras, the delivery of commodities intended for use soon after they reached their destination. Two such handles preserving impressions of Tutankhamun's *prenomen* were excavated at the frontier post of Tell el-Borg on the Sinai peninsula,[5] showing that Egyptian troops continued to man the fortress (which is not at all surprising).

By contrast, architectural remains and the reliefs that once decorated them are evidence of more than just business as usual. As might be expected, Thebes, the home of Tutankhamun's heavenly father Amun, furnishes a wealth of material documenting building projects initiated during the king's reign. But some other sites, from as far south as Upper Nubia (Republic of Sudan), preserve significant remains of structures commissioned under Tutankhamun, while to the north there are remnants of royal monuments attesting his reign in the environs of Memphis.

Projects in Nubia

The recent discovery at Jebel Barkal of evidence for Tutankhamun's Nubian viceroy Huy has been mentioned in Chapter 3, pp. 39–40. Until now neither restoration work nor construction projects at Jebel Barkal have come to light that might be attributable to a commission of the king. But it would not be surprising should the on-going excavations there eventually produce such documentation. For now, Kawa, about 90 km upstream from the Third Cataract, is the southernmost site where building activity undertaken in Tutankhamun's name has been archaeologically demonstrated.

Amenhotep III is presumed to have built at Kawa, which was called Gem-Aten in antiquity. Despite the reference in the town's ancient name to the solar disk at the heart of Akhenaten's religion, excavations have not yet turned up evidence for the 'heretic' himself or Aten worship at the site.[6]

Between 1929 and 1931, an expedition from the University of Oxford under the direction of F. Ll. Griffith uncovered the remains of a temple built by Tutankhamun; the relief decoration shows the king ministering to the gods Amun, Re-Horakhty, and Atum, Min, Isis, and Thoth.[7] In a relief from the temple, now in the Ashmolean Museum, Oxford, a deeply bowing figure identified by his name and title as Setepatenkhay, Superintendent of Southern Lands, carries a tall, staff-like bouquet in one hand and with the other leads a hefty, reluctant steer to the slaughter.[8] This same man makes an appearance in the paintings of the tomb at Thebes of his superior, the Nubian viceroy Huy. Here, at Kawa, pennants flutter from the ends of the steer's horns which are shaped like open hands, waving in acclamation. The effigy-head of a Nubian with a feather in his hair is fixed between them. Bulls with horns decorated in a similarly elaborate fashion are depicted in Huy's tomb and in the festive procession on the walls of the Colonnade Hall of Luxor Temple (see further, below) where, however, the men leading them do not bow as deeply as Setepatenkhay in the scene at Kawa. Figures were depicted bowing in the presence of their betters and of the king in particular since the Old Kingdom, but the posture is especially conspicuous in the art of the Amarna Period when even the bodyguards of the royal couple stoop while sprinting alongside the king and queen in their chariots.

The most remarkable aspect of the cult celebrated in the temple at Kawa was worship of the deified Tutankhamun as an incarnation of Amun,[9] with whom he shared an epithet identifying them both as a lion.[10] In Nubia, Tutankhamun enjoyed the status of a god, like Amenhotep III before him and, subsequently, Ramesses II who ordered the usurpation of Tutankhamun's cartouches at Kawa in his own favor.

Faras, about 25 km inside Egypt's contemporary border with Sudan, has already been mentioned in the previous chapter, since sculptures commissioned by Tutankhamun were discovered at the site, reused in the significantly later Meroitic cemetery. The archaeologists who excavated the statues also cleared segments of an enclosure wall of the fortified town[11] called in antiquity Sehetep-netjeru, 'Propitiating the gods' – a phrase forming part of Tutankhamun's Gold Horus name. During the king's reign the administration of Nubia under his viceroy Huy was apparently centered at Faras. Here, as at Kawa, the king enjoyed the status of a divinity; within the confines of the fortress, the plan of a temple devoted to his worship could be traced. Meager fragments of the inscribed reliefs which once decorated its walls were recovered, like the statuary, from the Meroitic cemetery.

A mud-brick chapel at Faras dedicated to Huy's memory by 'his sister' Taemwadjsy had stone fittings decorated with reliefs which also reflected the worship of the sovereign. Huy was shown paying homage to a pair of feather-topped cartouches enclosing Tutankhamun's personal and throne names.[12] Taemwadjsy herself was active in the cult of the divinized Tutankhamun at Faras, as was Huy's brother, who bore the title Second Prophet of Nebkheperure.

The only site between Faras and Thebes, far downriver, where any evidence for royal construction work during Tutankhamun's reign has been found, is in Wadi Abbad on a route to the Red Sea, 20 to 25 km east of Edfu. In 1902, 'during a hasty visit to the vicinity of El Kab', F. W. Green remarked on the ruins of a Roman way station there.[13] Eight decades or so earlier, John Gardiner Wilkinson passed by the site on one of his reconnoiters in the Eastern Desert, as did Richard Lepsius.[14] All these visitors reported seeing Tutankhamun's cartouches on sandstone blocks at the site. The damage to the king's name as recorded by Lepsius was not intentional, nor was there any indication suggesting usurpation was planned. Where the structure from which these blocks originated stood before they were requisitioned for reuse, ultimately being transported to the wadi in Roman times, is anyone's guess.[15]

Projects at Western Thebes

In Tutankhamun's reign, if not already during the reign(s) of his immediate predecessor(s), the stonemasons and artisans who lived in the village at the foot of the eastern mountain

. will have been sent back to Thebes and to the settlement of Deir
st bank of the Nile where they had lived with their families before
sion. Perhaps they were put to work undertaking the projects of
.ioned in Chapter 3, but it is doubtful that the order to start work on a
.ew king was issued immediately (see Chapter 6, pp. 87–8, 91).

.r of tombs in the Theban necropolis are known which belonged to officials
st-Amarna Period.[16] Until 1989, when archaeologists from the University of
.erg discovered the tomb of a man who served as High Priest of Amun during
Tutankhamun's reign, the most noteworthy among them was that of the Nubian viceroy
Huy. This man has been mentioned immediately above, and in Chapter 3, pp. 39–40, in
connection with his sovereign's commissions in Nubia. In the mid-nineteenth century,
the draftsmen of the Prussian expedition under Lepsius's direction copied the then
well-preserved paintings in the tomb; the same paintings, much the worse for wear,
were published in facsimile about 75 years later by Nina M. Davies.[17] One of the scenes
shows Huy's investiture as viceroy by an unnamed overseer of the treasury (presumably
Maya, cf. p. 67 above and 80, below) while Tutankhamun observes the ceremony from
a baldachin;[18] in another scene, Huy presents Nubian tribute to the king.[19]

No representation of Tutankhamun is preserved in the decoration of the tomb discovered
by the team from Heidelberg, but the king's name, subsequently altered to read Horemhab,
attests to the earlier dating of the tomb and of its owner who was named Parennefer-
Wenennefer. This man was probably the first person appointed to serve as High Priest of
Amun following Akhenaten's death and the re-endowment of the god's cult at Karnak, as
outlined in the text of the Restoration Stela. The first part of the priest's two-part name –
Parennefer – refers to Akhenaten, which explains why it was erased where it occurred in the
inscriptions of the tomb at some point after attacks began on Akhenaten's memory.[20]

Only about one-third of the original decoration of the tomb, which was executed not
only in painted plaster (as in Huy's tomb) but also in relief, has survived. Among the
subjects shown is a scene of desert plants and animals awakening at sunrise as described
in Akhenaten's hymn to the sun god. Before the discovery of Parennefer's tomb, only
royal parallels for this motif were known – scenes in the Aten temple at Karnak and in
Akhenaten's own tomb at Amarna.[21] Other scenes in Parennefer's tomb also take their
inspiration from the royal repertory of Amarna. Egyptologists eagerly await the
publication of this fascinating tomb. Could Parennefer and his contemporaries select
whatever sites they liked for their tombs and the themes to be depicted in the decoration
without royal sanction in the aftermath of Akhenaten's reign? The same questions are
posed by the tombs of post-Amarna officials at Saqqara, the necropolis of the
administrative capital Memphis (see further, below).

Currently, there is no definitive evidence on the west bank of the Nile at Thebes
for new construction officially commissioned in Tutankhamun's name. A single

inscribed architectural fragment from the 'palace city' built by Amenhotep III at Western Thebes provides a tantalizing clue for connecting Tutankhamun to the site. His presence there would not be surprising, given the efforts made elsewhere to associate him with Amenhotep III. The palace precinct, known today by its Arabic name Malqata, occupied more than 225,000 sq. m.[22] A mission from the MMA conducted excavations there in the second decade of the twentieth century. Monumental inscribed items – as opposed to small objects like faience ring bezels, seal impressions, and so forth – were few and fragmentary. In the 1916/17 season the archaeologists explored a structure which they identified as a temple of Amun.[23] Finds from the area indicated that the building had played a role in the second of three 'jubilees' which Amenhotep III celebrated in the final decade of his reign. Like other buildings at Malqata, it was made of mud-brick with furnishings (offering tables, stelae, and statuary), as well as doorjambs and lintels, of stone. When the archaeologists concluded their work in 1920, a sandstone fragment which they believed belonged to a massive doorjamb was among the finds they reburied at the site. The partially preserved text on it includes most of a cartouche enclosing the name of King Horemhab, but the hieroglyphs are clearly secondary. Many years after the archaeologists from the MMA had departed Malqata, William C. Hayes published the inscription using the notes and photographs they had made, but without access to the original.[24] He concluded that Horemhab's name in the inscription on the fragment replaced the personal name of the palace's founder, Amenhotep III.

It is certainly true that cartouches with the personal name Amenhotep were attacked during the Amarna Period at Malqata, as elsewhere. But do the remains of the original hieroglyphs here belong to Amenhotep III's name? On the photograph, traces of vertical signs are discernible in the basket-hieroglyph (*heb*) at the bottom of Horemhab's cartouche; these could well correspond to the three hieroglyphs in the writing of the epithet 'ruler of Upper Egyptian Heliopolis' which regularly follows Tutankhamun's personal name in exactly this position, at the bottom of his cartouche. Furthermore, a comparable example of Horemhab replacing 'Amenhotep' with his own name is not documented, whereas instances of his usurpation of inscriptions naming Tutankhamun are legion. Perhaps the MMA expedition which resumed work at Malqata in 2008 will uncover new evidence for Tutankhamun at the site – or re-excavate the fragment so that the cartouche can be examined.

Tutankhamun at Karnak[25]

On the east bank of the Nile, at both Karnak and Luxor Temples, major construction was undertaken during the reign. The program pursued in Tutankhamun's name was first and foremost oriented towards projects which had originated with Amenhotep III. The single exception seems to be the decoration in relief of the exterior wall of the courtyard between Pylon VII, on the north–south axis of Karnak Temple, and the enclosure wall of the temple house, properly speaking.[26]

The subject of the relief commissioned here for Tutankhamun alluded to the king's role in ensuring the uninterrupted supply of sustenance for the gods worshipped in the temple.[27] In the center of the composition, Hapi, a corpulent fecundity figure personifying the inundation of the Nile, brings a tray laden with offerings to the enthroned goddess of the harvest Renenutet, depicted as a snake-headed woman. To the right and left, Tutankhamun approaches the Theban triad – Amun, Mut, and their son Khonsu; the king raises one hand in a gesture of address while the other grasps the crook and flail. His head is lost but the tall feathered crown above is preserved. (Plate XIV illustrates that part of the composition which remains *in situ* on the wall, just to the left of the doorway providing access through a courtyard to the main temple.) The cartouches identifying the pharaoh no longer name him as Tutankhamun but rather Horemhab, who ordered their usurpation when he became king. Once the relief gleamed brilliantly in the sun, for it was originally gilt; many small holes for attaching thick gold foil with pegs to the wall remain to attest its former glory.

The neighboring area around the Sacred Lake was devoted to provisioning the cult practiced in Amun's temple.[28] Probably priests lived here during the Eighteenth Dynasty, as excavations have revealed to have been the case in much later times. Warehouses where the supplies for the offering tables were stored stood here during the New Kingdom. Perhaps there were bakeries as well, producing bread and cakes fit for the gods. Texts from the time of Thutmose III leave no doubt that a poultry yard and a pond for waterfowl were located in this area for the ducks and geese that ended on the altars. There was no more appropriate place for a relief focusing on providing the cult with the products of the fields and river than this spot where the offerings were taken to be consecrated though the adjacent doorway into the main part of the temple with its Holy of Holies.

Two sandstone fragments come from a large royal stela, decorated on both sides, which may well have once stood nearby.[29] The exact find spot of the larger fragment within the precinct is not known, but the smaller was discovered in debris of the so-called cachette court, behind the wall with Tutankhamun's relief showing the personification of the inundation and the goddess of the harvest just described. With an estimated original height of about two meters the stela will have been only slightly smaller than the Restoration Stela. A large cartouche, topped with double plumes and a sun disk, heads up a design in sunk relief which runs down the middle of both small sides. The combination of emblems here refers to the celebration of endless jubilee festivals. The lower termination is a clump of the heraldic plants of Upper and Lower

Egypt. (The small sides of the Restoration Stela are similarly decorated.) The plumed cartouche on one side has been re-carved to contain Horemhab's throne name;[30] the other has been erased, but never re-cut.[31]

Both larger lateral surfaces of the stela are decorated; one of them was carved entirely in raised relief while the other combined raised relief with provision for inlays.[32] At some point the stela was split down the middle; now only the figures of Amun and Mut in raised relief on one surface of the larger fragment are well preserved. All that remains of Tutankhamun before them is his hand proffering 'truth' in the shape of the hieroglyph depicting the squatting figure of the goddess Maat. The earliest depictions of this ritual which asserted the king's role in maintaining world order (Egyptian: *maat*) date to the co-regency of Queen Hatshepsut and her step-son/ nephew Thutmose III. (The presentation-of-*maat* tableau was one among several iconographic innovations that were apparently introduced into the repertory of temple decoration at that time.) During the earlier years of Akhenaten's reign, the presentation of *maat* was a very common motif. In Emily Teeter's study of the ritual, she draws attention to the mention in the inscription on the Restoration Stela of Tutankhamun's claim to have restored *maat* as it had obtained in primordial times, while noting that later kings made the same claim following periods of 'real or conceptualized political distress'.[33]

The zone below the feet of the figures was to have been filled with a frieze of pinioned lapwings, raising their human hands in adoration of centered cartouches of Tutankhamun – another feature this stela shared with the Restoration Stela – but the carving was never completed; nor does it seem that a text was ever inscribed below.[34] Indeed, the stela was left unfinished, and its usurpation in Horemhab's favor abandoned.

When it came to construction activity during Tutankhamun's reign, the area near the Sacred Lake was, however, the venue of a 'side-show', not the site of major construction activity. This was undertaken in Tutankhamun's name at the entrances to the precinct where Amenhotep III had also been active.

Tutankhamun at the Third Pylon[35]

Amenhotep III's master plan for Karnak envisioned a monumental colonnade with seven pairs of columns, analogous to the colonnade in front of the Solar Court of Luxor Temple, which would flank the approach to the temple from the Nile quays. Processions passing through it would enter the precinct via his pylon (now Pylon III), the main entrance in his day. But only the foundations for the lateral walls of the colonnade had been laid and construction work barely initiated when Amenhotep III died. Akhenaten did not pursue the project as planned by his father. In front of Amenhotep III's pylon his son erected instead a grand peristyle court on a foundation of undecorated *talatat*.

The reliefs on some 68 piers, which were also constructed of *talatat*, showed Nefertiti worshipping Aten. French archaeologists have argued that this peristyle court was demolished during Tutankhamun's reign; the undecorated *talatat* of the foundations were left in place while the decorated blocks with the depictions of Nefertiti were reused, as fill in an initial phase of construction work on a new pylon (today's Pylon II) commissioned by Tutankhamun. In other words, here, at the entrance to the temple, Tutankhamun (and/or his advisors) sought to associate himself with Amenhotep III, not only adding his own, if diminutive, figure to the reliefs on Pylon III, as well as restoring them (see Chapter 3, p. 42), but also by carrying forward and even expanding Amenhotep III's program to glorify Amun. Unfortunately for Tutankhamun, work had not progressed very far at all when his death intervened, leaving the pylon and its decoration to be completed by Horemhab.

Tutankhamun at the Tenth Pylon

Amenhotep III had built not only the pylon on the east–west axis of the temple, providing access for processions approaching Amun's sanctuary from the Nile, but his reign also witnessed the beginning of construction on a pylon at the southern end of the temple's north–south axis (today Pylon X). This would have opened onto the processional route leading south from Amun's sanctuary to the temple of the god's consort Mut with its U-shaped sacred lake.

The text on the statue depicting a Seventeenth Dynasty king enthroned beside the goddess mentioned in Chapter 4, p. 56, provides the earliest evidence which has come to light so far associating Mut with Isheru as her precinct was known in antiquity. Queen Hatshepsut built here during her co-regency with Thutmose III; he, too, is represented in the reliefs she commissioned. The queen's building program included a monumental gateway (now Pylon VIII), where processions departed Karnak when proceeding south to Isheru, passing shrines erected along the route.[36]

Amenhotep III's pylon on the north–south axis of Karnak Temple would certainly have eclipsed that of Hatshepsut (and Thutmose III), if the king had not died after only eight courses had been laid. Akhenaten did not continue work on this project of his father. Because large sandstone blocks with Akhenaten's reliefs and inscriptions were found here – some reused as fill in the pylon and others nearby – some specialists have suggested that he did commission a structure in the vicinity, but others have cast doubt on this idea, attributing the blocks instead to a building of Akhenaten's located elsewhere at Karnak.[37]

Tutankhamun's name is unquestionably associated with the avenue of ram-headed sphinxes that lined the processional avenue from the Tenth Pylon begun by Amenhotep III to Isheru (Plate XV): elements of his titulary can be read on the bases

Figure 23 a Headless sphinx from the Processional Avenue between Pylon X, Karnak Temple, and the Mut Precinct.
b – c Sphinx with the head of Nefertiti, converted to a ram-headed sphinx with a statue of Tutankhamun added between the paws.

of many of them, even if Horemhab did usurp the cartouches. When archaeologists first began to work in this area, the sphinxes presented a sorry sight (Figure 23a). All were headless and the inscriptions were weathered. Study by French Egyptologists working at the Centre franco-égyptien du temples de Karnak clarified the history of these sculptures; towards the end of the last century, the sphinx avenue became the subject of a conservation project initiated by the SCA. The sphinxes were commissioned neither by Tutankhamun nor Amenhotep III, but by Akhenaten, as part of his plan to turn Karnak into a temple for the veneration of his god Aten.[38] (Depictions of Akhenaten as a sphinx and bases for sphinxes at his temples in Tell el-Amarna show that he was not averse to this statue type, at least during the earlier years of his reign.) Originally the sphinxes were of two types – the human heads of one series depicted Akhenaten wearing the *nemes* head-cloth while those of the other series showed Queen Nefertiti with a tripartite wig (Figure 23b). Where they stood at Karnak is not known. But they were not only the largest sphinxes comprising an avenue associated with the temple; they were also the most numerous.

Sculptors working for Tutankhamun 'beheaded' the sphinxes; ram heads provided with integral tenons were fitted into slots cut in the leonine bodies. Small standing statues of Tutankhamun, his arms crossed on his chest and his hands grasping crook and flail, were inserted between the paws of each recumbent animal (Figure 23c). Sphinxes of this kind, incorporating the figure of a diminutive king, had been introduced by Amenhotep III;[39] the choice of this genre may well have been yet another conscious effort to associate Tutankhamun with his illustrious predecessor. Tall bases bearing Tutankhamun's titulary were provided for the reworked sphinxes when they were erected in their new setting. It is only logical to suppose that Tutankhamun also ordered work to be resumed on the pylon where the sphinx avenue started.[40]

The appropriation of Akhenaten's sphinxes does not necessarily imply animosity towards him. However, the discovery of blocks which show undeniable and purposeful damage to Akhenaten's figure and names inside the Tenth Pylon, directly on top of the last course laid under Amenhotep III, makes it very likely that Tutankhamun's reign witnessed the first officially sanctioned attacks on Akhenaten's memory. But here, too, Tutankhamun's death left the work to be completed by his second successor King Horemhab. Figures of Pharaoh in the reliefs decorating the pylon and the inscriptions identifying them as Horemhab are original, unlike the inscriptions on the bases of the sphinxes.

The traces of hieroglyphs under Horemhab's *prenomen* and personal name in those inscriptions on the bases of the sphinxes at the southern end of the avenue do not, however, read Nebkheperure Tutankhamun, Ruler of Southern Heliopolis, but rather Kheperkheperure Ay, Father of the God. Here, as elsewhere, when Ay succeeded Tutankhamun, he continued his predecessor's project; both their roles were then conclusively and irrevocably usurped by Horemhab.

The Colonnade Hall of Luxor Temple

Work on Amenhotep III's ambitious vision for Luxor Temple also came to a halt with his death. The construction of the Colonnade Hall (Plate XVI) with its central aisle of fourteen massive columns, Phase III of Amenhotep III's plan for the site, was completed but none of the relief decoration had been carved when he died. Tutankhamun took up this project and nearly saw it to completion before he, too, went the way of all mortals.

The principal subject of the reliefs executed in Tutankhamun's name on the interior walls of the Colonnade Hall was the procession which took place on the occasion of the annual Festival of Opet.[41] The primary purpose of the temple, deduced from the inscriptions and decorative program of the structure as a whole, may have been to provide a stage for the celebration of this festival which reaffirmed the sacred legitimacy of the reigning king.[42] The god at the center of the cult celebrated here was Amun, who covered the distance to Luxor Temple from his home at Karnak in his sacred bark, accompanied by his consort Mut and their son Khonsu, also traveling the distance in their barks. Tutankhamun and Ankhesenamun in separate boats joined the procession for the journey south. Many individual vignettes included in the depiction of the procession have parallels in scenes of festivities in other temples – for example, the scenes of musicians and dancers, troops running with their standards, and butchers dismembering sacrificial oxen in the lowest registers. Booth-like constructions depict temporary shrines along the route of the procession where offerings were made. Not only is the series here the fullest and most detailed known from any temple, it is also of high artistic quality, executed in fine low relief which is the hallmark of Tutankhamun's reign.

This style of carving is exemplified by the depictions of the king cut on the south face of the portal opening into the Colonnade Hall.[43] At either side of the doorway Tutankhamun is shown as if entering the temple and approaching Amun. Here and in the episodes of the Opet Festival itself on the lateral walls, Tutankhamun is depicted not as a child but as a young adult, lending support to the supposition that the reliefs were carved later in his reign, rather than earlier.

Tutankhamun's images are virtually the same in both scenes flanking the portal, but his figure on the west jamb is somewhat better preserved (Plate XVII). With one hand, he elevates an arm-like censer, its handle terminating in a falcon's head topped by a sun disk, while with the other he pours a libation. His traditional costume includes the Blue Crown with uraeus, and, over the projecting panel of his knee-length kilt, a sporran-like accessory suspended from his belt. In the center of the frieze of uraei that borders the lower edge of the sporran is a small cartouche with his *prenomen*. The crew of workmen responsible for erasing all but the sun disk in it so that it could be replaced with Horemhab's *prenomen* did not do a thorough job, by contrast to their work of altering the large pair of cartouches above the figure: as throughout the colonnade, that label now identifies the king as Horemhab.

A remarkable feature of the reliefs is the prominence of Amenhotep III in the texts and scenes executed under Tutankhamun. In some scenes of the procession, a statue of Amenhotep III is depicted on board Amun's bark, but in the reliefs on the monumental columns, figures of Tutankhamun and Amenhotep III alternate in the scenes showing Pharaoh performing his duties in the cult. Ray Johnson suggests that the association of the two kings seems to amount to more than recognition of the older king's role in the initial planning of the temple to replace a modest structure of the mid-Eighteenth Dynasty. He compares their relationship as depicted in the reliefs to what might be expected of father/son co-regents.[44] A familial relationship between them is undeniable, but even if Tutankhamun had been the son of Amenhotep III, it would have been chronologically impossible for them to have ruled together. Rather, their association in the reliefs is symbolic of the official policy of Tutankhamun's reign which linked him to the pre-Amarna past, as if his immediate predecessors had never existed.

Tutankhamun at Tell el-Amarna?

The only definitive evidence for Tutankhamun's reign which has been excavated at Tell el-Amarna is provided by faience ring bezels and molds for their manufacture. Typically, those inscribed with the *prenomen* Nebkheperure far outnumber those with his personal name, Tutankhamun. (It is worth repeating that not one instance of the earlier *nomen* Tutankhaten has been found at Tell el-Amarna – cf. p. 20.) Down until the present no building at Tell el-Amarna is attributable to his reign. But it cannot be categorically ruled out that he commissioned some construction work at the site, since activity during King Horemhab's tenure on the throne is documented at Akhenaten's capital not just by the blocks from the structures demolished at his orders, which were taken to Hermopolis for reuse in his building projects there,[45] but by a few fragments of sculpture inscribed with his titulary, excavated by the EES at Tell el-Amarna itself.[46]

A partially preserved wall painting in a house on West Street in the Workmen's Village may depict Tutankhamun as king, rather than Akhenaten.[47] Its original location in the house is not certain. As plausibly reconstructed by Fran Weatherhead, the figure wears the Nubian wig with a uraeus. The representation of a king in the decoration of a workman's home is indeed remarkable, even if the fragments of painted plaster came from the middle room of the dwelling, rather than from the front room where they were found. (It was in the front room of the houses that animals were sometimes kept.)

Tutankhamun at Memphis

At Saqqara, the necropolis of the administrative capital Memphis, as in Western Thebes, a number of tombs were commissioned by Tutankhamun's contemporaries. The most famous among them are those built for the 'generalissimo' and king's deputy Horemhab before he ascended the throne, and for Maya, head of the treasury whose career continued right down into Horemhab's reign. Both tombs were visited in the nineteenth century when reliefs and statuary were carried off to Europe, but it was only in the mid-1970s that a joint expedition of the EES, London, and the Rijksmuseum, Leiden, began to search for them. In the wake of locating and scientifically excavating both sanded-up, temple-like tombs, the archaeologists also unearthed a number of smaller tombs built by contemporaries. Some of the best-preserved reliefs removed in the nineteenth century are now in the Leiden collection. One scene from Horemhab's Saqqara tomb shows Tutankhamun accompanied by Ankhesenamun (both figures now headless) rewarding the tomb owner for distinguished service in a type of scene which had become popular in the decoration of officials' tombs during Akhenaten's reign:[48]

the king and his queen stand at the Window of Appearances to shower the general with gifts of gold.[49]

Remarkable finds continue to be brought to light by French as well as English archaeologists exploring those parts of the Saqqara necropolis where tombs were sited by the families of influential courtiers and officials who served the crown for the decades following Akhenaten's death.[50] The proper understanding and appreciation of this material will occupy scholars for years to come. Other specialists have made significant discoveries by 'excavating' in museums – in exhibition galleries accessible to the general public, as well as in storage facilities. Such work has resulted in the identification and dating of reliefs and funerary equipment removed long ago from their original contexts, leading in turn to insights into the administration of the country at this crucial period. For example, Beatrix Gessler-Löhr has identified a fragmentary relief in the collection of the Kunsthistorisches Museum, Vienna, as deriving from the tomb of one of the men who served as mayor of Memphis in the post-Amarna Period, Sakeh by name.[51] His titles are appropriate for an influential confidant of the king – but which king? Gessler-Löhr persuasively argues on the basis of stylistic and iconographic details in favor of Tutankhamun.

The text of the Restoration Stela makes it clear that Tutankhamun was living at Memphis when it was promulgated, in a palace founded at the beginning of Dynasty XVIII by Thutmose I. Three adjoining relief-decorated blocks recently unearthed by chance beneath a contemporary dwelling in a village to the north of Saqqara were at first tentatively identified as perhaps belonging to the decoration of a palace that Tutankhamun himself built in the vicinity of Memphis.[52] To the right, Tutankhamun is depicted in the age-old pose of the victorious pharaoh, about to deliver the *coup de grâce* to captives held fast by their hair. In the smaller-scaled scene to the left, Tutankhamun, seated on a well-cushioned stool, shoots an arrow at a target while Ankhesenamun squats at his feet. Zahi Hawass was quick to note the similarity of this composition to one of the vignettes on the small golden shrine (Obj. No. 108) found in the king's tomb.[53] However, the blocks do not come from a palace, but from a tomb where they belonged to a scene showing the Window of Appearances in a palace. Reliefs (and paintings) depicting relief and/or painting are not common in Egyptian art, and especially not in the tomb of a private individual. Whether these scenes accurately reflect the appearance of a wall in the palace where Tutankhamun and Ankhesenamun resided at Memphis is by no means certain, but the presence of the archery tableau demonstrates that the scene's reference was not to Tutankhamun's existence in the Hereafter.[54]

Precious little evidence has survived for any royal projects of Tutankhamun's reign in the Memphite area.[55] Only a single royal commission has come to light *in situ*, in the cemetery at Saqqara. The discovery goes back to the early days of Egyptian archaeology, and the mid-nineteenth century when the Frenchman Auguste Mariette followed up a hunch concerning the likely location of the burials of the sacred Apis bulls. These animals, which often attained huge proportions, were closely associated with the cult of Ptah, the primary god worshipped at Memphis. Mariette's exploration of the westernmost sector of the necropolis led to his discovery of the Serapeum, a precinct encompassing a series of 'greater' and 'lesser' vaults where Apis bulls were laid to rest in stone sarcophagi for centuries, down into Ptolemaic times. A few isolated burials in subterranean chambers with relief-decorated chapels above ground pre-dated the creation of the first of these galleries for multiple burials towards the middle of Ramesses II's reign. The earliest of the individual interments was made under Amenhotep III, while Tutankhamun was responsible for the third. Like the other Apis burials, it had been robbed in antiquity with only remnants of the original equipment left for Mariette to recover. These included three faience pendants inscribed with Tutankhamun's *prenomen* and pieces of a wooden coffin, as well as the standard set of canopic jars (four vessels, made of limestone, for internal organs removed during mummification). All the items excavated by Mariette went to the Louvre.[56] The stoppers of the jars depict rather bland human heads (without beards) wearing shoulder-length striated wigs pushed back behind the ears.[57]

A so-called stole made of faience beads found in Tutankhamun's tomb (Obj. No. 269o; Figure 24), appears to be an actual example of a liturgical garment like the one Ramesses II wears in a double scene painted on the walls of the tomb of the Apis burials at Saqqara, dating to his reign.[58] The ornament consists of seven strands of disc-shaped, blue-green faience beads with regularly inserted gilt spacers. Little *ankh*s dangle from the gold plaques at each end displaying Tutankhamun's cartouches, the *prenomen* qualified 'beloved of Sokar' and the *nomen*, 'beloved of Ptah'. Perhaps Tutankhamun wore it at the obsequies for the Apis buried during his reign, if not at some other religious ceremony at Memphis.

Figure 24 'Stole' made of faience beads from the tomb of Tutankhamun, Obj. No. 269o; Egyptian Museum, Cairo, JE 61961.

At Abusir, the northernmost sector of the Saqqara necropolis, the cult of the lioness goddess Sakhmet was celebrated in the funerary temple of the Fifth-Dynasty king Sahure at least as early as the time of Amenhotep III.[59] No certain evidence of royal patronage under Tutankhamun exists here – only the mention of his name in the title of a scribe who had a stela carved at the bottom of a wall in the sanctuary.[60] There is, however, a relief depicting Tutankhamun with Sakhmet which once decorated a structure very probably erected in the environs of Memphis; another which surely comes from the region has been provisionally associated with the king. In both cases, Sakhmet accompanies Ptah, the god *par excellence* of Memphis, and it is he who takes precedence over his consort in the scenes.

The relief with a secure, though secondary Memphite provenance showing a king with Sakhmet, which may be attributable to Tutankhamun's initiative, is one of two limestone 'slabs' from among debris near the chapel of Seti I.[61] Both are nowadays in the local museum, and it is quite possible that they originate from one and the same structure where they once served as lintels.[62] The symmetrical composition on the less well-preserved piece showed a king before Ptah inside his characteristic kiosk, with Sakhmet, depicted as a lion-headed woman, standing behind him. The heads of all four figures, along with the upper edge of the block, are not preserved; the figure of the king in the right-hand scene is very damaged, and the condition of the relief is, in general, poor. The second block also shows symmetrical scenes, but this time Ptah is not accompanied by Sakhmet.[63] The king is engaged in a ritual race: to the left, he wears the White Crown and grasps an oar in one hand and a 'steering device' in the other; at the right, wearing the Red Crown, he runs with libation vessels in both hands. All the cartouches identifying the ruler in both scenes have been hacked out, and at the left his face was attacked as well. Stéphane Pasquali assigns both lintels to Tutankhamun or, perhaps, Ay, with responsibility for the defacement attributed to Horemhab.[64]

There can be no doubt that the king depicted in the third scene before Ptah and Sakhmet is indeed Tutankhamun. The group occupies the left-hand half of yet another limestone lintel. In the early twentieth century, the German nobleman Baron Friedrich Wilhelm von Bissing purchased it at Giza; in 1920, he sold it to the Egyptian Museum in Berlin (Figure 25).[65] The gods whom Tutankhamun approaches in the right-hand half of the symmetrical composition are Amun and Mut. All four deities are enthroned, and in both scenes Ankhesenamun accompanies her spouse. The queen's modius is topped with double feathers and sun disk; she shakes a sistrum in one hand and, at the left, grasps a *menat* in the other. There is a sun disk with uraeus atop Sakhmet's leonine head; Mut's headgear includes the Double Crown worn above the vulture headdress, and she raises her right hand in a gesture of greeting. At the left, Tutankhamun appears in the *nemes* head-cloth and presents a conical loaf of bread while at the right he holds a small vessel in each hand and his headgear is the Blue Crown. The inscription on the small portion of the integral doorjamb preserved at the right reads 'son of [the sun god] Re of his body . . .'; at the left, there is only 'perfect god, lord of the two lands . . .'

The surface is not well preserved at all, but the right-hand side has suffered more seriously than the left, which suggests weathering as well as purposeful damage. The

Figure 25 Lintel from a structure of Tutankhamun: provenance not known; Egyptian Museum, Berlin, ÄgM 21840.

accomplished carving of the figures at the right compares well to that at the left, attesting the hands of two different sculptors. The cartouches of the royal pair have been intentionally hacked, even if it seems that the queen's name at the left was not as severely attacked as her husband's. The sun disk at the top of the king's cartouche with the *prenomen* has been left standing, as would be expected if usurpation had been planned. The near obliteration of the queen's figure at the right-hand edge was probably not as purposeful as it looks now. In any case, it is obvious that an attack on the names has taken place.

Yet another limestone lintel with symmetrical scenes depicting a king before deities has been attributed to Tutankhamun's reign. Labib Habachi recognized that the cartouches which now label this king Horemhab have been usurped, and he was the first to propose that the king who commissioned the relief was Tutankhamun.[66] Each half showed the king kneeling, a sun disk encircled by uraei above his head, to present offerings to funerary deities. In the poorly preserved left half, it is Osiris enthroned, with Isis and Nephthys standing behind him; at the right, Hathor, in a manifestation specific to Memphis, accompanies Sokar-Osiris, the falcon-headed god of the Memphite necropolis (Figure 26). The funerary character of these gods and the smaller dimensions of the lintel set it apart from the two lintels just described.[67] In any case, there is no reason to suppose that all three lintels derive from a single structure. This one was found inside the enclosure of the Ptah Temple, where it had been incorporated into a tomb built for the son of a Dynasty XXII pharaoh. At the time of reuse, the original

Figure 26 Detail; lintel from a structure of Tutankhamun, reused in the tomb of Prince Sheshonk at Mitrahineh; Egyptian Museum, Cairo, JE 88131.

composition was supplemented to both left and right with a kneeling figure of the tomb owner carved on adjacent blocks. The entire ensemble can be seen today re-erected in the garden of Cairo's Egyptian Museum.

The last piece of indisputable evidence for projects commissioned by Tutankhamun in the north comes from Giza.[68] It is a limestone doorframe, now also in the Egyptian Museum, Cairo, which was excavated about eight decades ago from a building made of mud-brick located to the southeast of the valley temple of Chephren's pyramid.[69] The decoration of the architrave amounts simply to a panel with the names of Tutankhamun and Ankhesenamun, 'beloved of Hauron'. This Canaanite deity, whose cult was introduced to Egypt in the Eighteenth Dynasty not later than the reign of Amenhotep II, was at home in the desert where he provided protection against snakes and scorpions. At the Giza plateau he was identified with Harmachis, a falcon god embodied in the great sphinx.[70]

Both jambs of the doorframe bear cartouches of Ramesses II, and it is that pharaoh's name which was cut into a layer of plaster, applied over the panel inscribed with the names of Tutankhamun and his wife, to claim the doorframe for his own. After the plaster separated from the limestone, only traces of the secondary hieroglyphs remained, along with those of the plumes with sun disks surmounting the larger cartouches of Ramesses II. The absence of the epithet 'chosen one of Re' from the king's throne name suggests that the usurpation of the doorframe may date to the beginning of his reign when other sources document Ramesses II's activity at Giza.

The Giza plateau was one place where the pharaohs of the New Kingdom indulged in the sport of hunting desert fauna. Apparently this provided the rationale for initially identifying the building where the doorframe was installed as a 'rest house' where a royal hunting party might take a break from the chase or spend the night. Now it seems likely that the structure was instead one of several New Kingdom chapels dedicated to Hauron in this part of the Giza necropolis.[71]

Hunting equipment deposited in Tutankhamun's tomb could be interpreted as evidence for his love of the chase. One scene on the lid of the painted box (Obj. No. 21) depicts the king pursuing desert game from his chariot.[72] But, like other paintings on the box showing him hunting lions and vanquishing Egypt's enemies to the north and south, this scene is hardly the record of actual events but rather intended to demonstrate the pharaoh in his ideological role subduing chaos. By contrast, the inscription down the handle of a fan (Obj. No. 242) localizes an expedition of the king to bag ostriches to supply the feathers for it: the hunt took place in the desert to the east of Heliopolis.[73]

One theory supposes that Tutankhamun died as a result of a hunting accident, but before commenting on this and other suggestions about the cause of his death in Chapter 7, the preparations made in advance for his burial are reviewed in the next chapter.

Tutankhamun's Funerary Temple, his Tomb, and the Sarcophagus Found in It

Egyptologists presume that a king began preparing for his continued existence in the Hereafter soon after his accession, choosing a site for his tomb and initiating work on a funerary temple.[1] There is ample data in support of this idea, ranging from year dates painted on blocks quarried for building the pyramids of the Old Kingdom, to texts on shards of pottery, limestone flakes, and papyrus citing events in the lives of the stonemasons, sculptors, draftsmen, and painters who cut and decorated the royal tombs of the New Kingdom centuries later in the Valley of the Kings at Western Thebes. Specialists on the Amarna Period long suspected that Akhenaten was no exception; speculation centered on KV 25 (see immediately below, p. 93), a tomb in the western branch of the Valley of the Kings where his father, Amenhotep III had been buried. It seems that some progress had been made as well on a funerary temple for Akhenaten at Thebes, before the decision was taken to begin work on both a tomb and a funerary temple at his new capital in Middle Egypt.[2]

Evidence does exist, however, that not all kings were preoccupied with awareness of their mortality when they acceded to the kingship.[3] As many as 15 months may have elapsed after the accession of the Twentieth-Dynasty king Ramesses IV before a site was selected for his House of Eternity, while Seti II of Dynasty XIX did not initiate work on his tomb until at least eight-and-a-half months after he became king. These and other similar exceptions were the result of unusual circumstances – for example, Seti II had to contend with a usurper. An equally exceptional situation obtained when Tutankhaten became king after the deaths of perhaps as many as three rulers in less than four years at most. And he was just a boy who might have been expected to live for years; thoughts of his death would have been far from the minds of those who were effectively in control of the country. If, on the other hand, he was frail (but evidence supposedly supporting this idea is contested) or should a plague account for the demise of his immediate predecessors (as some theorize[4]), then plans for a funerary temple and tomb would not have been out of place. Sound conclusions deducible from the meager data preserved are hard to come by; no definitive answer can be given to the question of when plans for Tutankhamun's burial began to be made, even if one item of the king's funerary equipment – the sarcophagus in which the king was laid to rest[5] – provides grounds for entertaining the possibility that no preparations at all were made in advance for the inevitable.

The sarcophagus in Tutankhamun's tomb (Plate XVIII)

A stone sarcophagus may well have been at the very top of a pharaoh's list of priorities when it came to contemplating his death, outranking even a tomb. More than 75 years ago, William C. Hayes, in his study of the royal sarcophagi of the Eighteenth Dynasty made prior to the Amarna Period, called attention to the fact that all of them (except for the sarcophagus in KV 42, whose ownership is disputed[6]) are finished, even though the tombs where they were found are not. Early on, Akhenaten ordered a sarcophagus as well as a canopic chest with figures of the solar god as a falcon at the corners, its wings enveloping the contents.[7] Both were taken along to Tell el-Amarna, but only the design of the sarcophagus was altered before it and the canopic box were put to use for Akhenaten's burial in the Royal Wadi there. Alterations are also evident in the decoration and texts on the basin of the sarcophagus in which Howard Carter found the three nested coffins containing Tutankhamun's mummy, but none at all are discernible on the lid.

The sarcophagus's lid

The lid and basin of the sarcophagus in Tutankhamun's tomb are made of different kinds of stone. Down through the reign of Thutmose IV, Eighteenth-Dynasty royal sarcophagi were carved from quartzite. Akhenaten ordered one made of granite, perhaps following the example of his father, but we cannot be sure, since only the granite lid of Amenhotep III's sarcophagus, which was once gilded,[8] was found in his tomb; the basin is missing. The material of the lid of the sarcophagus in Tutankhamun's tomb is also granite, but the basin is made of dark red quartzite, by contrast to the dull, yellow color of its Eighteenth-Dynasty predecessors which were stained red only after they were sealed in the course of the burial. Perhaps Tutankhamun's sarcophagus once had a lid of quartzite that was somehow damaged, so that a replacement had to be ordered.[9] Regardless, there can be no doubt that the granite lid was intended for use with the quartzite basin since the fit is perfect, and the form, which imitates a sloping shrine roof, is well suited to the design of the sarcophagus as a whole.

Two of the three columns of text on the top of the lid invoke Anubis and Thoth, orthodox funerary deities who officiated at the ceremony of judging the deceased. The third text is a recitation of the falcon god Behdety, who uniquely assumes the role here customarily played by the sky goddess Nut, protecting the corpse by enveloping it in her winged arms. The sole figural decoration of the lid is Behdety's icon – a winged sun disk – on the front.

The basin of the sarcophagus

Unlike the pristine inscriptions naming Tutankhamun on the lid of the sarcophagus, the texts on the basin, as well as its decoration, show unmistakable signs of alteration (Figure 27; Plate XIX). Wings were added to the arms of the figures of the goddesses who stand at the corners, and there are sporadic traces of hieroglyphs belonging to erased texts and the register lines that once bordered them. Furthermore, the carving of the decoration is unfinished, with the state of completion diminishing towards the foot end; there, details of the goddesses' jewelry were executed in paint, rather than in relief, and the frieze of *djed*-pillars and *tjt*-knots in the dado below their feet was blocked out but no details were carved. In the original design, only the goddesses' outstretched arms interrupted the texts which otherwise covered the lateral surfaces of the basin.

The secondary, altered inscriptions on the basin now name Tutankhamun as the beneficiary of the protection provided by the traditional tutelary goddesses at the corners – Isis, Nephthys, Selket, and Neith – and by the Four Sons of Horus, demigods associated with the internal organs removed from the corpse during mummification who are invoked in the texts. Modifications of the original design affected not only the inscriptions which were erased, leaving only minimal traces of individual hieroglyphs identifiable today. The addition of wings to the arms of the goddesses effectively and significantly reduced the surface area available for re-inscription; indeed, this may have been intentional, in the interest of expediency, if the alterations were first undertaken only when Tutankhamun died as I believe likely.

The design of the basin, incorporating female figures at the corners, associates it with the sarcophagi commissioned for Tutankhamun's successors Ay and Horemhab, but

Figure 27 South side and foot end of the sarcophagus in the tomb of Tutankhamun.

also with Akhenaten's sarcophagus after it had been altered to show Nefertiti standing at all four corners. It has been deliberately shattered, but archaeologists were able to recover fragments from his tomb and its vicinity in the Royal Wadi at Tell el-Amarna. The basin was reconstructed in the 1930s and then a second time around 1970; since then, it has stood inconspicuously in the grounds of the Egyptian Museum in Cairo, at the left side of the building. In 1998 Marc Gabolde published a new reconstruction on paper of the basin.[10] Earlier attempts at reconstructing the design of the basin showed the figures of Queen Nefertiti at the corners facing towards the middle of both sides, like the goddesses in the design of the later royal sarcophagi of Ay and Horemhab. Gabolde could demonstrate, however, that all four figures of Akhenaten's queen faced forward, towards the head end of the basin, just like the figures of the goddesses on the sarcophagus in Tutankhamun's tomb.

Could the sarcophagus in Tutankhamun's tomb then have been made for Akhenaten very early in his reign, even before his sarcophagus that was taken along to Amarna? An argument that could be made in favor of this idea might cite the proportions of the goddesses at the corners. Gay Robins has demonstrated that the figure of Isis at the head end reflects the orthodox canon, rather than the altered canon of proportions introduced during Akhenaten's reign but which did not long survive him. However, the figures of Selket and Nephthys display some features – longer necks and larger heads – which Robins suggests could be remnants of the Amarna canon.[11] Such anomalies may well reflect sculptors working simultaneously according to different traditions on the basin, just as the use of both sets of proportions in the decoration of the Burial Chamber can be explained by supposing that some painters were quicker to return to the 'old' way of designing figures than others.[12]

Furthermore, the architectural design of the sarcophagus in which Akhenaten was laid to rest differs from that of the basin in KV 62. The lid of the former includes a cavetto cornice, but in the design of the latter and of the sarcophagi of Kings Horemhab and Ay as well, this element is incorporated into the basin. If the development of sarcophagus design was linear, it is very unlikely that Akhenaten commissioned the KV 62 basin before he ordered the sarcophagus used for his interment in the Royal Tomb at Amarna.

The architecture and decoration of the sarcophagus in KV 62 – which are appropriate only for the sarcophagus of a ruler – place its manufacture between Akhenaten's modified sarcophagus from the Royal Tomb at Tell el-Amarna and those of Ay and Horemhab. Some experts have argued that the KV 62 basin was made for Tutankh**aten** soon after his accession, with the alterations necessitated when his name was changed to Tutankh**amun**. But this is unlikely, since all the texts were erased and new inscriptions carved, not just the cartouches with his personal name.[13] The new texts reading

Tutankhamun are also arranged differently, within new register lines. This would have been necessary if the 'icon' of the radiant Aten was conspicuous in the original decoration, and the god's name in cartouches prominent in the texts, as on Akhenaten's sarcophagus from the Royal Tomb. But that, too, seems unlikely, because the original design included the traditional, orthodox funerary goddesses at the corners of the basin with hieroglyphs identifying them atop their heads.

For whom was the basin commissioned, if not for Akhenaten or Tutankhaten?

The prime candidates for original ownership of the basin include Tutankhamun's predecessors: King Smenkhkare and the ruling queen who bore the epithet 'beneficial for her husband'. Nor can it be categorically ruled out that one of them commissioned a sarcophagus for the reburial of Akhenaten at Thebes in accordance with orthodox ritual, since there is evidence – the magical bricks inscribed for the Osiris Akhenaten, as well as the coffin and canopic jars found in KV 55 which were initially adapted for his use (see Chapter 1, p. 8) – that traditional funerary equipment was prepared with his reburial in mind, even if it never actually took place.

In my study of the sarcophagus, I considered and dismissed the idea that it could have belonged to a female pharaoh who followed Akhenaten on the throne, since in 1993 no funerary equipment made for such a woman had been identified. But then Marc Gabolde demonstrated that items made for her burial were subsequently reworked for Tutankhamun's use. In other words, it is today plausible that she commissioned a sarcophagus for herself as Pharaoh. The appropriation of her equipment, such as the miniature coffins intended to contain her viscera, for Tutankhamun's use makes it unlikely that she was accorded a pharaoh's burial.

The amount of time needed to remove the inscriptions naming the original owner from the basin of the sarcophagus, to carve wings for the goddesses and new texts naming Tutankhamun as its owner, can be estimated at about 800 man hours. If a team of four men, one at each lateral surface, worked for at least eight hours each day, they could have completed the appropriation of the basin in Tutankhamun's favor in a month. In other words the job could have been finished within 70 days, the standard period, according to tradition, for completing the mummification process. If so, it follows that no sarcophagus was commissioned for the king early on – as was customary – and perhaps no preparations at all were made for his burial until he died. This would explain why a tomb inappropriate for the burial of a pharaoh had to be enlarged and items of funerary equipment belonging to others adapted for his use. Nowadays I consider this a likely possibility, but admittedly there is no proof; the sarcophagus could have been reworked earlier, at any point after the king's *nomen* was changed to Tutankhamun.

A tomb in the Valley of the Kings?

If a search was conducted during Tutankhamun's lifetime for a suitable location for his tomb it will have centered on the Valley of the Kings, since the existence of a funerary temple for his immediate predecessor on the west bank of the Nile at Thebes (see p. 20, above) implies that his/her tomb was sited there, rather than in the Royal Wadi at Tell el-Amarna.[14]

The tomb which Carter discovered in 1922, KV 62, was not originally intended for Tutankhamun's interment – nor, for that matter, for the burial of any pharaoh.[15] Its plan does not meet the requirements for a king's tomb that had evolved from Thutmose III's reign down through the time of Amenhotep III, and which the Royal Tomb at Amarna also exemplifies. In KV 62, there is no succession of descending stairways and corridors that characterize such tombs, no piers in the burial chamber, and no so-called tomb robbers' shaft (or 'well room') – all features retained in the plan of Akhenaten's tomb.[16] Instead, KV 62's original plan (cf. Figure 28) conformed to the modest type of tomb

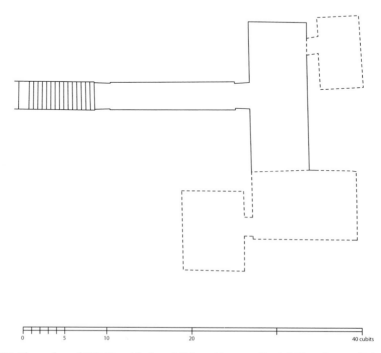

Figure 28 Floor plan of KV 62, with the additions (Annexe, Burial Chamber, and Treasury) to the original, single chamber (Antechamber) indicated by broken lines.

suitable for lesser members of the royal family – kings' sons and daughters, as well as wives – given burial in the Valley of the Kings during the Eighteenth Dynasty. (Stairways typified the entrance to such tombs whereas shafts provided access to the burial chambers of tombs for commoners who were granted burial in the Valley of the Kings; neither type was decorated nor did the owners possess sarcophagi.) Perhaps KV 62, like KV 61 (a single-chambered tomb accessed via a shaft), had never been used but sealed empty, in anticipation of allocation. But it is also possible that the burial of a previous owner was cleared from KV 62 before the tomb was enlarged to accommodate Tutankhamun and his equipment (see Chapter 7, p. 106). I consider it more than likely that the work was undertaken only after Tutankhamun died, during preparations for his funeral.

Evidence is still lacking to support the claim of any of the sites in the Valley of the Kings which Egyptologists have proposed as a tomb once intended for Tutankhamun. A location in the western branch of the Valley of the Kings could have appealed to the king (and/or his advisors), since Amenhotep III, with whom the official policy of the reign sought to associate him closely, lay there, in KV 22.

West Valley A, a single small chamber at the bottom of a short stairway, is about 60 m south of KV 22. A Japanese expedition from Tokyo's Waseda University cleared it in connection with work in Amenhotep III's tomb. In a report on the clearance, Jiro Kondo interprets the meager finds to suggest that the chamber probably served as a storeroom prepared in connection with Amenhotep III's interment in KV 22, rather than as a tomb intended to receive a burial.[17]

Some Egyptologists have proposed identifying KV 23, the only other tomb in the western branch of the Valley known to have been used during the Eighteenth Dynasty for a burial, as initially planned for Tutankhamun. This sepulcher is located some distance from KV 22; its decoration and the sarcophagus found there within the makeshift burial chamber claim it for Tutankhamun's successor King Ay.[18]

A tomb used for a group of non-royal interments during the Third Intermediate Period, many decades after Tutankhamun's death and burial, KV 25, is close to KV 23. During the New Kingdom only a stairway and a descending corridor were completed when work ceased. The architecture of the entrance, the dimensions, and the proportions are definitely kingly; in a lineal succession of royal tomb plans, KV 25 should date after Amenhotep III's tomb.[19] As mentioned in passing above, it was perhaps initiated by Amenhotep IV/Akhenaten during the earlier, Theban phase of his reign, before he took the decision in his fifth regnal year to found a new capital city in Middle Egypt and to fly in the face of tradition by choosing a site for his tomb on the east, rather than the west bank of the Nile there.

With Akhenaten interred at Tell el-Amarna, KV 25 would have been available for appropriation by his immediate successor(s), for whom construction of a funerary temple at Thebes was initiated. According to the scenario that I consider plausible, when death intervened, the burial of Akhenaten's male successor was made (without a sarcophagus, it may be added) in the valley proper, in KV 55. Perhaps on that occasion, the nearby sepulcher KV 62 came to the attention of those officials involved with the interment, who recalled its location a decade later when a tomb was needed for Tutankhamun's burial.

A funerary temple for Tutankhamun at Medinet Habu?

Specialists once supposed that Tutankhamun had commissioned the mortuary complex which lies at Medinet Habu immediately to the north of the funerary temple of the Twentieth-Dynasty king Ramesses III. Excavations at the site in the 1930s, conducted by Chicago's Oriental Institute under the direction of Uvo Hölscher, uncovered nine foundation deposits, but the objects in them bear Ay's name as Pharaoh, not Tutankhamun's. Plenty of documentation exists for Horemhab's usurpation of the temple from King Ay. The 'evidence' offered in favor of Tutankhamun's original ownership of the temple amounted to colossi found there which supposedly resembled him, even though there was no trace of his names in the inscriptions: only traces of King Ay's names could be discerned under the hieroglyphs in the cartouches laying claim to the sculptures for Horemhab. The best preserved among them are two quartzite colossi depicting a striding king, one now in Cairo and the other in Chicago's Oriental Institute Museum, and a limestone bust from a colossal seated statue which Richard Lepsius brought to Berlin in the mid-nineteenth century. All three preserve the body type and the physiognomy of King Ay, not Tutankhamun.[20]

The only object bearing Tutankhamun's name which derives from the vicinity of Medinet Habu is a 'burned reused mud brick with the stamp of Nebkheperure [Tutankhamun's *prenomen*], found in the rubbish of Ramesses III's "Western Fortified Gate".[21] Huge quantities of bricks stamped with the cartouche of Amenhotep III were found reused at Medinet Habu by the archaeologists from Chicago. They come from the older king's nearby palace complex at Malqata where Tutankhamun's reign may well have witnessed construction activity (see Chapter 5, p. 73). The brick with Tutankhamun's throne name could derive from some building erected during his reign at Malqata. It would have then come to Medinet Habu along with the bricks of Amenhotep III when, beginning in Dynasty XX, the structures at Malqata were systematically demolished to obtain building material for reuse.[22]

Nowadays discussion of Tutankhamun's funerary temple centers on inscribed architectural elements – architraves, doorjambs, segments of piers, lotiform columns, and cornices – and wall reliefs retrieved from secondary contexts in and around the

Karnak and Luxor Temples; others have been discovered in significantly later contexts, reused on the west bank[23] as well as beyond the city limits of contemporary Luxor.

The 'Mansion of Nebkheperure'

The honor of having recorded the first relief attributable to a funerary temple for Tutankhamun goes to the French savant Achille C. Prisse d'Avennes. His drawing of a block which he saw in Karnak Temple (Figure 29) was published in 1847.[24] The complete scene showed a king spanning his bow while hunting from his chariot in the desert. Although the cartouches are not completely preserved, enough unmistakable traces remained to identify the pharaoh as Tutankhamun. Ray Johnson has provided an overview of all the inscribed and/or decorated blocks attributable to the Mansion which had been located down to the beginning of this century, and he discusses some problems of interpretation associated with them.[25] Ray and Marc Gabolde, who illustrates and considers several scenes in his unpublished dissertation on Ay,[26] are currently preparing a comprehensive joint publication of the corpus.

The sandstone used for the architectural elements and wall reliefs of the Mansion was not quarried in post-Amarna times, but rather at Akhenaten's command, to construct and decorate structures he erected at Karnak Temple before the move to Tell el-Amarna. Some blocks reused in the construction of the Mansion are of traditional size, measuring *c.* 65 cm tall by 150 cm wide, such as were used in the earliest phase of Akhenaten's construction work at Karnak; most are, however, *talatat*.[27]

In the corpus compiled by Marc and Ray, Tutankhamun's titulary figures prominently in the inscriptions on the architraves; on the piers, he is depicted as Pharaoh in the presence of various gods and goddesses, and in the wall reliefs his figure occurs in a variety of contexts (some notable scenes are described below). Ay is also present in

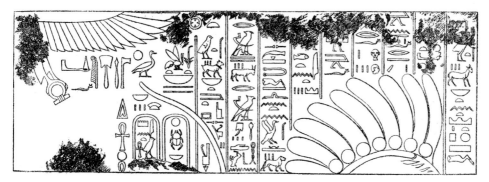

Figure 29 Block from a hunting scene in the Mansion of Tutankhamun, Karnak. Present location not known.

word and deed, but in two different capacities – as a courtier in the following of his sovereign Tutankhamun, and as a king in full panoply, honoring the memory of his young predecessor (whom the dedicatory texts on some architraves style 'his son'). Ay's figures in the former context have been carefully erased and plastered over. His royal titulary in the inscriptions on the architraves, asserting his role in 'making' the monument for Tutankhamun, were also carefully erased in apparent preparation for usurpation, but this was never carried out, nor was Tutankhamun's titulary on the same architraves touched (Figure 30). By contrast, the figures of both Tutankhamun and Ay as kings on the piers and in the wall scenes have been attacked; in the associated cartouches, all but the names of the gods Amun and Re have been hacked out (Figure 31a–b).

The architectural elements and segments of wall relief composed of reused blocks were themselves reused again, as fill inside the Second and Ninth Pylons, built by King Horemhab after he succeeded Ay. Finally, during medieval times, both pylons, and the Tenth Pylon as well, served as 'quarries' for local building projects and also for construction at other sites in the environs of Luxor.

Some Egyptologists (including myself, initially) thought that these blocks bearing the names and figures of Tutankhamun and Ay derived from two different buildings, since two different names are mentioned in the inscriptions they bear.[28] Resolution of this issue in favor of a single structure called 'Mansion-of-Nebkheperure, beloved-of-Amun, Founder-of-Thebes', sometimes shortened to 'Mansion-of-Nebkheperure-in-Thebes',[29] entails the supposition that it was begun while Tutankhamun still reigned – at

Figure 30 Architrave from the Mansion of Tutankhamun showing the erasure of Ay's *prenomen* above Tutankhamun's.

a   b

Figure 31 a   Segment of a pier from the Mansion of Tutankhamun showing the hacking of
Tutankhamun's cartouches, save for the names of the gods Amun and Re.
b   Segment of a pier from the Mansion of Tutankhamun showing the hacking of a king's
figure (Ay?).

a time when Ay's role was that of a loyal courtier – but completed by Ay when he
himself acceded to the kingship after Tutankhamun's death.[30] This idea is consonant
with the techniques of the reliefs. Those depicting Ay in the service of King Tutankhamun
are carved in raised relief. Down through the Eighteenth Dynasty, Egyptian sculptors
employed this technique for spaces with limited sources of light – above all, for the
innermost rooms of a temple, where the select few practiced the cult. Such rooms were
built and decorated first, taking precedence over more generally accessible parts of a
temple. (Those raised reliefs showing Ay as Pharaoh, like the scenes of warfare and
hunting featuring King Tutankhamun, will have decorated the walls under the roofed
ambulatory surrounding the courtyard in the plan of the Mansion proposed by Marc.)

There can be no doubt that King Ay did in fact complete the Mansion-of-
Nebkheperure, beloved-of-Amun, Founder-of-Thebes, fulfilling the time-honored
obligation of a new ruler to his predecessor and, perhaps not coincidentally, affirming
his legitimacy as successor.[31] But did Tutankhamun intend this building at its inception
to function eventually as his funerary temple? Nowadays, I don't think so. I suppose,
rather, that Tutankhamun commissioned it as a chapel in connection with the worship
of Amun, possibly at Karnak, or as a way station – for example, along the Processional
Avenue leading south to the Mut Precinct or to Luxor Temple – with depictions of Ay
in the reliefs as his loyal retainer.[32]

With an initial phase of construction, I would associate a plan to furnish the Mansion
with the series of statues depicting members of the Theban 'ennead' discussed in
Chapter 4, pp. 62–3. Marc has found the names of seven of these gods in the labels
identifying figures in the reliefs on the piers of the ambulatory.

When the structure – along with the sculptures to furnish it – was left unfinished at
Tutankhamun's death, it could have then been converted at Ay's behest into a funerary

temple for his predecessor. In that connection, the figures of Ay as a courtier in the reliefs would hardly have been appropriate.[33] In other words, it is possible that Ay himself ordered such raised-relief images of himself to be carefully erased and plastered over after he became king.[34]

The way Ay's figures were treated in the scenes showing him as fan-bearer in attendance on Tutankhamun is in marked contrast to the hacking out of the images of King Ay (and Tutankhamun, too, along with the names of both kings), which is doubtless attributable to Horemhab's command.

The question of the structure's original location remains, if it was intended as a funerary temple from its inception. Did it stand on the west bank of the Nile, in the series of funerary temples sited along the edge of the cultivation by earlier rulers of Dynasty XVIII?[35] Or, as I consider more likely, on the east bank in immediate proximity to Karnak Temple? Martina Ullmann reviews the pros and cons of both sites in her discussion of the Mansion, deciding in favor of the likelihood that it stood near Karnak, where the blocks were found.[36] Those who prefer the west bank must reckon with ferrying blocks from Akhenaten's structures at Karnak across the Nile for reuse in building the Mansion there, and then only a decade or so later, their return to the east side and Karnak where they were re-employed once more, in the construction of Horemhab's Pylons II and IX. The transport of blocks from Western Thebes to Karnak for reuse is documented, but with certainty only beginning in Dynasty XX. Transport of blocks to and fro as would be required for a west-bank location of the Mansion-of-Nebkheperure-in-Thebes is possible but, in my opinion, less than probable.

Depictions of Pharaoh in the reliefs of Tutankhamun's Mansion

The sunk-relief decoration of the piers surrounding an open courtyard behind the *c.* 20 m wide façade conformed to tradition. The king – Ay, as well as Tutankhamun – stands under the protective wings of the solar falcon Behdety or of Nekhbet's vulture, facing a goddess or a god (most frequently, Amun). The divinity embraces the king, holds an *ankh*-sign to his nose, or clasps him by the hand.

The scenes so far documented in the decoration likewise derive from the standard repertory found in temples of the gods during the New Kingdom. These include presentation of offerings, rites of purification, processions on land and on the river with large and small divine barks, etc., paralleling closely the decoration of the Colonnade Hall of Luxor Temple.[37]

One of the conventional themes is the presentation of *maat*. In the reliefs of the Mansion the king proffers a small squatting figure of the goddess Maat with a feather – her distinctive attribute – atop her head; presumably the recipient was Amun, but the adjoining block has not yet been located. Nor can the king whose figure has been damaged by hacking – Tutankhamun or Ay? – be identified in the absence of a label.[38]

Another traditional but much older theme in the reliefs of the Mansion is 'driving the calves' (Plate XX). Because the scene comes from Karnak, Amun should be the god in whose honor this rite was performed. Arno Egberts has traced this subject with its agrarian/pastoral origins back to at least as early as the Fifth Dynasty:[39] fragments of relief from King Sahure's funerary temple at Abusir belonged to such a tableau. Most, though not all later examples come from gods' temples, rather than a funerary context. Beginning in the New Kingdom driving the calves is coupled with the scene of 'consecrating the *meret*-chests', another rite affirming the ruler's legitimacy.

Complete scenes of Pharaoh driving the calves into the presence of a god show the animals depicted in four sub-registers, one above the other, in front of the king. Labels distinguish the calves by color: black, white, red, and dappled. The block from the Mansion illustrated here preserves part of two calves. The remaining two calves are partially preserved on other blocks belonging to the scene, as is the figure of the king driving them, followed by the smaller figure of the royal *ka* (the embodiment of Pharaoh's 'life force').

The blue painting of Amun's skin preserved here contrasts with the color of his figure in scenes created before the Amarna Period.[40] Few depictions of the god survived the iconoclastic phase of Akhenaten's reign and fewer still retain their original color, but so far only one has been documented with traces of blue painting; the others show the god with red-brown skin like that of other males. The relief from the Mansion showing Amun with blue skin epitomizes his new, post-Amarna coloring; by the time of Seti I, scarcely more than three decades later, a figure of Amun with red-brown skin was a thing of the past. Blue was the most prestigious color in the Egyptian palette; Egyptologists have often explained Amun's blue skin color as a reference to his role as a god of the heavens. Regardless, it clearly distinguished representations of Amun from mortals – including the king – as well as from other gods.

The blocks comprising the scene of driving the calves were decorated on both sides; because the king kneeling in front of Amun on the other side is labeled Ay, he, rather than Tutankhamun, may well have been the king driving the calves before the Lord of Karnak. This type of scene, with the complimentary scene showing the rite of consecrating *meret*-chests, is documented at other sites with either Tutankhamun or Ay as Pharaoh officiating – for example, with Tutankhamun before Min and Isis in his temple at Kawa.[41]

There can be no doubt, however, that Tutankhamun is the king hunting in the desert from a chariot in another scene that can be assembled from several blocks. The pair of his cartouches and the text describing the hunt are included in the drawing of the block made by Prisse d'Avennes in the nineteenth century already mentioned and illustrated in Figure 29. The king in his speeding chariot takes aim with his drawn bow at desert game, including (according to the inscription) lions as well as varieties of antelope. Apparently this scene included various kinds of desert game, unlike in the decoration of the painted box from Tutankhamun's tomb (Obj. No. 21) where the pursuit of lions was relegated to a separate scene. Another block from a hunting scene in the Mansion shows a wild bull, felled by one of the king's arrows, lying beneath the cab of the king's speeding chariot (Plate XXI). Such tableaux express the ideological role of Pharaoh, subduing the forces of chaos manifest in wild animals.

The cartouches preserved in scenes of two military campaigns on the walls of the roofed ambulatory formed by the piers in the Mansion also leave no doubt that the victorious pharaoh featured in them is Tutankhamun. There is nothing unconventional about the king's adversaries in these encounters – on one side of the courtyard he engages in battle against the traditional foes to the south, and on the other he confronts 'Asiatic' adversaries at home to Egypt's northeast.[42] In traditional fashion, each series of scenes of warfare concluded with the obligatory presentation of the spoils, including prisoners of war, to Amun in gratitude for his vouchsafing victory to the king.

Some unusual details have tempted Egyptologists to suggest that these scenes could well depict actual events – military campaigns undertaken in Tutankhamun's name if not actually led by him on the battlefield. The detailed depictions of foreign prisoners included in the decoration of the tomb which Horemhab built at Saqqara while still serving Tutankhamun faithfully as generalissimo[43] are cited in support of the idea that the reign witnessed warfare with the king, at least nominally, engaging southern as well as northern foes. The sequence of scenes of a campaign against Asiatic foes would then 'illustrate' military campaigns alluded to in contemporary (or nearly contemporary) cuneiform documents.[44] But for now, I remain skeptical, since none of the blocks so far identified as belonging to these scenes in the Mansion of Nebkheperure bears any remains of an historical text to substantiate the supposition.

One of the vignettes, unique down until the present, that has excited comment shows a prisoner suspended in a cage above the deck of a ship (Figure 32). The long, draped robe of the captive sets him apart from the Egyptians and identifies him as a foreigner from Syria–Palestine. Is he a prisoner taken captive in a real campaign being transported back to Egypt, perhaps for ceremonial execution?[45]

Another detail shows Egyptian infantrymen marching along with severed hands skewered on their lances, providing graphic illustration of a gruesome feature of Egyptian warfare: the severing of the hands of the defeated as trophies paraded and presented for a commensurate reward.[46] Four pits containing severed hands, discovered at a palace in the Delta at Tell el-Dab'a and datable towards the end of the Second Intermediate Period (or about 1550 BC), corroborate the mention of this practice in texts from the beginning of the New Kingdom.[47] (Later, Ramesside war reliefs include

Figure 32 Captive in a cage suspended above the deck of a ship; relief from the Mansion of Tutankhamun.

piles of penises to the same purpose.) One scene from the walls of the Mansion shows a soldier stooping to chop off the hand of a dead (or dying?) Nubian lying under the wheels of Pharaoh's chariot,[48] and the same deed is included in a battlefield scene on the painted box from Tutankhamun's tomb.

This and other scenes from the Mansion give every appearance of uniqueness, but that is not necessarily proof that they refer to actual, historical events rather than documenting instead the imaginative talent of a gifted draftsman. Regardless, as Ray Johnson has noted, the presence of such scenes in the decoration of the Mansion shows that the origins of narrative relief predate the accession of the Ramessides. Continuing excavations of a mortuary temple at Abydos of King Ahmose, first king of Dynasty XVIII, may well push back the origins even further.[49]

The scenes in the decoration of the Mansion associated specifically with funerary rites – in particular, a series depicting episodes involving statues of the deceased ruler – all feature Tutankhamun. They parallel reliefs in the funerary temple of Thutmose II on the west bank of the Nile which that king's son Thutmose III completed for his father.[50] These ritual scenes evoke the solar destiny of the deceased king – Tutankhamun was no longer among the living.

Tutankhamun's Death and Burial

Widely differing answers have been given to the questions of when, where, and under what circumstances Tutankhamun died. That the king lived to experience the grape harvest of the ninth year after his accession is demonstrated by six dockets of Year 9 on the amphoras filled with wine stored in the Annexe of his tomb. When Jaroslav Černý published the hieratic inscriptions from KV 62, he believed that the single docket of Year 10 was 'in all probability' also Tutankhamun's,[1] but other specialists were hesitant to accept a decade-long reign for the king. Then, in 1996, Pierre Tallet argued convincingly that the date referred to wine of Akhenaten's tenth year. Noting that wines in ancient times might not have been as perishable as we tend to believe, he proposed that the wine of Akhenaten's Year 10 was included with the burial because of the prestige value of the year's vintage, like the wine in another amphora from the Annexe labeled Year 31 which must refer to the reign of Amenhotep III.[2]

Thanks to the bouquets, garlands, wreaths, and floral collars found in the tomb and in the cache of materials associated with the burial of the king excavated from KV 54 (see further below, pp. 114–15), the time of year when Tutankhamun died can be estimated. Assuming that the blossoms and fruit were freshly picked for the purpose and that the time from the king's death until he was buried amounted to the textually well-documented ideal of 70 days, then he died in January or early February.[3] Perhaps a somewhat longer interval is more likely,[4] and of course, there is no telling whether unusual circumstances might have delayed the obsequies after the mummification of the king's body had been completed.

Specialists who have examined the mummy over the years have thought they could recognize a number of anomalies[5] – for example, in the position of the arms (crossed horizontally across the body rather than angled upwards) and the location of the embalming incision.[6] And then there is the amount of resins and oils poured over the mummy, regularly described as excessive, to be accounted for. But no hard and fast standards for royal mummies are discernible before Dynasty XIX,[7] and the remains found in KV 55 – the closest 'mummy' in time to Tutankhamun's – are equally problematic of interpretation: one arm lies across the body with the other extended down alongside the trunk (which contributed to its initial identification as female) while its 'skeletonized' state can be attributed at least in part to an inadequate amount of just those oils and resins that were used in excess on Tutankhamun's corpse.[8]

Clues are also lacking about the whereabouts of the king when death struck. He may have been in a palace at Memphis or carrying out a religious obligation at the site of a major temple in Upper Egypt, underway on a tour of inspection or participating in a hunting expedition. And if he led the Egyptian army into battle,[9] he may even have died abroad. But as Darnell and Manassa conclude, 'we may never know whether Tutankhamun actually rode his chariot into battle ...',[10] and I for one find it unlikely.

The cause(s) of Tutankhamun's death

Theories about what led to Tutankhamun's death are legion, with no end to speculation in sight. Some of the suggestions are grounded on scientific analyses of his mummy; others (like those attempting to identify what might have 'ailed' Akhenaten) are inspired by the representations of the king in relief and painting – which have been incorrectly interpreted as showing him to be frail or even crippled.[11] Regardless, the results are inconclusive. About the only definitive statement that can be made is that the mummy provides no evidence for supposing that he was murdered by a blow to the head.[12] But the alternative cause, or rather the combination of causes the study of Hawass et al. proposes (considered immediately below) is by no means uncontested.

F. J. Rühli, head of the Centre for Evolutionary Medicine at the University of Zurich, and Salima Ikram, an Egyptologist at the American University in Cairo specializing in the study of ancient Egyptian human as well as animal mummies, have co-authored a critical review of the many theories, published through March 2013, about why Tutankhamun died when he did.[13] Since the initial 'autopsy' of the king's body at the time KV 62 was cleared, it has been examined in detail four times. On the last occasion, Zahi Hawass oversaw the removal of the mummy from the tomb, by contrast to the three previous examinations which took place inside it, where the mummy had reposed within the outmost coffin in the basin of the quartzite sarcophagus. Following on the extraction of DNA (the resulting conclusions have been discussed above, in Chapter 1) and CT scans, the pitiable remains of the king were returned to KV 62 and placed in the controlled environment of a lighted glass case at the south end of the Antechamber.

One goal of the review that Rühli and Ikram achieve with spectacular success is highlighting 'the complexities of palaeopathology: how a single individual ... studied in detail by so many groups, can yield so many and sometimes contradictory results ...'.[14] The only issue on which experts can be said to agree is the king's age at death – he was between 17 and 19 years old when he breathed his last.

Hawass's team could rule out some of the multitude of pathological conditions, traumas, and physical defects from which Tutankhamun purportedly suffered while simultaneously identifying new afflictions such as Köhler's Disease II and a club foot. The team's own conclusion – that 'the most likely cause' of Tutankhamun's death was 'avascular bone necrosis in conjunction with a malarial infection'[15] – has not met with an enthusiastic reception in the scientific community, let alone among Egyptologists.[16] For example, even if it be conclusively demonstrated to everyone's satisfaction that Tutankhamun did have malaria, there is no way of determining whether he succumbed to it or recovered instead.[17]

A persistent shortcoming of many scientific/medical studies, which is not discussed by Rühli and Ikram, is the failure of their authors to consult experienced, well-informed Egyptologists. A glance at the footnotes of the *JAMA* article reveals the extent of this problem (and coincidentally raises questions about the peer-review system). Citations in error and/or incomplete references for books by Egyptologists and articles in 'non-scientific' publications are many, while some pertinent titles are simply missing. For example, to bolster the theory that Tutankhamun experienced difficulty walking, the reference is Reeves's *Complete Tutankhamun*, without any page number cited. Furthermore, the reader will find no support for the idea that Tutankhamun needed a cane or crutches in the overview of the sticks and staves found in the tomb that Reeves provides.[18] On the other hand, Hawass et al. do not include a reference to Ali Hassan's monograph on such standard items of Egyptian funerary equipment (since the Old Kingdom!) that do not provide any clue about the physical health of the owners.[19] Similarly, Renate Germer's monograph on the extensive plant remains found in the tomb[20] is cited, again without page references, as if she proposes that the king took along a supply of medicine to the Hereafter for relief from his many purported ailments. And if Hawass and his collaborators had looked at the publication of the small golden shrine (Obj. No. 108) from KV 62, they might have thought twice about citing scenes showing Tutankhamun seated while hunting and fishing – contexts in which they think he should be standing – as documenting his physical weakness.[21] The comparative evidence demonstrates that the seated posture, like the bow Tutankhamun uses in one such scene, is related to prestige and status, not a reflection of a frail constitution.[22]

Rühli and Ikram conclude: 'However, even with the best medical and Egyptological forensic work, it is doubtful that all aspects of Tutankhamun's health and possible causes for his death will ever be known due to the absence of the indispensable direct medical practitioner-patient interaction, and the limited amount of body tissue [available for study].'[23] In other words, only the court physician might possibly have been in a position to tell us why Tutankhamun died.

Funerary equipment 1: canopics, mummy 'trappings,' pectorals

If the king had been ailing for some time, as Hawass and his team conclude, arrangements should have been somewhat advanced for his burial when he passed away. By contrast, I have speculated in the previous chapter that few if any provisions for Tutankhamun's afterlife preceded the king's death. Be that as it may, a flurry of activity will have resulted when news of the king's demise became known at the royal residence in Memphis. There was plenty to do while the body was being readied for burial. His personal effects had to be packed – everything he might have used in this life and require for the next, from clothing and jewelry, furniture and linens, to his hunting gear and chariots, etc. – and lists drawn up for a token supply of food and drink to satisfy his hunger and thirst in perpetuity.

More importantly, the one-chambered tomb in the Valley of the Kings selected for the burial had to be enlarged (cf. Figure 28). A crypt was cut at the north end of the single room to a depth of nearly a meter below the original floor level to serve as the Burial Chamber; from its east end opened a smaller room that Carter would call the Treasury. Near the southeast corner of what had become KV 62's Antechamber, a third room was added, its entrance at floor level. Tentative plans for decorating the tomb needed to be made as well and a schedule drawn up for stocking it.

Simultaneously, the equipment indispensable for a pharaoh's burial and survival in the Hereafter had to be assembled. The inscriptions on many items that had been made for his predecessors (the ruling queen in particular) could be altered to name Tutankhamun, but others had to be commissioned for him. In the last chapter, I argued that the sarcophagus in KV 62 was not made for Tutankhamun but rather for a predecessor, quite possibly the ruling queen, even if no trace of her name survives. By contrast, the inlaid gold bands (so-called trappings) that were placed like bindings around the mummy (Obj. Nos 256b 1–4) and the little gold coffins, four in number, for the organs removed from the body during mummification (Obj. Nos 266g 1–4) preserve unequivocal traces of the cartouche with her special epithet 'beneficial for her husband'.[24]

The gilded figures of the tutelary goddesses (Isis, Nephthys, Selket, and Neith, all subsumed under Obj. No. 266) whose outstretched arms 'protected' the canopic shrine around the chest of Egyptian alabaster were designed in conformity with the 'Amarna canon' (Figure 33). Gay Robins has also remarked that the pleated garments they wear are inappropriate attire for goddesses;[25] like the crimped sash knotted under their breasts such clothing belonged to a queen's wardrobe, familiar from representations of Nefertiti. Possibly these features are holdovers from Akhenaten's reign; alternatively, the figures were made after Akhenaten's death but before Tutankhamun came to the throne to depict a queen and were only subsequently adapted for traditional use by affixing the goddesses' emblems to their heads.

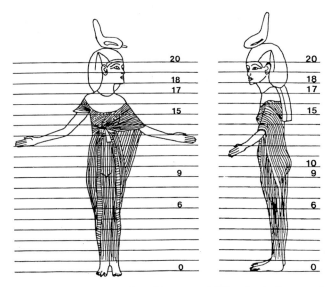

Figure 33 Drawing demonstrating that the statue of Selket from the canopic shrine in Tutankhamun's tomb (Obj. No. 266) was designed according to the Amarna canon.

The position of two of the goddesses' figures in relation to the shrine provides an example of the carelessness of those who carried out the burial: the statue of Selket was attached to the sled where Nephthys should have stood and vice versa.[26] Also noteworthy is the damage to the lids of the four compartments of the canopic chest. Both vulture and uraeus at the forehead on one lid (Obj. No. 266c) were broken off, and the vulture's beaks of Obj. Nos 266e and 266f were chipped, while the king's nose of the last had been so inexpertly mended as to disfigure the face.[27] Aidan Dodson terms the claim that the lids do not 'look like' Tutankhamun subjective and dismisses it.[28] Each lid depicts the king wearing the royal *nemes* head-cloth with a vulture's head and a uraeus at his brow. The pairing, which is found both earlier (in the design of the stoppers of Amenhotep II's canopic chest) and later (for those of King Horemhab), conforms to specifically funerary imagery. As in the design of all three coffins from KV 62, the vulture and cobra fronting the king's headdress do not represent the goddesses of Upper and Lower Egypt, as repeatedly incorrectly described. Rather they embody Isis and Nephthys, respectively, who join forces to protect their brother Osiris with whom the king in death was assimilated.[29]

The sisters appear on many items of funerary equipment from the tomb as does the sky goddess Nut, depicted as a winged woman; texts frequently express the wish that she protect the deceased king with her embrace.[30] She is featured in the design of a pectoral (Obj. No. 261p(1)) where traces of the original texts show that it, too, once belonged to the ruling queen.[31] The jewel was found in the portable shrine (Obj. No. 261) surmounted by a recumbent figure of the jackal god Anubis which stood in the doorway between the Burial Chamber and the Treasury. Another of the seven pectorals found with it (Obj. No. 261p(3)) had also been appropriated from a predecessor of Tutankhamun, possibly Akhenaten.[32]

Funerary equipment 2: 'Statuettes-in-shrines' and shabtis

Claims have been made from time to time that the second coffin, the second and third shrines erected around the sarcophagus, some of the funerary figurines (shabtis), and a few of the so-called statuettes-in-shrines were not commissioned for Tutankhamun but intended for the burial of a predecessor. There are certainly anomalous pieces among the last that deserve more attention than Friedrich Abitz gave them in his study.[33] Over thirty of these figures depicting the king and deities were found in the tomb. A few were free-standing, but most were sealed in shrine-shaped boxes. Five of them are illustrated here in Plate XXII.

One of the statuettes-in-shrines (Obj. No. 289b) depicts a striding king atop a panther's back. The modeling of the torso with its feminine breasts led to the suggestion that it belonged to the funerary equipment commissioned for a woman. Other noteworthy features include the eyes' lack of a cosmetic strip and the pointed, rather than squared-off ends of the eyebrows, unlike those of the companion piece, found in the same shrine (Obj. No. 289a), and of the other figures depicting the king among the statuettes-in-shrines. A belt is missing from the kilt, and the apron-like accessory lacks the feather-pattern shown on the others. And, finally, the sandals worn by the figure are set into the base, not attached to the top of it, as in the design of the remaining statuettes.[34] Add to these anomalies the fact that the proportions of Obj. No. 289a are closer to those of the traditional canon.[35] The conclusion seems inescapable that Obj. No. 289b was not made for Tutankhamun.

Among the statuettes there are two figures of the falcon-headed demigod Duamutef, a deity responsible for protecting the internal organs removed during mummification. One of them (Obj. No. 304b) and the companion figure of Qebehsenuf (Obj. No. 304a), found in a shrine with it, differ in workmanship from all the other statuettes of mummiform gods. Their eyes (and the falcon-markings around them on Obj. No. 304b) are simply painted on (by contrast to the inlaid eyes of the other figures), and their broad collars are much less detailed than those worn by the remaining mummiform gods. They are not identified by an inscription as the others are, and the seal used to secure the shrine containing them is virtually unique in Tutankhamun's tomb. They, too, belonged in all likelihood to the equipment prepared for another ruler.

Most of the gilded figures reveal evidence of haste: the black painting of the bases was slapdash, and the texts naming the gods (and the king's cartouche as well) were sloppily added. A ritual of some kind was probably involved with draping the figures in linen before sealing them in the shrines,[36] a procedure that was not without incident. The front of the statuette depicting the lion-headed goddess Sakhmet enthroned had to be sawn off so that the figure would fit into her shrine; perhaps that was when she lost her scepter. The missing attribute is one more indication of the carelessness with which the burial was carried out.

One theory proposes that the primary role of the statuettes-in-shrines was played during the funeral[37] while Abitz argued that they guaranteed the rebirth of the rejuvenated king in the Hereafter. An ostracon from the Valley of the Kings which dates to the time of the nineteenth-dynasty pharaoh Merenptah supports the idea that the statuettes' function was in the next world, rather than at the funeral. The text documents the transport of 'the gods of Merenptah' into his tomb, witnessed by a group of officials; this took place about three years before the king's death.[38] In other words figures of gods were among the items stocked in the tomb long before Merenptah died. Thus I consider it likely that the 22 sealed shrines with statuettes which Carter found in the Treasury were among some of the first items deposited in Tutankhamun's tomb – after the king's death but in advance of the funeral. No inscription, not even a quickly scribbled hieratic note in paint, revealed what each sealed shrine held; for this reason it is doubtful that the relative position of the shrines followed a strict, predetermined plan with a special meaning for the arrangement. The several paragraphs I have devoted here to the statuettes-in-shrines are intended to demonstrate the potential for research on just one group of objects even decades after the tomb's discovery.

The same might be said about the shabtis. Tutankhamun was well supplied with such figurines, which were expected to substitute for him should he be called upon to do manual labor in the Hereafter. Such 'deputies' belonged to the standard burial equipment of king and commoner alike. Tutankhamun's shabtis were made of many different materials – from various hard and soft stones, like quartzite and Egyptian alabaster; wood, both completely and only partially gilded (Plate XXIII); and the ubiquitous faience, varying in color from blue-green to deep indigo. Most depict him wearing a pharaoh's headgear (a crown or royal head-cloth) with a uraeus at the brow. Some of the larger, well-made pieces pair the uraeus of Nephthys with the vulture's head of Isis, as in the design of the canopic coffinettes, but a few examples lack any royal insignia at all.[39]

Tutankhamun's predecessors Amenhotep III and Akhenaten did not lack this type of funerary accessory. Many shabtis are known for both even if their tombs were plundered; only a single shabti of Akhenaten's survived antiquity intact. Their shabtis, too, were made of a variety of materials and depicted the subject wearing several different head coverings. The text on Amenhotep III's shabtis was especially created for him while Akhenaten's bore only his name. The larger, well-made shabtis from KV 62 carry the standard shabti text from Chapter 6 of the Book of the Dead in full; others bear only an excerpt from it. Some smaller figures were inscribed with just one or both of Tutankhamun's cartouches, and seven faience shabtis have the appropriate spell but lack the name of any owner. Inscriptions on six shabtis – one of them an unusual type depicting the king lying on a bier – attest their dedication by two high-ranking officials of the reign.

Tutankhamun's readily identifiable facial features are not reproduced consistently even among the large, well-modeled shabtis, let alone among the faience figurines made in series. This has led to speculation that some were made not for him, but for a predecessor. However, as Geoffrey T. Martin has observed, a comparable amount of deviation is discernible in the features of Akhenaten's shabtis, all certainly created for him alone.[40]

Funerary equipment 3: shrines, coffins, mummy mask, skullcap

The suggestion was first made decades ago that the second of the four gilded shrines surrounding the sarcophagus was not commissioned with Tutankhamun in mind. The color of the gold inside the cartouches, which differs from the surrounding gilding, aroused the suspicion that Tutankhamun's name replaced another.[41] In the meantime, Tutankhamun's original ownership of the third shrine has also been questioned, and Harris has cited additional criteria in support of the idea that both were made for someone else.[42]

Earlier theories proposed Smenkhkare as the owner of the second shrine, but Harris suggests that Akhenaten commissioned both the second and third shrines. He calls attention to the presence in the texts of the royal title 'perfect ruler' (rather than the traditional 'perfect god') and the epithet 'appearing in the White Crown', both especially associated with Akhenaten. But as noted above (Chapter 1, p. 8), 'perfect ruler' was introduced only in the *later* years of Akhenaten's reign; its use is incompatible with the orthodox funerary beliefs expressed in the texts and iconography of the shrines. The inscriptions on the inlaid ebony throne attest the retention of 'perfect ruler' for a time, however brief, after the accession of Tutankhaten. An immediate successor of Akhenaten should be the original owner of the second shrine (if there was one), a person who placed faith in orthodox funerary deities and texts while not rejecting all of Akhenaten's innovations.[43] Determining for whom the second shrine was commissioned is important for the study of Egyptian religion since the texts include the earliest example of the so-called 'enigmatic netherworld book' with its synthesis of solar and Osirian beliefs.[44] Clearly, detailed study of all four shrines from iconographic and stylistic points of view needs to be undertaken.[45] The excellent high-resolution digital images made by master photographer Sandro Vannini[46] could be put to scholarly use in such a study.

The dissimilarity of the facial features to the idealized likeness of Tutankhamun has been cited as a reason to doubt that the second coffin was made for the king's burial. Claude Vandersleyen, for example, has referred to the 'disquieting unlikeness' of the face's 'very peculiar [square] shape' and its harsh, sullen expression.[47] As others have also remarked, the second coffin resembles the usurped canopic coffinettes in design and technique, but it is hardly a duplicate of them, for there are differences in detail, and I cannot recognize the purported similarity of physiognomy. Until now, no claim has been made that the texts naming Tutankhamun on the second coffin are not original.[48] If the second coffin can indeed be convincingly dissociated from Tutankhamun, then the question would arise whether either (or both) of the two other coffins belonged to him, since the fit of all three inside each other is so very snug. Aidan Dodson's forthcoming study of the coffins may yet bring some new evidence to bear on these theories, if not provide a definitive answer to the question of their ownership.

Nicholas Reeves has proposed that the face of the famous gold mask (Obj. No. 256a), undoubtedly an official likeness of Tutankhamun, replaced the face of the ruling queen when the mask, too, was adapted for the king's use.[49] The section of Spell 151 of the Book of the Dead, which guaranteed the mask's ability to function as the face of the deceased, is inscribed on the back. Both the basin of the third, innermost gold coffin and its lid bear the same text, positioned precisely so that the head of the king's mummy wearing the mask rested directly underneath as well as on top of the spell.[50] Regardless of whether the mask was made or adapted for the king from a previous owner, the presence of the text in immediate proximity to the mummy is another indication of the trust placed in the efficacy of traditional funerary beliefs.

A beaded skullcap (Obj. No. 256tttt) lay directly on the king's shaved head below a curious ornament (Obj. No. 256qqqq+rrrr) combining a vulture with outspread wings and a uraeus (again presumably emblematic of Osiris's sisters Isis and Nephthys). Set into the bodies of four cobras decorating the skullcap were pairs of cartouches bearing what seems to have been a unique variant of the earlier so-called didactic name of Akhenaten's god Aten. Since the cap cannot be found today, discussion of the possible meaning of the variant name and its reference relies on Carter's copies of the hieroglyphs and Harry Burton's photographs. Years ago Desroches-Noblecourt proposed an imaginative explanation for the mention of the solar god in immediate proximity to the mummy: for her the skullcap was evidence of Tutankhamun's abiding faith in Akhenaten's beliefs, with Ay seeing to the departure of his young predecessor from this life wearing 'the mark of the well-beloved Globe'.[51] In the interim Harris has asked rhetorically if the name of Aten uniquely documented here might be read as a reference to the location of Akhenaten's tomb at Amarna.[52] And he adds that it does show 'that some pieces at least of tomb equipment intended for Akhenaten were later pressed into use' for Tutankhamun's burial.[53] But this conclusion begs the question of whether the skullcap was indeed an item of funerary equipment made for Akhenaten. Could it have been made instead between Akhenaten's death and Tutankhaten's accession for a ruler who used epithets associated with Akhenaten at a time when theology had evolved to allow the re-association of Re-Horakhty, mentioned in the cartouches of the skullcap, with Aten?[54]

Until conclusive evidence proves otherwise, a list of those items essential for the orthodox funeral of a king that were commissioned for Tutankhamun includes: the first and fourth shrines from around the sarcophagus; the outer gilded coffin and the solid gold innermost coffin; the (face of the) gold mask; the canopic chest, canopy, and shrine (but not the coffinettes nor, in all probability, the figures of the tutelary goddesses 'protecting' it); the shabtis; most of the statuettes-in-shrines; the three theriomorphic biers (see p. 118); amulets and amuletic jewelry made of gold sheeting found on the mummy; the 'magic bricks' in the niches in the Burial Chamber; the model boats for journeying in the Hereafter; the life-size statues 'guarding' the entrance to the Burial Chamber; and the oars from the floor of the Burial Chamber, along with various other sundry small items.

Stocking the tomb[55]

With a single exception, the boxes found in the tomb belonged to the furnishings of the palace(s) where the king lived, requisitioned for transporting his possessions to Thebes. When a box was packed, a scribe hastily listed its contents on the lid. Upon arrival at an assembly point, probably on the west bank of the Nile (perhaps near the entrance to or even in the Valley of the Kings itself), the boxes will have been opened and the contents checked against the list made at the departure point. Christian E. Loeben suggests that when the boxes were repacked before eventually being deposited in the tomb, haste and carelessness – regularly attributed to those cleaning up after a robbery in antiquity – could have resulted in the disparities between the lists and the contents.[56]

The only box made especially for Tutankhamun's burial is a large, gable-lidded chest provided with carrying poles (Obj. No. 32).[57] Men carrying the same kind of portable chest are shown in scenes of the cortege in two non-royal tombs of the Old Kingdom, demonstrating the continuity of funerary traditions over nearly a millennium. Tutankhamun, labeled Osiris, is depicted in a panel on the front of the box worshipping Wenenefer (a hypostasis of Osiris). The texts inscribed in the strips of ebony framing each side and on the lid call upon a veritable army of deities who are enjoined to provide every benefit of consequence in the Hereafter for the king. At discovery, the box contained cups and small vessels made of stone, faience, and glass, seven stone knives, and lumps of resin and incense – items that probably saw ritual use at the funeral. The chest's position in the Antechamber accords with the conclusion that it will have been among the items brought into the tomb only after the blocking of the doorway to the Burial Chamber was built, plastered, and sealed by the necropolis officials.

Many of the other objects found in KV 62 which had no recognizable (at least for us) role in the actual funeral could have been taken into the tomb as soon as the work of enlarging it was completed. Of course, the Antechamber had to remain empty, since it provided access to the Burial Chamber and the Treasury beyond, as well as space for assembling the parts of the three larger shrines that would surround the sarcophagus. In the Treasury itself, the items lined up against the walls to the left and right of the entrance – two dismantled chariots, statuettes-in-shrines (provided they had no role in the obsequies, which I believe to have been the case), and boxes with shabtis topped with boat models – could have been brought in early. A sufficiently wide path was left open for introducing the canopic equipment which would reach the tomb with the funeral procession to be set up in its place according to tradition at the foot of the sarcophagus. (The small nested anthropoid coffins subsumed under Obj. No. 320 – the innermost, containing a lock of hair, inscribed for Queen Tiye – and a box with the coffined mummies of two stillborn female fetuses,[58] Obj. No. 317, will have been piled on top of the shrines in the far corner at some point, perhaps as an afterthought.)

The Annexe, too, could be stocked with amphoras of wine and oil, baskets filled with dried fruit, legumes, and grain, and the remaining boxes of shabtis (the Book of the Dead stipulated that they be at the head and foot of the mummy, accounting for their division between the Treasury and the Annexe). Some furniture was also brought in and stacked rather precariously against the left-hand wall, but other pieces were held back for later deposition in the Antechamber.

The quartzite sarcophagus basin will have occupied its appointed place in the Burial Chamber well in advance of the funeral. (The two pieces of the granite lid probably were also in KV 62, lying on the floor at the south end of the Antechamber.) This conclusion follows from the fact that Howard Carter discovered the first sarcophagus made for Hatshepsut in the unfinished Wadi Gabbanat el-Qurud tomb which was commissioned for her as Thutmose II's queen.[59] It had been installed in the tomb early on – long before it would have been needed, and before the queen's plans for her eventual interment were altered to foresee burial as Pharaoh in the Valley of the Kings.

Horst Beinlich has proposed a reconstruction of Tutankhamun's funeral, based on the scenes depicting funerals in some nearly contemporaneous non-royal tombs in the Theban necropolis.[60] These, he is convinced, reflect royal ritual. Whether any episodes took place in the mortuary temple of the king as Beinlich supposes is moot. Regardless, the actual obsequies began with the journey by boat to the west bank of the Nile and continued with a procession bearing the king's mortal remains (mummy and canopic equipment) to the tomb.

Gay Robins has explained how the distribution of the paintings in the Burial Chamber of KV 62 is related to the crucial episodes of the funeral and Tutankhamun's successful passage from this world to the next.[61] The abbreviated version of the 'journey to the west' on the east wall (Plate XXIV) shows only the sled bearing the mummy beneath a canopy; the canopic chest is absent. The traditional 'nine friends' towing the sled are joined by the viziers of Upper and Lower Egypt[62] and a twelfth figure whose preeminence is signaled by his costume as well as his immediate proximity to the mummy. Furthermore, like King Ay on the adjacent wall, he is shown with an 'Amarna foot' (see p. 12) suggesting perhaps an especially close relationship to the royal family.[63] The figure is often presumed to depict Horemhab,[64] who called himself Tutankhamun's 'regent' or deputy.

The canopic chest is not the only omission from the abbreviated depiction of the cortege in Tutankhamun's tomb. No mourning women, conspicuous features of such scenes in non-royal tombs, accompany Tutankhamun to the cemetery. Probably too much importance should not be ascribed to the absence of the widow. The limited space available demanded economy that went so far as to limit royal funerary texts on the west wall of the Burial Chamber to the first hour of the Amduat, which in its entirety charts the progress of the sun god's journey through the hours of darkness.

The scene showing Ay as Tutankhamun's successor performing the Opening of the Mouth on the king's mummy at the east end of the north wall follows logically on the procession, around the corner from the east wall.[65] In the sequence of scenes in non-royal tombs this rite takes place at the entrance of the tomb. If that were so in Tutankhamun's case, then a funerary tent could have been erected in the Valley of the Kings near KV 62's entrance to accommodate the personnel and equipment. Beinlich proposes that the three animal biers and the three larger shrines surrounding the sarcophagus in the Burial Chamber were used one after the other over three successive nights (and four days) of essential rites before the actual interment took place. (In his scenario, the fourth, smallest shrine sheltered the mummy in the procession.) The idea that the shrines saw use outside the tomb and were subsequently taken down and then re-erected in the Burial Chamber makes sense, even if it cannot be proved. Like the animal biers, they preserve evidence of mishandling and careless assembly.[66]

It was perhaps after the closure of the third and final coffin, when the priests had concluded the essential rituals accompanying that act and withdrawn, that the debris left over from the mummification of the king was deposited along with floral collars, animal bones, and pottery in KV 54, a pit located at some distance from KV 62. This deposit, discovered at the end of 1907, is customarily described as an embalming cache (for which there are many examples found outside the Valley of the Kings[67]) including not only the typical little sacks of natron, balls of linen bandages, and so forth left over from the mummification of Tutankhamun, but also what was long understood as the remains of a funerary banquet, along with the pottery used on that occasion and the floral garlands worn by the guests. Both the interpretation of those items as deriving from a meal and the idea that the material was once actually stored in the corridor of KV 62[68] have been called into question,[69] but not that the contents were in some way connected to the burial of Tutankhamun.

The priests may not have needed much time to perform the essential rituals, but the actual work of closing the coffins, one after the other; lowering the ensemble into the sarcophagus; maneuvering the pieces of the lid into place; and camouflaging the break will not have been accomplished quickly nor without incident.[70] Simultaneously the stocking of the Treasury had to be finished before beginning the work of setting up the four shrines (and the framework for the pawl between the fourth, outermost shrine and the third) around the sarcophagus in the confines of the Burial Chamber. The sides of each shrine, beginning with the largest, were brought in and leaned against the appropriate walls, one after the other. Then the smallest was assembled, followed by the second smallest and so forth. A problem posed by this process was that some elements of the shrines were simply too large to pass though the opening from the Antechamber into the Burial Chamber. The same pieces had already caused difficulties when they were brought into the tomb. A variant of the solution for this initial problem – the final six steps of the stairway, along with the jambs and lintel of the doorway opening into the Antechamber were cut away[71] – was put into practice here: a chunk was simply knocked out of the northwest corner of the Antechamber large enough to admit the pieces to the Burial Chamber.

With the shrines in place, the partition wall could be built up between the Burial Chamber and the Antechamber with a small opening left for the painters to exit when they were finished. Their task was made doubly difficult by the cramped quarters and poor lighting in the Burial Chamber, which could have contributed to the rather mediocre quality of the paintings in general and resulted in some anomalous proportions of the figures on the north wall – their larger heads in particular – which conform to neither the traditional nor the Amarna canon.[72] Other features of the paintings that suggest a period of transition include the crimped sash (a typical accessory worn by Amarna queens with their elaborately pleated gowns) here incongruously in combination with the simple sheath dress of the goddesses, and the 'Amarna foot' of the god Anubis.

After the painters exited the tomb, the priests could perform the very last rituals in the Burial Chamber. These included sealing the 'magic bricks' in the niches cut for them. Each niche was closed with a splinter of limestone, plastered over, and painted.[73]

Maria Rosa Guasch Jané proposes that there is a connection between the contents of the niches and the three empty wine amphoras found in the Burial Chamber (Figure 34).

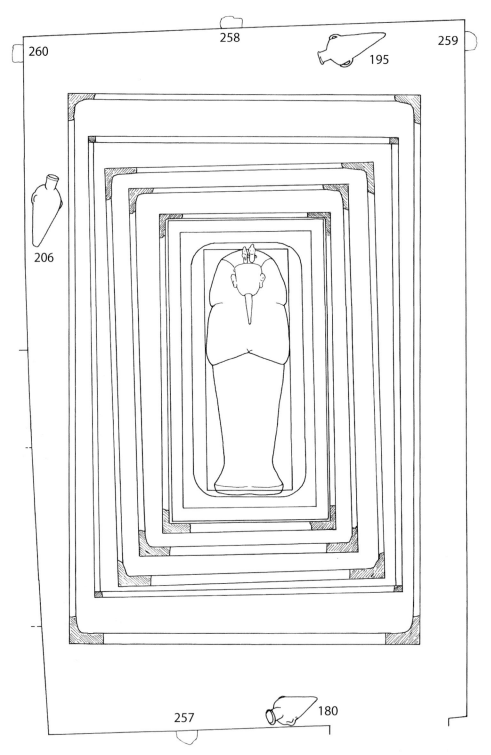

Figure 34 Floor plan of K V 62's Burial Chamber showing the positions of the wine amphoras, Obj. Nos 180, 195, and 206, in relation to the niches for magic bricks Obj. Nos 257–60.

State-of-the-art analysis of the residue showed that the amphoras once contained three different types of wine (like the unopened amphoras in the Annexe, according to their labels).[74] Jané interprets spells from the Book of the Dead to propose that the red wine in the amphora at the west wall (Obj. No. 195) aided 'Tutankhamun's transfiguration as Osiris-Ra' and the white wine contained in the amphora at the east wall (Obj. No. 180) his 'transfiguration as Ra-Harakhty', while the prized *sedeh*-wine in the amphora at the south wall (Obj. No. 206) helped him with 'the most difficult step in his transformation, his nocturnal trip through the southern sky'. But who drank this wine insuring Tutankhamun's 'transformations'?[75]

Jané brings her interpretation of the amphoras' contents to bear on what she believes to be a problem posed by the figures in the niches (Obj. Nos 257–60): their orientation does not correspond to the stipulations in the Book of the Dead.[76] In fact only a single figure was oriented 'correctly' and, furthermore, there was an extra figure (of Osiris), and no text on the brick supporting the figure of Anubis. Jané argues that these discrepancies resulted from an intention 'to enhance an Osirian protection ritual following the new beliefs at the end of the Amarna period [*sic*]'.

Jané does not claim to be either the only person or the first to identify Osirian references in the burial of Tutankhamun. Three decades ago Alix Wilkinson published two articles on this theme.[77] Ikram, too, suggests that perhaps the anomalies she recognizes in the king's mummification were 'a literal transformation' of his body into Osiris, speculating that 'at this delicate historical/religious time, it was thought that the usual modes for the transformation . . . were not sufficient, and so the priest-embalmers prepared the body in such a way so as to literally emphasize the divinity of the king and his identification with Osiris'.[78] I remain leery of this and similar theories of my colleagues who would discover a religious meaning behind what they consider irregularities in burials in general, not just in Tutankhamun's case. As Howard Carter observed:

> Tradition holds that in burial customs each article belonging to the tomb equipment has its prescribed place in the tomb. However, experience has shown that no matter how true the governing conventions may be, seldom have they been strictly carried out. Either the want of forethought with regard to requisite space, or the want of system when placing the elaborate paraphernalia in the tomb-chambers, overcame tradition. We have never found any strict order, we have found only approximate order.[79]

I am convinced that the many instances of carelessness and poor planning observable in Tutankhamun's burial are not at all exceptional but the rule. I suspect that while not necessarily intentionally skimping on ritual, the Egyptians were on the whole nevertheless eager to be over and done with the burial of their kings during the New Kingdom, if not throughout pharaonic history.

Final activities

With the doorway to the Burial Chamber walled up and sealed, the remainder of the funerary equipment could be brought into the tomb and the completion of the stocking undertaken in earnest. I imagine this process was hurried; the end was finally in sight of a process which must have already occupied some days, if not considerably longer. The animal biers were lined up against the far wall of the Antechamber, and various pieces of furniture placed on top of and under them, along with prepared meat and fowl in purpose-made whitewashed boxes. The placement of the 'guardian statues' of the king facing each other at either end of the north wall made no secret of the fact that the Burial Chamber lay beyond. Simultaneously, boxes and more pieces of furniture were passed hand to hand down the stairs and corridor into the tomb, which will have resulted in damage to some items while providing the opportunity for pilfering.[80] The gilded chariots were probably the last items to be brought into the tomb, perhaps as an afterthought; they were deposited just inside and to the left of the Antechamber's entrance. Then masons were called in to block that doorway, the corridor was filled with rubble,[81] and a final wall was built up to block the entrance at the bottom of the steps descending from the floor of the Valley of the Kings. When the necropolis officials had pressed their seals into the plaster smeared on that wall and the last chips had topped up the stairwell, the entrance to the tomb would have been indistinguishable from its surroundings. Tutankhamun was consigned to the world of the dead and buried.

Epilogue

The paintings in the Burial Chamber of KV 62 leave no doubt that Ay claimed responsibility as Tutankhamun's successor for the king's funeral; as Pharaoh in priestly regalia he performs the Opening of the Mouth ceremony on the deceased king's mummy. Nor can there be any question that Ay was followed on the throne of Egypt in turn by Horemhab, whose reign would usher in the Ramesside era. Speculation about the relationship of these two men to Tutankhamun as well as to each other continues.[1] In Horemhab's own words inscribed on his pre-royal as well as royal monuments, he asserted his role as Tutankhamun's 'deputy', but royal monuments from the reign of the king do not mention him. By contrast, Ay was depicted as fan-bearer in the following of his predecessor in the reliefs that decorated the Mansion of Nebkheperure.[2] This circumstance suggests that his claim superseded any pretensions to the kingship Horemhab may have harbored.

The high status Ay enjoyed during Akhenaten's reign when he attained the rank of fan-bearer was attributable at least in part to the role of his wife Tiy as Queen Nefertiti's wet-nurse. There are specialists who argue in favor of his being linked by blood to the ruling family as well, although there is no hint of this in the texts and representations of the spacious tomb he commissioned as a commoner at Amarna.[3] Under Tutankhamun Ay retained his privileged role. The idea that he added vizier to his titles during his predecessor's reign and that this aided his accession to the kingship cannot be credited, based as it is on the reading of a title plus epithet on one scrap of gold foil found in the Valley of the Kings (KV 58).[4] There may be little reason to doubt that Ay is the person who bore the title in question, but Jaroslav Černy pointed out long ago that the reading of it as 'vizier' is not enough to add that office to those well documented for Ay.[5]

The idea that Ay married Tutankhamun's widow Ankhesenamun to bolster a claim to the throne is similarly tenuous. The presence of his throne name beside hers in the design of a glass ring suggests little more than that she survived the death of Tutankhamun and that some understanding existed between her and his successor.[6] The paintings in Ay's royal tomb are unequivocal: unusual as the appearance of a wife in a king's tomb may be, Tiy's presence beside Ay in the scenes[7] shows she retained until Ay's death the status documented for her before his accession in the tomb they had planned to share at Amarna.

Ay continued projects initiated during Tutankhmun's reign, left unfinished when he died, at Luxor Temple[8] as well as at Karnak. The notion that Ay was a partisan of Akhenaten's religious ideas in opposition to a pro-restoration clique led by Horemhab[9] is irreconcilable with the traditional iconography which continued to be employed at Ay's remit for these projects to honor the orthodox gods. Evidence for restoration work at his own initiative is sparse,[10] but then again, his reign was comparatively brief, amounting to a little more than three complete years.

The pre-royal career of Horemhab is not traceable with confidence back into the reign of Akhenaten;[11] he could not have been a young man at his accession, though hardly as old as Ay. One theory supposes that Horemhab's absence from Egypt on a military campaign when Tutankhamun died put an end to any hopes he may have had as 'king's deputy' to succeed the young pharaoh.[12] But as commander of the army, would Horemhab not have had the means to remove Ay from the throne, if he had so desired? Perhaps, however, he could no longer call upon the loyalty of the troops, had he already been replaced as generalissimo by the 'king's son' Nakhtmin even before Ay's accession.[13]

Regardless, Horemhab does indeed seem to have been absent from the limelight for the intermezzo of Ay's reign. Tutankhamun is the only king documented in the reliefs and inscriptions of his pre-royal tomb at Saqqara. The pharaoh initially presumed to be Ay depicted officiating at a fragmentary scene of awarding Horemhab the Gold of Honor in the second courtyard turns out to have been Tutankhamun instead.[14] Mention of King Ay is limited to his name on a few small finds from the tomb.[15]

Nicholas Reeves has discussed factors in support of the idea that Ay was duly laid to rest as pharaoh in KV 23 in the western branch of the Valley of the Kings.[16] Another factor that can be cited in favor of this conclusion is the fact that the walls of the makeshift burial chamber are decorated. In KV 62 the paintings were executed only after the sarcophagus was closed and the shrines had been erected around it.

Eventually, however, Horemhab's official policy towards his immediate predecessor underwent a significant change. Ay's monuments were usurped, and preparations were made to replace his titulary with Horemhab's wherever it occurred in the reliefs of Tutankhamun's funerary temple, the Mansion of Nebkheperure at Thebes. But subsequently, the wish (or need?) to distance himself from the 'Amarna' pharaohs led Horemhab to deny any connection to Tutankhamun as well. Instead of proceeding as planned to fill the role that Ay as king had occupied in the texts and decoration of the Mansion, masons were enjoined to attack the figures and names of Tutankhamun, if less thoroughly than those of Ay, before the building was pulled down and the blocks reused to fill the pylons Horemhab built at Karnak.[17] Tutankhamun's cartouches survived untouched on only very few of the other monuments he commissioned.

At precisely which moment the desecration of Ay's burial was mandated is not known, but just possibly it was simultaneous with the moves to usurp Ay's inscriptions and figures at Karnak. If later, rather than earlier in Horemhab's reign, with attacks on Tutankhamun later still,[18] that might explain why KV 62 was left untouched, allowing the boy-king and his 'treasure' to experience a very different fate more than 3,200 years later.

Map with Sites Mentioned in the Text

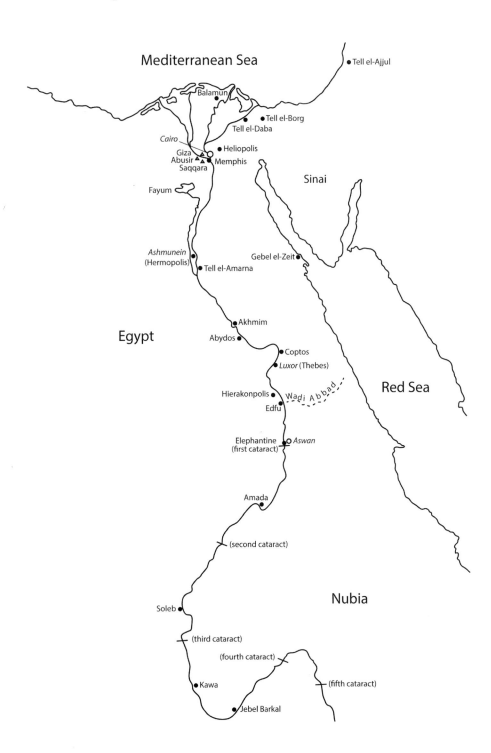

Mediterranean Sea

● Tell el-Ajjul

Balamun
●

● Tell el-Borg
Tell el-Daba

Cairo
Giza
Abusir
Saqqara
● Heliopolis
● Memphis

Sinai

Fayum

Ashmunein
(Hermopolis)
● Tell el-Amarna

Gebel el-Zeit ●

● Akhmim
Abydos ●

Egypt

● Coptos
● *Luxor* (Thebes)

Hierakonpolis ●
Edfu ●

Wadi Abbad

Red Sea

Elephantine
(first cataract)
● ○ *Aswan*

Amada ●

(second cataract)

Nubia

Soleb ●

(third cataract)
(fourth cataract)

Kawa ●

(fifth cataract)

● Jebel Barkal

Chronology*

Early Dynastic Period	*c.* 2900–2545
Dynasty III	*c.* 2592–2544
Djoser	*c.* 2592–2566
Old Kingdom	*c.* 2543–2120
Dynasty IV	*c.* 2543–2436
Cheops	*c.* 2509–2483
Chephren	*c.* 2472–2448
Dynasty V	*c.* 2435–2306
Sahure	*c.* 2428–2416
First Intermediate Period	*c.* 2118–1980
Middle Kingdom	*c.* 1980–1760
Dynasty XI	*c.* 2080–1940
Nebhepetre-Montuhotep II	*c.* 2009–1959
Dynasty XII	*c.* 1939–1760
Senwosret I	*c.* 1920–1875
Amenemhet III	*c.* 1818–1773
Second Intermediate Period	*c.* 1759–1539
Dynasty XV [Hyksos]	????–1539
Khamudi	????–1539
New Kingdom	1539–1077
Dynasty XVIII	1539–1292
Ahmose	1539–1515
Amenhotep I	1515–1494
Thutmose I	1494–1483?
Thutmose II	?1482–1479
Thutmose III	1479–1426
[Queen] Hatshepsut	1479–1458
Amenhotep II	1425–1400
Thutmose IV	?1399–1380
Amenhotep III	1379–1342
Amenhotep IV/Akhenaten	1341–1325
Smenkhkare	1324–1323
[Queen] Ankh[et]kheperure-Neferneferuaten	?1323–1322
Tutankhamun	1322–1314

Ay	1313–1310
Horemhab	1309–1296?
Dynasty XIX	?1295–1191
Seti I	1290–1279
Ramesses II	1279–1213
Merenptah	1213–1203
Seti II	1202–1198
Dynasty XX	1190–1071
Ramesses III	1187–1157
Ramesses IV	1156–1150
Ramesses V	1149–1146
Third Intermediate Period	1076–723
Dynasty XXII	943–746

*Courtesy of Rolf Krauss; revised and adapted after Erik Hornung, Rolf Krauss, and David A. Warburton, *Ancient Egyptian Chronology* (Leiden and Boston: Brill 2006), pp. 490–5. Dates are provided solely for orientation and only for dynasties and kings cited in the text. In general, all dates should be understood as subject to change. The chronology of the late Eighteenth Dynasty in particular is currently in flux due to controversies surrounding Akhenaten's successor(s) and the length of Horemhab's reign.

Abbreviations

A & L	*Ägypten und Levante: Internationale Zeitschrift für ägyptische Archäologie und deren Nachbargebiete* (Vienna)
ASAE	*Annales du Service des Antiquités de l'Égypte* (Cairo)
AUC	American University in Cairo
BACE	*Bulletin of the Australian Centre for Egyptology* (North Ryde, Australia)
BIFAO	*Bulletin de l'Institut français d'archéologie orientale du Caire* (Cairo)
BiOr	*Bibliotheca Orientalis* (Leiden)
BSEG	*Bulletin de la Société d'Égyptologie de Genève* (Geneva)
BSFE	*Bulletin de la Société française d'égyptologie* (Paris)
CdE	*Chronique d'Égypte* (Brussels)
CSA	Conseil Suprême des Antiquités (Cairo)
EAO	*Égypte Afrique & Orient* (Avignon)
EES	Egypt Exploration Society (London)
ENiM	*Égypte Nilotique et Méditerranée – Une revue d'égyptologie sur Internet* (Montpellier)
GI	Griffith Institute, Oxford
GM	*Göttinger Miszellen* (Göttingen)
IFAO	Institut française d'archéologie orientale du Caire (Cairo)
JAMA	*Journal of the American Medical Association* (Chicago)
JARCE	*Journal of the American Research Center in Egypt* (New York)
JEA	*Journal of Egyptian Archaeology* (London)
JEH	*Journal of Egyptian History* (Leiden)
JNES	*Journal of Near Eastern Studies* (Chicago)

JSSEA	*Journal of the Society for the Study of Egyptian Antiquities* (Toronto)
Kmt	*Kmt. A Modern Journal of Ancient Egypt* (San Francisco)
MDAIK	*Mitteilungen des Deutschen Archäologischen Instituts, Kairo* (Mainz)
MMA	Metropolitan Museum of Art, New York
NARCE	*Newsletter of the American Research Center in Egypt* (Princeton, New Jersey)
OLZ	*Orientalistische Literaturzeitung* (Berlin)
RdE	*Revue d'Égyptologie* (Louvain)
SAK	*Studien zur altägyptischen Kultur* (Hamburg)
SCA	Supreme Council of Antiquities (Cairo)
ZÄS	*Zeitschrift für ägyptische Sprache und Altertumskunde* (Leipzig)

Notes

Introduction

1 Gauthier, *Le livre des rois d'Égypte* v. II (Cairo: IFAO 1912), pp. 365–73.

2 Maspero, 'Note on the Life and Reign of Touatânkhamanou', in Theodore M. Davis et al., *The Tombs of Harmhabi and Touatânkhamanou* (London: Constable 1912), pp. 111–23.

3 Carter and Mace, *The Tomb of Tut.ankh.Amen* v. I (London: Cassel 1923), p. 171.

4 The complete record was first published only years later by F. Filce Leek, *The Human Remains from the Tomb of Tutankhamun* (Oxford: GI 1972).

5 Howard Carter, *The Tomb of Tut.ankh.Amen* v. II (London: Cassell 1927), pp. 153–4.

6 My article, 'Impact of the Discovery of KV 62 (the Tomb of Tutankhamen)', *Kmt* 25: 1 (Spring 2014), pp. 29–37, reviews the difficulties associated with the clearance of the tomb and the subsequent history of scholarship focusing on the treasure. For a different perspective on the discovery see Donald M. Reid, 'Remembering and Forgetting Tutankhamun – Imperial and National Rhythms of Archaeology', in William Carruthers, ed., *Histories of Egyptology: Interdisciplinary Measures* (London and New York: Routledge 2015), pp. 157–73 with additional bibliography.

7 For a well-illustrated article discussing the science and technology involved in the project see the anonymous contribution 'Exact Facsimile of the Burial Chamber of KV 62 Gifted to Egypt', *Kmt* 24: 1 (Spring 2013), pp. 50–63.

8 For a significantly higher price of admission, tourists can still visit KV 62.

9 The master plan for the Grand Egyptian Museum, now scheduled to open in 2018 at Giza, includes a section devoted exclusively to the finds from the tomb of Tutankhamun.

10 *Tutankhamun's Painted Box,* reproduced in colour from the original in the Cairo Museum by Nina M. Davies with an explanatory text by Alan H. Gardiner (Oxford: GI 1962); cf. Gardiner's comments in his autobiography, *My Working Years* (London: Cornet 1962), p. 39.

11 Prints of Burton's photographs are also on file in the Egyptian Department of the MMA, New York.

12 Desroches-Noblecourt, *Tutankhamen: Life and Death of a Pharaoh* (New York: New York Graphic Society 1963).

13 'Toutankhamon et son temps', on view through July 1967.

14 Vandier, 'Toutânkhamon, sa famille, son règne', *Journal des Savants* (1967), pp. 65–91.

15 The catalogues of both exhibitions – identically titled *Treasures of Tutankhamun* (London: Trustees of the British Museum 1972; New York: MMA 1976) – were the work of I. E. S. Edwards, who was Keeper of Egyptian Antiquities at the British Museum when the exhibition was shown in London.

16 Rolf Krauss, 'Tutanchamun zwischen Revolution und Restoration', in Jurgen Settgast, ed., *Tutanchamun* (Mainz: von Zabern 1980), pp. 28–55.

Chapter 1

1 One candidate who can be ruled out straightaway is the 'King's Mother Meritre,' mentioned from time to time only to be rejected – recently, for example, by Ute and Andreas Effland, *Abydos: Tor zur ägyptischen Unterwelt* (Darmstadt: Wissenschaftliche Buchgesellschaft 2013), p. 31. The throne name of Meritre's son, written alongside hers on a scarab discovered at Abydos by Auguste Mariette in the mid-nineteenth century, is Nebkheper**enre**, not Tutankhamun's Nebkheper**ure**: see, e.g., Otto J. Schaden, *The God's Father Ay* (Ann Arbor: University Microfilms 1977), p. 152; p. 203 n. 50.

2 Van Dijk, 'The Noble Lady of Mitanni and Other Royal Favourites of the Eighteenth Dynasty', in van Dijk, ed., *Essays on Ancient Egypt in Honour of Herman te Velde* (Groningen: STYX 1997), pp. 37–9; 45 (figs 3a–b); Marc Gabolde, 'La parenté de Toutânkhamon', *BSFE* 155 (2002), pp. 32–48; fig. 7; for references to earlier literature, see ibid. p. 40 n. 17. Van Dijk suspects that the text is palimpsest; Gabolde's rendering also includes traces of other signs, although he does not comment in his text on the possibility that the prince's name replaced another on the block. In fact, the traces van Dijk and Gabolde thought they recognized on the photographs in the excavation report are in all likelihood illusory. None are included in Johnson's rendering (Figure 1c) nor are any visible in the recent color images of the block that I have seen.

3 http://weekly.ahram.org.eg/2008/929/he2.htm (accessed 2 June 2011; now no longer available online).

4 Hawass, *Discovering Tutankhamun – from Howard Carter to DNA* (Cairo and New York: AUC Press 2013), p. 163 (top).

5 I am deeply indebted to Ray for permitting me to illustrate his drawings of the block here.

6 Tut*ankhu*aten is a unique full writing of the king's personal name; see Chapter 2, p. 28.

7 Gabolde, 'Baketaton, fille de Kiya', *BSEG* 16 (1992), pp. 27–40.

8 Gabolde, *BSFE* 155, pp. 41–3. In a recent study of Akhenaten's reign, Dimitri Laboury follows Gabolde's interpretation of this scene and his identification of Nefertiti as the prince's mother: *Les grands pharaons: Akhénaton* (Paris: Pygmalion 2010), p. 317 and *passim*.

9 Geoffrey Thorndike Martin, *The Royal Tomb at El-Amarna* v. II. *The Reliefs, Inscriptions, and Architecture* (London: EES 1989), pp. 37–41; fig. 7; pls. 58–60; 42–45; figs 8–10; pls. 63, 65.

10 Van Dijk, 'The death of Meketaten', in Peter Brand and Louise Cooper, eds, *Causing his Name to Live: Studies in Egyptian Epigraphy and History in Memory of William J. Murnane* (Leiden, Boston and Cologne: Brill 2009), pp. 83–8 with a postscript noting that John R. Harris had published a similar thesis in an article, in Danish, in 2004. Neither van Dijk nor Harris was the first to voice this theory; see, for example, Murnane's review article, 'The End of the Amarna Period Once Again', *OLZ* 96 (2001), col. 15. By contrast, James P. Allen, 'The

Amarna Succession', also in Brand and Cooper, eds, *Causing his Name to Live*, pp. 9–20, proposes that the group depicts Princess Meritaten and her daughter, sired by Akhenaten. This cannot be the case: royal children were suckled by wet-nurses, not by their mothers, and the coiffure of the woman in the scene is a wet-nurse's enveloping wig, inappropriate for a daughter of Akhenaten and Nefertiti.

11 Martin, 'The Dormition of Princess Meketaten', in David Aston, ed., *Under the Potter's Tree* . . . (Fs Janine Bourriau; Louvain, Paris and Walpole, Mass.: Peeters 2011), pp. 633–44.

12 In the text on the front of the backrest of the gold throne from KV 62 (here Plate V): M. Eaton-Krauss, *The Thrones, Chairs, Stools, and Footstools from the Tomb of Tutankhamun* (Oxford: GI 2008), p. 32; fig. 6.

13 Cf. M. Eaton-Krauss and E. Graefe, *The Small Golden Shrine from the Tomb of Tutankhamun* (Oxford: GI 1985), p. 29. Marc Gabolde, 'L'ADN de la famille royale amarnienne et les sources égyptiennes', *ENiM* 6 (2013), pp. 186–7, points out that the existence of the title 'great one of the "harem" of Nebkheperure' is attested during Tutankhamun's reign which suggests that the king had other wives.

14 According to Jaana Toivari, 'Marriage at Deir el-Medina', in Christopher J. Eyre, ed., *Proceedings of the 7th International Congress of Egyptologists, Cambridge, 3–9 September 1995* (Louvain: Peeters 1998), p. 1161, marriage among non-royals was an on-going process, not a specific act, by contrast to divorce which was effected by a formal, public oath on the part of either husband or wife.

15 Dodson, *Amarna Sunset – Nefertiti, Tutankhamun, Ay, Horemheb, and the Egyptian Counter-Reformation* (Cairo and New York: AUC Press 2009), *passim* and esp. p. 23; reiterated in his *Amarna Sunrise – Egypt from Golden Age to Age of Heresy* (Cairo and New York: AUC Press 2014), pp. 118–19.

16 *Amarna Sunset*, p. 17.

17 Allen, 'The Amarna Succession', in Brand and Cooper, eds, *Causing his Name to Live*, pp. 13–14.

18 See Christian Bayer and M. Eaton-Krauss, 'The Amarna Triad', *RdE* 63 (2012), pp. 30–32; pl. IV.

19 In this connection, note that six years earlier, Hawass was quoted as saying 'DNA tests prove nothing; the royal mummies are precious assets. To experiment with them is a crime' (see Stephen J. Glain, 'Effort to unwrap lineage of mummies hits wall', *Wall Street Journal*, 1 May 2001; accessed 20 July 2014 at www.wsj.com/article/SB 988669015926705186).

20 Hawass et al., 'Ancestry and Pathology in King Tutankhamun's Family', *JAMA* 303 (12 Feb. 2010), pp. 638–47 + eAppendix and other supplementary material, available online to subscribers.

21 Medical experts' criticisms and rejection of various conclusions of the article, as well as the rejoinder of three of Hawass's team members, were published in *JAMA* 303 (13 June 2010), pp. 2471–5. See also the interview with Frank Rühli, who had previously been a collaborator of Hawass, published under the title 'Akte Tut, Ungelöst', *SonntagsBlick Magazin* 11 (21 March 2010), pp. 26–8.

22 Forbes, 'Tutankhamen's Family Tree – Full of Knots!' *Kmt* 21: 2 (Summer 2010), pp. 19–35; cf. my comments, 'Mummies (and Daddies)', *GM* 230 (2011), pp. 29–35.

23 So Carl Zimmer, 'DNA Double Take', *The New York Times,* 17 September 2013 (accessed 17 September 2013 at www.nytimes.com/2013/09/17/science/dna-double-take.html).

24 For his monuments, see Dietrich Wildung, 'Le frère aîné d'Ekhnaton: Réflections sur un décès premature', *BSFE* 143 (1998), pp. 10–18.

25 Grimm, 'Goldsarg ohne Geheimnis', in Sylvia Schoske and Grimm, eds, *Das Geheimnis des goldenen Sarges: Echnaton und das Ende der Amarnazeit* (Munich: Staatliches Museum Ägyptischer Kunst 2001), pp. 101–20. To date, Allen ('The Amarna Succession', in Brand and Cooper, eds, *Causing his Name to Live*, p. 13) is alone in accepting Grimm's conclusions. Gabolde (who believes the body is that of Akhenaten) tells me that he shares my rejection of Grimm's thesis; see now also Dodson, *Amarna Sunset*, pp. 41–2; 146 n. 70; but cf. idem, *Amarna Sunrise*, p. 197 n. 52 where his comment is equivocating.

26 For the Nubian wig and who wore it, see Eaton-Krauss, 'Miscellanea Amarnensia', *CdE* 56 (1981), pp. 252–8.

27 See I. Munro, 'Zusammenstellung von Datierungskriterien für Inschriften der Amarnazeit nach J. J. Perepelkin "Die Revolution Amenophis' IV" Teil 1 (russ.), 1967', in *GM* 94 (1986), p. 87; cf. my *Thrones,* pp. 45; 82, and Dodson's comments, 'The Canopic Coffinettes of Tutankhamun', in Mamdouh Eldamaty and Mai Trad, eds, *Egyptian Museum Collections around the World: Studies for the Centennial of the Egyptian Museum, Cairo* (Cairo: SCA 2002), p. 281.

28 On the Discovery Channel (in the USA) in two parts, 21 and 22 February 2010. At one point team member Carsten Pusch remarked that the cranial sutures of the KV 55 skull suggested 'a younger individual rather than an older one' while Ashraf Selim, another team member, said that the person was 'quite mature. . . at least 45–55, possibly even as old as 60'.

29 Note 'b' to the chart, on p. 640 of the *JAMA* article.

30 Edward F. Wente and James E. Harris, 'Royal Mummies of the Eighteenth Dynasty: A Biologic and Egyptological Approach', in C. N. Reeves, ed., *After Tutankhamun: Research and Excavation in the Royal Necropolis at Thebes* (London and New York: Kegan Paul International 1992), p. 17 n. 7. The authors of the *JAMA* article overlooked this publication.

31 Smith, *The Royal Mummies* (Cairo: IFAO 1912), pp. 51–6.

32 Joyce Filer, 'The KV 55 body: the facts', *Egyptian Archaeology* 17 (2000), pp. 13–14.

33 For example, by Allen, 'The Amarna Succession', in Brand and Cooper, eds, *Causing his Name to Live*, p. 13.

34 Strouhal, 'Biological Age of Skeletonized Mummy from Tomb KV 55 at Thebes', *Anthropologie: International Journal of the Science of Man* (Prague) XLVIII/2 (2010), pp. 97–112. I am indebted to Geoffrey Martin for providing me with photocopies of this article and that of Corinne Duhig, 'The Remains of Pharaoh Akhenaten are not yet identified . . .', pp. 113–15, in the same issue of *Anthropologie*.

35 Harrison, 'An Anatomical Examination of the Pharaonic Remains purported to be Akhenaten', *JEA* 52 (1966), pp. 95–119.

36 See n. 34.

37 Dodson, 'How old is that mummy in the coffin?' *Ancient Egypt* (Manchester) 10: 2 (October/November 2009), pp. 66–7.

38 Dodson, *Amarna Sunset*, pp. 13–17; idem, *Amarna Sunrise*, pp. 88; 130.

39 Gabolde, *BSFE* 155, pp. 32–48.

40 Schlögl, *Nofretete. Die Wahrheit über die schöne Königin* (Munich: C. H. Beck 2012), pp. 97–107; 113–18.

41 Gabolde, *ENiM* 6, pp. 177–203.

42 Schlögl cites neither the title of Fletcher's book – *The Search for Nefertiti: The True Story of an Amazing Discovery* (London: Hodder & Stoughton 2004) – nor the storm of protest which greeted its appearance (see, e.g., Mark Rose, 'Where's Nefertiti', online at www.archaeology.org/online/reviews/nefertiti/index.html, accessed 6 October 2014).

43 Smith, *Royal Mummies*, pp. 40–2.

44 This is simply stated in the unpaginated section 'Pathology of the Royal Mummies' in the supplementary online content/eAppendix to the *JAMA* article; 'Traumatic events (face, calvarium) (assumed cause of death)' is entered in the slot for 'Pathologies and diseases' on the fact sheet for the mummy. No data is cited in support of this claim, just as the authors do not publish the data on which their estimate of the age at death of the remains from KV 55 are based (see above, p. 9). Note that Fletcher and her team, *Search for Nefertiti*, p. 377, considered the damage to be post-mortem.

45 Cf. Eaton-Krauss, 'Reprise: Akhenaten, Nefertiti, Amarna', *CdE* 88 (2013), p. 76. In the interim, the graffito citing her by name in Akhenaten's 16th regnal year has been published: Athena Van der Perre, 'The Year 16 graffito of Akhenaten in Dayr Abu Hinnis: A Contribution to the Study of the Later Years of Nefertiti', *JEH* 7 (2014), pp. 67–108.

46 Taemwadjsy's name and titles are the same as those of the well-documented sister/wife of Huy, Tutankhamun's Nubian viceroy; see Chapter 5, p. 71. Gabolde calls attention to a like-named sister of the wife of the governor of Elephantine during the reign of Amenhotep III: *ENiM* 6, p. 186–7 n. 41. Most recently the name of a Princess Taemwadjsy has turned up among the debris in KV 40 (mentioned by Salima Ikram, 'Nile Currents', *KMT* 25:3, Fall 2014, p. 7). This tomb seems, initially at least, to have been the burial place for a number of family members of Thutmose IV and Amenhotep III; see now Susanne Bickel's account of the discovery, 'Surprising Discovery in the Valley of the Kings: The Tomb of 18th Dynasty Princesses and Princes', *Kmt* 25:3 (Fall 2014), pp. 22–32.

47 Gabolde, *BSFE* 155, p. 41 and fig. 8.

48 Alfred Grimm and Hermann A. Schlögl, *Das thebanische Grab Nr. 136 und der Beginn der Amarnazeit* (Wiesbaden: Harrassowitz 2005), pp. 37–8; pl. XLVIII.

49 See Barry J. Kemp, *The City of Akhenaten and Nefertiti: Amarna and its People* (London: Thames & Hudson 2012), pp. 119–21.

50 Friederike Seyfried advises me that she has prepared an article demonstrating this.

51 Rainer Hanke's conclusion that the piece is modern is cited in Rolf Krauss's obituary of him, *GM* 225 (2010), pp. 107–9; cf. also the reservations I expressed in a review of Grimm and Schlögl's book, *BiOr* 63 (2006), col. 526.

52 Brock, 'Tutankhamun in the "King's House" at Amarna? Cairo SR 11575/20647', *BACE* 9 (1998), pp. 7–17.

53 Eaton-Krauss, 'Tutankhaten in the Paintings of the King's House at Amarna?' *BACE* 10 (1999), pp. 13–17.

54 For the 'Amarna foot' see E. R. Russmann, 'The Anatomy of an Artistic Convention: Representations of the Near Foot in Two Dimensions through the New Kingdom', *Bulletin of the Egyptological Seminar* 2 (1980), pp. 57–81.

55 Cf. now Fran Weatherhead, *Amarna Palace Paintings* (London: EES 2007), pp. 131–8 with fig. 68.

56 For them, see Catharine H. Roehrig, 'Senenmut, Royal Tutor to Princess Neferure', in Roehrig, ed., *Hatshepsut: From Queen to Pharaoh* (New York, New Haven, and London: MMA and Yale University Press 2005), pp. 112–16.

57 This title is not included in the labels identifying her figure as queen of Egypt, i.e., after Ay's accession.

58 Illustrated by Cyril Aldred, *Akhenaten and Nefertiti* (New York: Brooklyn Museum and Viking Press 1973), p. 119 (no. 35).

59 Bayer and Eaton-Krauss, *RdE* 63, pp. 30–32; pl. IV.

60 Zivie, *La tombe de Maïa: mère nourricière du roi Toutânkhamon et grande du harem* (Toulouse: Caracara Ed. 2009).

61 Gabolde, *D'Akhenaton à Toutânkhamon* (Lyon: Boccard 1998), p. 124 n.1012.

62 So initially Cynthia Sheikholeslami, ed., *The Egyptian Museum at the Millennium*, Cairo: SCA 2000), p. 114 (no. 123); subsequently Grimm and Schlögl, *Das thebanische Grab*, pp. 36–7, pls LII and LIII; and Jacobus van Dijk, 'A Cat, a Nurse, and a Standard-Bearer: Notes on Three Late Eighteenth Dynasty Statues', in Sue H. D'Auria, ed., *Offerings to the Discerning Eye: an Egyptological Medley in Honor of Jack A. Josephson* (Leiden and Boston: Brill 2010), pp. 326–30. Note that damage to the penis has led some to describe the child as a girl.

63 For the pectoral, see Earl L. Ertman, 'Types of Winged Scarabs: Tutankhamun's Use of the H-winged Scarab', in Eldamaty and Trad, eds, *Egyptian Museum Collections*, pp. 33–43.

64 Edith Bernhauer assigned the statue initially to earlier Dynasty XVIII, but now puts it into the post-Amarna Period: *Innovationen in der Privatplastik der 18. Dynastie und ihre Entwicklung* (Wiesbaden: Harrassowitz 2010), pp. 273–5. She dates the paleography of the inscription (which she thinks is secondary) to Dynasty XIX while van Dijk (who considers the text original) assigns it unequivocally to the post-Amarna Period. Ertman, 'H-winged Scarab', in Eldamaty and Trad, eds, *Egyptian Museum Collections*, p. 339, cites the opinion of Joann Fletcher (working from photographs) that the nurse's wig dates the group to Dynasty XIX or later.

65 Ockinga, *A Tomb from the Reign of Tutankhamun at Akhmim* (Warminster: Aris & Phillips 1997).

66 The second being 'A Prince or a God at el-Amarna? Reconsideration of an earlier opinion', *Amarna Letters* 1 (1991), pp. 86–93. The exact provenance is not recorded in the files of the EES excavations nor is the piece mentioned in the excavation reports.

67 Cf. Anna Stevens, *Private Religion at Amarna: the material evidence* (Oxford: Archeopress 2006), p. 143.

68 Ockinga, *Tomb from the Reign of Tutankhamun*, p. 56.

Chapter 2

1   For a review of most issues involved see Van der Perre, *JEH* 7, pp. 77–101 and cf. now
    Dodson, *Amarna Sunrise*, pp. 27–52.

2   An exception is Barry Kemp; see the oblique comment and chronological table in his *City of
    Akhenaten and Nefertiti*, pp. 15; 304.

3   Gabolde, *D'Akhenaton à Toutânkhamon*, pp.153–7. He notes that the epithet 'beneficial for
    her husband' was inspired by Akhenaten's name which translates 'Beneficial-for-Aten' and
    that it also calls to mind the description of the goddess Isis as the sister-wife of Osiris: 'she
    who is beneficial for her brother/spouse'.

4   Dodson, *Amarna Sunset*, pp. 38–47. For reservations and critique, see my review of *Amarna
    Sunset*, in *Egyptian Archaeology* 37 (2010), p. 35.

5   For example, Martin von Falck, 'Zwischen Echnaton und Tutanchamun. Eine neue
    nachgezeichnete Skizze', *Sokar* (Berlin) 25:2 (2012), pp. 86–97, who argues that the queen's
    spouse cited in the epithet is Smenkhkare.

6   'The Amarna Succession', in Brand and Cooper, eds, *Causing his Name to Live*, pp. 18–19.

7   Dodson's assertion that 'the majority view' identifies the letter writer as Tutankhamun's wife
    (*Amarna Sunset*, pp. 89–94) is partisan. For one recent exchange of salvos between the
    opposing camps, see Francis Breyer, 'Egyptological Remarks concerning Dahamunzu', *Ä & L*
    20 (2010), pp. 445–51 (in favor of dating the episode following Tutankhamun's death) and
    the rejoinder of Marc Gabolde, 'Ghost Egyptian-Hittite/Hittite-Egyptian Loan-words', *GM*
    233 (2012), pp. 109–13.

8   Cf. Jared C. Miller, 'Amarna Age Chronology', *Altorientalische Forschungen* 34 (2007),
    pp. 252–93, opting for Nefertiti as the letter writer. He comments (ibid. 255): 'The less
    certain a claim is, the more dogmatically the claim is held.'

9   For a translation of the pertinent passage in Horemhab's coronation inscription see
    William J. Murnane, *Texts from the Amarna Period in Egypt* (Atlanta: Scholars Press 1995),
    p. 231.

10 Christiane Desroches-Noblecourt, *Toutankhamon et son temps* (Paris: Ministère d'État
    Affaires Culturelle 1967), pp. 90–1.

11 I. E. S. Edwards, *Treasures of Tutankhamun* (London: Trustees of the British Museum 1972),
    cat. 44, noted the disparity in the texts on the caps, casting doubt on the idea that they once
    formed a set. But a larger-scaled set of crook and flail found together in KV 62 – Obj. Nos
    269d and e – shows an analogous disparity: *prenomen* and *nomen* (Tutankh*amun*) on the
    former, but the *prenomen* only on the latter.

12 Kawai, 'A Coronation Stela of Tutankhamun? (JE 27076)', in Eldamaty and Trad, eds,
    Egyptian Museum Collections, pp. 637–44.

13 Cf. Eaton-Krauss, *Thrones*, pp. 51–3.

14 Dodson, *Amarna Sunset,* p. 75. For the dating of the name change from Tutankhaten to
    Tutankhamun, see further below, pp. 30–1.

15 Mentioned in the so-called Pawah graffito on the wall of Theban Tomb 139: Murnane, *Texts
    from the Amarna Period*, pp. 207–8.

16 Initially discussed in detail by Beatrix Gessler[-Löhr] in her study of evidence from Memphis for the reign of Akhenaten, 'Akhenjati in Memphis', *SAK* 2 (1975), pp. 139–87; see now Valérie Angenot, 'A Horizon of Aten in Memphis?' *JSSEA* 35 (2008), pp. 7–26.

17 Gabolde, *D'Akhenaton à Toutânkhamon*, p. 283. His conclusion is based on analysis of the wine dockets recovered at the site.

18 John D. S. Pendlebury, *City of Akhenaten* v. III: Part 1. *The Central City and the Official Quarter* (London: EES 1951), pp. 3–4.

19 Eaton-Krauss, 'Mut and Tutankhaten', *GM* 235 (2012), pp. 17–18.

20 ÄgM 14197; first published by Adolf Erman, 'Geschichtliche Inschriften aus dem Berliner Museum', *ZÄS* 38 (1900), p. 113. For the proposed reading of the cartouche of the king as Tutankhaten on a stela of Seba, mayor of Thinis, in Cambridge's Fitzwilliam Museum, see my remarks, 'King Tutankhaten', *Orientalia* 80 (2011), p. 304 n. 23.

21 Often erroneously mentioned – most recently by Dodson, *Amarna Sunrise*, pp. 146; 148.

22 See Eaton-Krauss, *GM* 235, pp. 15–17.

23 For Carter's comment and the following discussion of Obj. No. 351 see my *Thrones*, pp. 75–91.

24 Carter, *Tut-ankh-Amen* v. III, p. 113.

25 See my *Thrones*, pp. 25–56.

26 Carter and Mace, *Tut-ankh-Amen* v. I, p. 118.

27 This issue has not been raised in connection with the ownership of the inlaid ebony throne, although it, too, is scaled for an adult.

28 *D'Akhenaton á Toutânkhamon*, pp. 291–2.

29 For an earlier version of the following paragraphs, with references, see Eaton-Krauss, *Orientalia* 80, pp. 302–4.

30 The texts on this staff and on all the other inscribed ones from the tomb have been translated by Dieter Kurth, 'Die Inschriften auf den Stöcken und Stäben des Tutanchamun', in Horst Beinlich, ed., *6th Symposium on Egyptian Royal Ideology: 'Die Männer hinter dem König'* (Wiesbaden: Harrassowitz 2012), pp. 67–86.

31 This segment of the text is visible in the photograph showing the top of the staff in T. G. H. James, *Tutankhamun: The Eternal Splendour of the Boy Pharaoh* (London and New York: Tauris Parke 2000), p. 261 (staff at the right).

32 Ibid. p. 263 includes an illustration of this palette.

33 Ronald J. Leprohon, *The Great Name: Ancient Egyptian Royal Titulary* (Atlanta: Society of Biblical Literature 2013), pp. 7–19, discusses the various elements of the titulary and its development over time. For convenience's sake, the translations of the elements of Tutankhamun's titulary given below are those of Leprohon, ibid. p. 106, unless otherwise specified.

34 For the variant writings of all five names of Tutankhaten/amun, see Eaton-Krauss, 'The Titulary of Tutankhamun', in Jürgen Osing and Günter Dreyer, eds, *Form und Mass. Beiträge zur Literatur, Sprache und Kunst des alten Ägypten* (Fs Gerhard Fecht; Wiesbaden: Harrassowitz 1987), pp. 110–23.

35 Heinrich Brugsch, *Geschichte Aegyptens unter den Pharaonen* (Leipzig: Hinrichs 1877), p. 434.

36 Gunn, 'The Name Tutankhamun', *JEA* 12 (1926), pp. 252–3.

37 Fecht, 'Amarna Probleme', *ZÄS* 85 (1960), p. 90: 'Vollkommen an Leben ist Jati'. I am indebted to Richard Parkinson for suggesting the English translation of the German.

38 As pointed out by John Ray, 'The Parentage of Tutankhamun', *Antiquity* 49 (1975), p. 46.

39 For the relationship between *kheperu* and *mesut*, see John Baines, '*Mswt* "manifestations"?' in *Hommages à François Daumas* (Montpellier: Université de Montpellier 1986), pp. 43–50.

40 So Nicholas Reeves, *The Complete Tutankhamun: The King. The Tomb. The Royal Treasure* (London: Thames & Hudson 1990), p. 35; he errs in stating that the Horus name is not found in association with Tutankhaten.

41 Alexandre Piankoff, *The Shrines of Tut-Ankh-Amon* (New York: Pantheon Books 1955), p. 16.

42 H. Assad and D. Kolos, *The Name of the Dead: Hieroglyphic Inscriptions of the Treasures of Tutankhamun Translated* (Mississauga, Ontario: Benben 1979), p. 30.

43 Carter and Mace, *Tut.ankh.Amen* v. I, 190 (caption for pl. XLVI, illustrating the so-called wishing cup, Obj. No. 14).

44 For example, in one of eight cartouches in the altered texts on the sarcophagus (Obj. No. 240) used for Tutankhamun's burial.

45 As I noted in remarks on the reading of the cartouche with the *nomen* on a stela in the Fitzwilliam Museum, Cambridge, *Orientalia* 80, p. 304 n. 23.

46 See now Hana Navrátilová, *The Visitors' Graffiti of Dynasties XVIII and XIX in Abusir and Saqqara* (Prague: Czech Institute of Egyptology 2007), pp. 77–9.

Chapter 3

1 CG 34183: Pierre Lacau, *Stèles du nouvel empire* v. 1 (Cairo: IFAO 1926), pp. 224–30, pl. LXX. For an English translation, see Murnane, *Texts from the Amarna Period*, pp. 212–14; 257. The series of slots down the middle of the stela dates to post-pharaonic times and represents an effort to split it in two for reuse.

2 CG 34184: Lacau, *Stèles du nouvel empire* v. 1, pp. 230–1.

3 Alexandre Varille, *Karnak* v. I (Cairo: IFAO 1943), p. 19; pl. 48.

4 Pointed out by John Baines, 'Presenting and Discussing Deities in New Kingdom and Third Intermediate Period Egypt', in Beate Pongratz-Leisten, ed., *Reconsidering Revolutionary Monotheism* (Winona Lake: Eisenbrauns 2012), pp. 48–50; fig. 4.

5 Gerhard Haeny, ed., *Untersuchungen im Totentempel Amenophis' III* (Wiesbaden: Steiner 1981), pp. 65–70; fig. 12; pl. 14. On this stela, the text is oriented leftwards, as are the lapwings. On the stelas of Amenhotep III and Tutankhamun the lapwings are arranged symmetrically, facing towards the center of the frieze.

6 Cf. Baines, 'Presenting and Discussing', in Pongratz-Leisten, *Reconsidering*, p. 50.

7 Eaton-Krauss, 'Akhenaten vs. Akhenaten', *BiOr* 47 (1990), col. 554 n. 97, refuting the suggestion that Ay, as a courtier, was originally shown here rather than the queen. There is no reason to suppose that her figure was squeezed in secondarily as Lacau, *Stèles du nouvel émpire* v. 1, p. 225, thought possible.

8   Cf., e.g., the scenes in the lunettes of the two monumental stelas from the king's funerary temple: Haeny, ed., *Totentempel Amenophis' III.*, pp. 70–83; folding plate 5a–c. *Pace* Baines, 'Presenting and Discussing', in Pongratz-Leisten, *Reconsidering*, p. 48, the composition is unrelated to scenes depicting Akhenaten and Nefertiti where the queen herself presents offering to Aten.

9   Gabolde, 'Ay, Toutankhamon et les martelages de la stèle de la restauration de Karnak (CG 34183)', *BSEG* 11 (1987), pp. 43–4.

10   Pointed out, e.g., by J. R. Harris, 'The Date of the "Restoration Stela" of Tutankhamun', *GM* 5 (1973), pp. 9–11 who went on to consider regnal year 4 'perhaps the least difficult restoration'; cf. Dodson, *Amarna Sunset*, p. 63: 'almost certainly Year 4'. A decade ago, Jacobus van Dijk revived the Year 1 option: 'De restauratiestéle van Toetanchamon', in R. Demarée and K. R. Veenhof, eds, *Zij schreven geschiedenis* (Leiden: Ex Oriente Lux 2003), pp. 235–6.

11   Baines, 'Presenting and Discussing', in Pongratz-Leisten, *Reconsidering*, p. 52.

12   Murnane, *Texts from the Amarna Period*, p. 75.

13   Ibid. p. 213.

14   The stela has been recorded again recently by Klaus P. Kuhlmann: 'El-Salamuni: Der Felstempel des Eje bei Akhmim', in Günter Dreyer and Daniel Polz, eds, *Begegnungen mit der Vergangenheit – 100 Jahre in Ägypten. Deutsches Archäologisches Institut 1907–2007* (Mainz: von Zabern 2007), p. 181; fig. 256. Marc Gabolde is preparing a new translation with commentary.

15   Murnane, *Texts from the Amarna Period*, pp. 232–3.

16   Franke, ' "Erinnern – Dauern – Denkmäler" – Restauration und Renaissance im Alten Ägypten', *Imago Aegypti* 2 (2008), pp. 38–65, and especially pp. 43–5.

17   So Murnane, *Texts from the Amarna Period*, p. 243 n. 22; cf. also Jan Assmann, *Ägypten: Theologie und Frömmigkeit einer frühen Hochkultur* (Stuttgart: Kohlhammer 1984), p. 266, tentatively suggesting that 'they' in the final sentence cited are the 'Amarna kings'.

18   As described in an inscription published by Claude Traunecker, 'Données nouvelles sur le début d'Aménophis IV et son oeuvre à Karnak', *JSSEA* 14 (1984), pp. 62–9. A decree of Tutankhamun's Year 8 on a stela in Liverpool (E. 583) called for the (re)establishment of offering in temples from Elephantine in the south to Balamun in the delta, as well as the imposition of taxes 'in the entire land': see Amin A. M. A. Amer, 'Tutankhamun's Decree for the Chief Treasurer Maya', *RdE* 36 (1985), pp. 17–20.

19   Remarkably, as late as 2012, Jan Assmann, considered by many the authority on Akhenaten's religion, continued to espouse this outdated idea – see his contribution 'A New State Theology – the Religion of Light', in Friederike Seyfried, ed., *In the Light of Amarna: 100 Years of the Nefertiti Discovery* (Berlin: Staatliche Museen zu Berlin 2012), p. 79.

20   The vulture goddess Nekhbet was also attacked, but her partner, the cobra goddess Wadjet, was left intact; cf., in general, Rolf Krauss, 'Akhenaten: Monotheist? Polytheist?' *BACE* 11 (2000), pp. 93–101.

21   Monuments – royal as well as non-royal – from the Memphite region which associate Tutankhmun with Ptah and his cult are few (cf. Chapter 5, pp. 82–4).

22   Franke, *Imago Aegypti* 2, p. 57.

23 Murnane, *Texts from the Amarna Period*, p. 213.

24 So John Coleman Darnell and Colleen Manassa, *Tutankhamun's Armies: Battle and Conquest during Ancient Egypt's Late Eighteenth Dynasty* (Hoboken, New Jersey: John Wiley & Sons 2007), p. 50.

25 Inscribed on the monumental stela erected in his funerary temple at Kom el-Heitan; for Betsy M. Bryan's English translation of the passage see Arielle P. Kozloff and Bryan, *Egypt's Dazzling Sun: Amenhotep III and his World* (Cleveland, Ohio: Cleveland Museum of Art 1992), p. 91.

26 Brand, 'Secondary Restorations in the Post-Amarna Period', *JARCE* 26 (1999), pp. 113–34; idem, *The Monuments of Seti I: Epigraphic, Historical and Art Historical Analysis* (Leiden, Boston, and Cologne: Brill 2000), pp. 45–118 *passim*.

27 Personal communication cited by Brand, *JARCE* 26, p. 117 n. 24.

28 So Robert Morkot, 'Nubia in the New Kingdom: the limits of Egyptian control', in W. V. Davies, ed., *Egypt and Africa: Nubia from prehistory to Islam* (London: British Museum Press 1991), pp. 294–301. For the archaeological record of the Amarna Period in Nubia, including finds of decorated *talatat*, see Dominique Valbelle, 'Egypt on the Middle Nile', in Derek A. Welsby and Julie R. Anderson, eds, *Sudan – Ancient Treasures. An exhibition of recent discoveries from the Sudan National Museum* (London: British Museum Press 2004), p. 98 and cat. nos. 78, 80, 84, 85, etc.

29 These individuals are considered in detail by Nozomu Kawai in his dissertation 'Studies in the Reign of Tutankhamun' (Johns Hopkins University, 2006) which he is revising for publication.

30 Timothy Kendall and El-Hassan Ahmed Mohamed, 'An Emerging Picture: A Report of the NCAM Jebel Barkal Mission 2013–14', forthcoming in J. R. Anderson and D. A. Welsby, eds, *The Fourth Cataract and Beyond, Proceedings of the 12th International Conference for Nubian Studies* (Leuven: Peeters), in press. I am very grateful to Tim for providing me with a pre-print of this article.

31 For the history of these lions (BM EA 1 and 2) see John Ruffle, 'Lord Prudhoe and His Lions', *Sudan and Nubia: The Sudan Archaeological Research Society Bulletin* 2 (1988), pp. 82–7.

32 My thanks to Marc, who years ago generously provided me with a copy of his unpublished dissertation on Ay in which he discusses the text on BM EA 2 in detail: 'Le père divin Aÿ. Corpus commenté des documents et état des questions', Montpellier 1992, pp. 150–1; cf. also Hourig Sourouzian's entry on the lion in Edna R. Russmann, ed., *Eternal Egypt : Masterworks of Ancient Art from the British Museum* (London: British Museum Press 2001), p. 130.

33 Murnane, 'Soleb Renaissance: Reconsidering the Temple of Nebmaatre in Nubia', *Amarna Letters* 4 (2000), pp. 6–19. See now his posthumously published article 'Amenhotep III and Akhenaten at Soleb', in Nathalie Beaux and Nicholas Grimal, eds, *Soleb* v. VI. *Hommages à Michela Schiff Giorgini* (Cairo: IFAO 2013), pp. 103–24.

34 See Bryan, in Kozloff and Bryan, *Egypt's Dazzling Sun*, pp. 219–20.

35 Brand, *Seti I*, pp. 113–14.

36 Hassan el-Achirie, Paul Barguet, and Michel Dewachter, *Le temple d'Amada* v. II. *Description archéologique* (Cairo: Centre de documentation et d'études sur l'ancienne Égypte 1967), p. 2.

37 Martin Bomas provides an overview of the damage ordered by Akhenaten at Elephantine: 'Akhenaten in the 1st Upper Egyptian Nome', in Annie Gasse and Vincent Rondot, eds, *Séhel entre Égypte et Nubie* (Montpellier: Université Paul Valéry, Montpellier III 2004), pp. 31–7; cf. also Werner Kaiser, et al., 'Stadt und Tempel von Elephantine, 23./24. Grabungsbericht', *MDAIK* 53 (1997), p. 179 n. 243.

38 *Pace* Brand, *Seti I*, p. 109; cf. ibid., pp. 110–13, where Brand contradicts himself when discussing one of the best examples, a face of Amun on a block now in the Louvre.

39 Cf. Brand, *Seti I*, pp. 108–9.

40 Cf. Eaton-Krauss, 'Restorations and Erasures in the Post-Amarna Period', in Zahi Hawass, ed., *Egyptology at the Dawn of the Twenty-first Century: Proceedings of the Eighth International Congress of Egyptologists, Cairo, 28 March – 3 April 2000* v. 2 (Cairo: AUC Press 2003), pp. 198–9, 202 nn. 44–51.

41 Murnane, 'The Bark of Amun on the Third Pylon at Karnak', *JARCE* 16 (1979), pp. 11–27. Arielle Kozloff, *Amenhotep III: Egypt's Radiant Pharaoh* (Cambridge: Cambridge University Press 2012), p. 83, suggests that these figures were not added by Tutankhamun but were commissioned by Amenhotep III to depict himself, 'shortly after' his fifth regnal year. She believes that he then ordered the alteration of the scene in the third decade of his reign, in preparation for his first jubilee, adding 'figures of superhuman size on either side of the [god's] barge' (ibid., p. 134). But what occupied the space now filled by these huge figures earlier? I am not convinced. Kozloff herself concludes her remarks by commenting that thorough art historical analysis may necessitate a reevaluation of her proposal.

42 Brand, *JARCE* 26, p. 121.

43 Lanny Bell called these examples to my attention many years ago; see Eaton-Krauss, 'Tutankhamun at Karnak', *MDAIK* 44 (1988), p. 2 with n. 6; cf. Brand, *JARCE* 26, p. 115 with fig. 1.

44 Brand, *Seti I*, p. 63.

45 Kozloff, *Amenhotep III*, pp. 82–7; 133–7, provides an overview of Amenhotep III's construction work here and his building program at Karnak in general.

46 Murnane, 'Tutankhamun on the Eighth Pylon at Karnak', *Varia Aegyptiaca* 1 (1985), pp. 59–68.

47 A block with part of this text was published by Otto Schaden, 'Tutankhamun–Ay Shrine at Karnak and the Western Valley of the Kings Project: Report on the 1985–1986 Season', *NARCE* 138 (1987), p. 13; fig. 10.

48 Tutankhamun was probably also responsible for restoring the reliefs of this building in its original location; see Charles C. van Siclen, 'Preliminary report of Epigraphic Work done in the Edifice of Amenhotep II: Seasons of 1988–89 and 1989–90', *Varia Aegyptiaca* 6 (1990), p. 78 and cf. Brand, *Seti I*, pp. 81–2 for a discussion of secondary restorations here.

49 Cf. Horemhab's treatment of Ay's inscriptions in Tutankhamun's 'memorial temple', Chapter 6, pp. 96, 98.

50 See Bickel's preliminary publication (considering both structures) on which the following remarks are based: 'Amenhotep III à Karnak, l'étude des bloc épars', *BSFE* 167 (2006), pp. 12–32.

51 Cf. Brand, *Seti I*, p. 99, noting secondary restoration in Luxor Temple of fecundity figures damaged under Akhenaten.

52 For this fragment, see my comments in *MDAIK* 44, pp. 1–2 nn. 1 and 7. It is mentioned in passing by Nathalie Favry, *Sésostris Ier et le début de la XIIe dynastie* (Paris: Pygmalion 2009), pp. 260; 314 n. 532; and by David Lorand, *Arts et politique sous Sésostris Ier. Littérature, sculpture et architecture dans leur context historique* (Turnhout : Brepols 2011), p. 342 n. 8.

53 Schaden, *NARCE* 138, p. 14.

54 For a single *semawy-menu* text of King Ay which Brand interprets as indicative of a secondary restoration mandated by Tutankhamun's successor, see *JARCE* 36, pp. 118–20.

55 Brand, *Seti I*, pp. 93–102.

56 M. Eaton-Krauss and B. Fay, 'Beobachtungen an den Memnonskolossi', *GM* 52 (1981), pp. 26–7.

57 MMA 05.4.2: Edouard Naville, *The XIth Dynasty Temple at Deir el-Bahari* v. III (London: Egypt Exploration Fund 1913), p. 3, pls. VI.1 and VIIIE.

58 See Susanne Bickel, *Untersuchungen im Totentempel des Merenptah in Theben* v. 3. *Tore und andere wiederverwendete Bauteile* (Stuttgart: Steiner 1997), p. 98 for rejection of the idea that Amenhotep III's temple had been severely damaged by an earthquake and her suggestion concerning why Merenptah ordered the demolition of this part of the older king's temple.

59 Ibid., pp. 94–6.

60 See Philippe Martinez, 'Restaurations Post-Amarniennes commanditées par Ramsès II: un cas d'école à Deir el-Bahari', *Memnonia* XVIII (2007), pp. 157–76.

61 Brand, *Seti I*, p. 90 n. 119, cites information provided by Jarusz Karkowski of the Polish Centre of Mediterranean Archaeology Research Centre in Cairo, concerning excavations and restoration work in the temple since the 1960s.

62 My thanks to Monika Dolinska, Senior Keeper of the Egyptian Collection at the National Museum, Warsaw, and her colleague Janina Wiercinska of the Polish mission who are working on this material (email dated 7 October 2011, superseding Dolinska's comment, 'Temples at Deir el-Bahari in the New Kingdom', in Ben Haring, ed., *Funktion und Gebrauch altägyptischer Tempelräume*, Wiesbaden: Harrassowitz 2007, p. 75 with nn. 51 and 52).

63 I am once again grateful to Ray Johnson for providing this information (email dated 31 October 2011). The Epigraphic Survey's record of this and other texts in this building will be published in *Medinet Habu* v. XI.

64 For the site and the excavations which turned up this evidence, see Donald. M. Bailey et al., *Ashmunein (1980)* (London: British Museum Press 1982).

65 Brand, *Seti I*, pp. 49–56.

66 For an overview see Anna Garnett, ' "The Like of which Never Existed": The Memphite Building Programme of Amenhotep III', in Judith Corbelli et al., eds, *Current Research in Egyptology 2009: Proceedings of the Tenth Annual Symposium* (Oxford and Oakville: Oxbow 2011), pp. 53–66.

67 Robert G. Morkot, '*NB-M3'T-Rc*-united-with-Ptah', *JNES* 49 (1990), pp. 323–37.

68 Betsy Bryan, in Kozloff and Bryan, *Egypt's Dazzling Sun*, p. 75.

69 Johnson, 'Re-used Amenhotep III blocks at Memphis', *Egyptian Archaeology* 9 (1996), pp. 3–5; idem, 'Monuments and Monumental Art under Amenhotep III: Evolution and Meaning', in David O'Connor and Eric H. Cline, eds, *Amenhotep III: Perspectives on his Reign* (Ann Arbor: University of Michigan Press 1998), p. 65.

70 For example, by Donald B. Redford, *Akhenaten, the Heretic King* (Princeton: Princeton University Press 1984), p. 59.

71 Cf. Lisa K. Sabbahy, 'The Mnevis Bull at "Horizon of the Disc"', *Amarna Letters* 4 (2000), pp. 36–43; Stefanie Porcier, 'Un taureau sacré Mnévis à Tell el-Amarna?' *EAO* 44 (2006), pp. 35–40.

72 Georges Daressy, 'Le tombe d'un Mnévis de Ramsès', *ASAE* 18 (1919), pp. 312–13.

73 So Dietrich Raue, *Heliopolis und das Haus des Re: Eine Prosopographie und ein Toponym im Neuen Reich* (Berlin: Achet 1999), pp. 312–13; 317, after reviewing the hypotheses of Daressy (who explained the damage to the gods' figures as evidence for Tutankhamun's 'change of heart') and Robert Hari's idea that Ramesses II was responsible for the damage inflicted, before the blocks were reemployed.

74 Consideration of them, accompanied by photographs, is included in Nozomu's dissertation. I am again indebted to him for discussing his conclusions with me and for permission to cite them here.

75 Manfred Bietak, 'Zur Herkunft des Seth von Avaris', *Ä & L* 1 (1990), p. 36 with fig. 2. Cf. also Labib Habachi's mention of 'a block, perhaps with the name of Akhenaton and claimed by Haremhab' found at Tell Basta that he believed was somehow associated with the Hyksos capital: Habachi and Eva-Maria Engel, eds, *Tell el-Dab'a and Qantir: The Site and its Connection with Avaris and Piramesse* (Vienna: Österreichische Akademie der Wissenschaften 2001), p. 47.

76 Discussed in the dissertation of Vincent Razanajao (Université Paul Valéry – Montpellier III, 2000), 'Recherches sur Tell el-Balamoun, capital du XVIIe nome de Basse-Égypte', pp. 39–42. I am grateful to Patricia Spencer for this reference.

77 School of Archaeology and Oriental Studies, University of Liverpool, E. 583: see Amin, *RdE* 36, pp. 17–20.

78 The complete statue of Amun published by Zahi Hawass, 'A Statue of Thutmose II and the God Amun – Genuine or Fake?' in Hawass, ed., *The Realm of the Pharaohs: Essays in Honor of Tohfa Handoussa* (Cairo: SCA 2008), pp. 269–82, is not ancient.

79 CG 42052: Matthias Seidel, *Die königlichen Statuengruppen* v. 1. *Die Denkmäler vom Alten Reich bis zum Ende der 18. Dynastie* (Hildesheim: Gerstenberg 1996), pp. 125–6; pl. 30.

80 For the Karnak 'cachette' and the possibility that it was created by Roman engineers as late as the fourth century AD, see Laurent Coulon, Emmanuel Jambon, and Cynthia Sheikholeshlami, 'Rediscovering a Lost Excavation: The Karnak Cachette', *Kmt* 22:2 (Summer 2011), pp. 18–32.

Chapter 4

1 A catalogue of these sculptures is included in my study of Amun statues created in the post-Amarna Period which is nearing completion. Some of them (along with a few statues attributed to Tutankhamun in error) are illustrated in Denis Forbes's article 'Beyond the Tomb: The Historical Tutankhamen. From His Monuments', *Kmt* 16:2 (Summer 2005), pp. 38–50.

2 Eaton-Krauss, 'Four Notes on the Early Eighteenth Dynasty', *JEA* 84 (1998), pp. 209–10.

3 MMA 50.6: Ambrose Lansing, 'A Head of Tutankhamun', *JEA* 37 (1951), pp. 3–4.

4 My sincere thanks to Ray Johnson who took a cast of the head, generously provided by the Department of Egyptian Art at the MMA, to Luxor for testing the join I proposed.

5 Rather than kneeling, an alternative proposed by William Kelly Simpson, 'On the statue group: Amun affixing the crown of the king', *JEA* 42 (1956), pp. 118–19; cf. Seidel, *Die königliche Statuengruppen*, p. 227.

6 Cited in Seidel's discussion of the head, ibid., pp. 226–7.

7 Lansing, *JEA* 37, p. 4, who considered the sculpture to be a coronation group, did not fail to mention that Atum usually crowned the king, but even so, he decided in favor of identifying Amun as the god in this group. Amun is also the god in the two post-Amarna groups of this type from the Luxor Temple 'cachette', now in the Luxor Museum of Egyptian Art J. 834 and J. 837: see Seidel, *Die königlichen Statuengruppen*, pp. 232–6.

8 CG 42097: Seidel, *Die königlichen Statuengruppen*, pp. 219–21.

9 Cf. Eaton-Krauss, *GM* 235, pp.15–16.

10 But with a vulture rather than a uraeus at her forehead: Suzanne Bickel, *Totentempel des Merenptah*, pl. 72.

11 Turin C. 767: Eleni Vassilika, *Masterpieces of the Museo Egizio in Turin. Official Guide* (Florence: Scala 2009), pp. 72–3 (illustrated).

12 Müller, 'Über die Büste 23725 in Berlin', *Jahrbuch der Berliner Museen* 31 (1989), p. 13.

13 So Seidel, *Die königlichen Statuengruppen*, p. 221.

14 Ibid., pp. 222–4; Seidel's drawing of the piece inadvertently omits the flail.

15 Note, however, that Seidel, ibid., p. 222, was not prepared to exclude categorically the possibility that the triad depicted two local, Nubian deities such as Hathor of Ibshek and Horus of Buhen. However, there is no trace of a tripartite wig on the shoulders of the male figure (to camouflage the juncture of a falcon's head with a man's body), which would be expected were he Horus of Buhen.

16 J. 67: James F. Romano, *Luxor Museum of Ancient Egyptian Art. Catalogue* (Cairo: American Research Center in Egypt 1979), pp. 136–7 (illustrated).

17 ÆIN 1285: Mogens Jørgensen, *Ny Carlsberg Glyptotek Catalogue. Egypt II (1550–1080 BC)* (Copenhagen: Ny Carlsberg Glyptotek 1998), pp. 164–5 (illustrated).

18 J. 198: Romano, *Luxor Museum*, pp. 126–7 (illustrated).

19 Seidel, *Die königlichen Statuengruppen*, p. 221 n. 360, mentions it in passing among the sculptures he would assign to Tutankhamun's reign.

20 Jennifer L. Klimpton et al., 'Preliminary Report on the Work of the Epigraphic Survey in the Temple of Khonsu at Karnak, 2008–2009', *JARCE* 46 (2010), pp. 113–24 and esp. pp. 117–24.

21 Ray Johnson located the head belonging to her figure in the Egyptian Museum, Cairo; see his article 'A Luxor Face Lift', *Egyptian Archaeology* 11 (1997), p. 22.

22 CG 38488: Georges Daressy, *Statues de divinités* (Cairo: IFAO 1906), p. 131. In 1899, the head came to light in perfect condition, seven years after fragments of the body.

23 Emily Teeter, 'Khonsu or Ptah? Notes on Iconography at Karnak', *Varia Aegyptiaca* 5 (1989), pp. 145–53, discusses how to distinguish representations of them in relief.

24 The idea that the moon achieved a remarkable degree of prominence during the reign of the Tutankhamun – so, for example, Eric Hornung and Elisabeth Staehelin, 'Das Tal der Könige in der 18. Dynastie', in André Wiese and Andreas Brodbeck, eds, *Tutanchamun: Das golden Jenseits* (Basel: Antiken Museum Basel and Sammlung Ludwig 2004), pp. 81–2 – is based on the frequent use of the lunar disk and crescent in the design of several jewels among the 'treasure' from the tomb – just the kind of documentation lacking for earlier, as well as later kings.

25 Georges Legrain, *Statues et statuettes des rois et de particuliers* v. 1 (Cairo: IFAO 1906), p. 54.

26 Cf. in particular the head illustrated by Dorothea Arnold, *The Royal Women of Amarna: Images of Beauty from Ancient Egypt* (New York: MMA 1996), fig. 50.

27 Eaton-Krauss, 'The Sydney Goddess', in K. N. Sowada and B. G. Ockinga, eds, *Egyptian Art in the Nicholson Museum, Sydney* (Sydney: Mediterranean Archaeology 2006), pp. 91–6. The head in Cairo is CG 38888.

28 Cf. Arnold, *Royal Women*, figs 68–9.

29 When I saw this statue in April 1994, I was told that it was reserved for publication by Abdel Hamid Marouf of the Centre franco-égyptien and Otto Schaden. To the best of my knowledge, their study has not appeared in the interim.

30 Louvre AF 2575: Christophe Barbotin, *Les statues égyptiens du nouvel empire. Statues royales et divines* (Paris: Éditions du Musée du Louvre 2007), v. 1 pp. 188–89; v. 2, pp. 344–7 (illustrations).

31 CG 42091–2: Legrain, *Statues et statuettes* v. I, pp. 53–4. A fragmentary base inscribed for Tutankhamun which preserves one foot of a striding figure wearing sandals has been tentatively ascribed to another, third statue of this type by Hassan Selim, 'Two Royal Statue Bases from Karnak in the Basement of the Egyptian Museum in Cairo', *BIFAO* 111 (2011), pp. 328–30.

32 Sandals in Egyptian art and in statuary in particular need to be studied. The chapter 'Footwear in Late [*sic*!] Egyptian Art' in Andre J. Veldmeijer, *Tutankhamun's Footwear: Studies of Ancient Egyptian Footwear* (Norg: DrukWare 2010), pp. 208–24 is hardly a start.

33 Louvre E 11609: Barbotin, *Statues royales* v. I, pp.130–32 (no. 73); v. 2, pp. 200–205 (illustrations).

34 CG 603: Desroches-Noblecourt, *Toutankhamon et son temps*, pp. 194–7.

35 Cf. the opinions on the dating of the statue cited by Catherine Chadefaud, *Les statues porte-enseignes de l'Egypte ancienne (1580–1085 avant J.C.)* (Paris: author 1982), pp. 76–8; she herself remains uncommitted.

36 BM EA 37639: Morris L. Bierbrier, ed., *Hieroglyphic Texts from Egyptian Stelae . . . in the British Museum* X (London: British Museum 1982), p. 9; Chadefaud, *Les statues porte-enseignes*, pp. 10–11.

37 Bierbrier mentions the possibility that the crude signs which are oriented (incorrectly) leftwards may not be ancient.

38 Although this type of navel does occur during the post-Amarna Period it is most characteristic of both reliefs and statuary of the Amarna Period itself; cf. Eaton-Krauss, *CdE* 56, 258–64.

39 Janusz Karkowski, *The Pharaonic Inscriptions from Faras* (Warsaw: Editions scientifiques de Pologne 1981), p. 140; Chadefaud, *Les statues porte-enseignes*, pp. 11–12.

40 Cf. Karkowski, *Pharaonic Inscriptions*, p. 72 n. 133, who simply cites the British Museum sculpture for comparison, without going into detail, and concludes that the identification as Tutankhamun is 'highly probable'.

41 Alexandra Verbovsek, *Die sogenannten Hyksosmonumente: Eine archäologische Standortbestimmung* (Wiesbaden: Harrassowitz 2006), pp. 110–14, would deny a relationship between the New Kingdom standard-bearing statues of kings and the sculpture from Kiman Fares in Cairo depicting Amenemhet III carrying two standards topped by falcon heads. Her attempt to identify the figure as a depiction of the king as the co-regent of his father Senwosret III, in the role of Horus and *iwn*-priest (?), does not convince.

42 Chadefaud, *Les statues porte-enseignes*, and Helmut Satzinger, 'Der heilige Stab als Kraftquelle des Königs', *Jahrbuch der kunsthistorischen Sammlungen in Wien* 77 (1981), pp. 9–43, have published studies of the genre.

43 CG 42194: Legrain, *Statues et statuettes des rois et de particuliers* v. III (Cairo: IFAO 1913), pp. 3–4.

44 Jacobus van Dijk, 'A Cat, a Nurse, and a Standard-Bearer', in D'Auria, ed., *Offerings to the Discerning Eye*, pp. 330–2.

45 BM EA 75: Eaton-Krauss, 'Tutankhamun Presenting Offerings', in Russmann, *Eternal Egypt*, pp. 148–50.

46 My thanks again to Nozomu for sharing this information with me and providing the museum reference number of the pieces (Temp. reg. 20/1/41/3) which Habachi recorded incorrectly.

47 Cf. the dyad depicting Amenemhet III and the comments of Verbovsek, *Hyksosmonumente*, pp. 42–7, concerning the genre.

48 A statuette in Florence, Museo Egizio Inv. No. 543: Helen Whitehouse, 'The fish-offerer in Florence', in Elizabeth Frood and Angela McDonald, eds, *Decorum and Experience: Essays in Ancient Culture for John Baines* (Oxford: GI 2013), pp. 180–4.

Chapter 5

1 A scarab excavated at Knossos and said to be inscribed with Ankhesenamun's name (cf. Jean Leclant, 'Fouilles et travaux', *Orientalia* 47, 1978, p. 315) should be deleted from the list of such objects until it can be examined first-hand by an Egyptologist – so P. R. S. Moorey (to whom the reading of the name was credited) in his response of 20 May 1991 to my inquiry.

2 William Matthew Flinders Petrie, 'Ancient Gaza, 1932–22', *Ancient Egypt* 1932, p. 101 (no. 31); idem, *Ancient Gaza: Tell El Ajjul* v. III (London: British School of Archaeology in Egypt 1933), p. 5; pls. VII, VIII: 2. Alegre Savariego informs me that the ring is in the collection of the Rockefeller Archaeological Museum, Jerusalem (Inv. no. 33.1708).

3 Isabelle Régen and Georges Soukassian, *Gebel el-Zeit* v. 2. *Le matériel inscrit: Moyen Empire – Nouvel Empire* (Cairo: IFAO 2008), pp. 81–2.

4 So, too, the scarab of 'Amen-Onkhs [=Ankhesenamun?], daughter of Akhenaten and married to Tutankhamun' from Lachish – Olga Tufnell et al., *Lachish (Tell ed Duweir)* v. II.

The Fosse Temple (London, New York, and Toronto: Oxford University Press 1940), p. 69 (no. 10); pl. XXXIIA and B (10).

5 James K. Hoffmeier and Jacobus van Dijk, 'New Light on the Amarna Period from North Sinai', *JEA* 96 (2010), pp. 201–2; figs. 14–15.

6 Cf. however the suggestion that Tutankhamun's temple at Kawa, discussed immediately below, may have originated as another of Akhenaten's temples in Nubia: W. Raymond Johnson, 'Akhenaten in Nubia', in Marjorie M. Fisher, ed., *Ancient Nubia: African Kingdom on the Nile* (Cairo and New York: AUC Press 2012), p. 93.

7 M. F. Laming Macadam, *The Temples of Kawa* v. II. *History and Archaeology of the Site* (Oxford: Oxford Univ. Press 1955), pp. 12–14; 31–40; figs. 5–9; pls. I–IV, XXXVII–XL. New excavations at the site under the direction of Derek A. Welsby of the British Museum have not turned up any new Dynasty XVIII material so far.

8 Acc. No. 1931.552: Helen Whitehouse, *Ancient Egypt and Nubia in the Ashmolean Museum* (Oxford: Ashmolean Museum 2009), p. 130 (illus.).

9 This phenomenon has been thoroughly investigated by Lanny Bell, 'Aspects of the Cult of the Deified Tutankhamun', in Paule Posener-Krieger, ed., *Mélanges Gamal Eddin Mokhtar* (Cairo: IFAO 1985), pp. 31–59.

10 For the reading of this epithet as 'Lion-upon-the-terrace', see Ivan Guermeur, *Les cultes d'Amon hors de Thèbes: Recherches de géographie religieuse* (Turnhout: Brepols 2005), p. 91.

11 See the review of earlier exploration and a catalogue of finds published by Karkowski, *Pharaonic Inscriptions*, esp. pp. 4–5; 69–73; 115–24; 130–6. There may well have been a pre-existing settlement at the site.

12 Julia Budka, *Der König an der Haustür* (Vienna: Afro-Pub 2001), pp. 227–9. Budka presumes the lady was Huy's wife, as does Nozomu Kawai in his dissertation.

13 'Notes on Some Inscriptions in the Etbai District', *Proceedings of the Society for Biblical Archaeology* 31 (1909), p. 248.

14 For Wilkinson and Lepsius see the references in Bertha Porter and Rosalind L. B. Moss, *Topographical Bibliography of Ancient Egyptian Hieroglyphic Texts, Reliefs, and Paintings* v. VII: *Nubia, the Deserts, and outside Egypt* (Oxford: GI 1951), p. 321.

15 Note that John Coleman Darnell, 'A Stela of the Reign of Tutankhamun from the Region of Kurkur Oasis', SAK 31 (2003), p. 85, would interpret these blocks as one indication of 'wide-ranging activity in the Eastern Desert under Tutankhamun'.

16 Friederike Kampp and Karl Joachim Seyfried, 'Eine Rückkehr nach Theben: Das Grab des Pa-ren-nefer, Hoherpriester des Amun zur Zeit Tutanchamuns', *Antike Welt* 26:5 (1995), fig. 2, locate six such tombs on their map of the Theban Necropolis.

17 Nina M. Davies and Alan H. Gardiner, *The Tomb of Huy, Viceroy of Nubia in the Reign of Tutankhamun* (London: EES 1926). Patricia Spencer drew my attention to a notice dated 2 December 2014 in *Ahram Online* reporting that the tomb is scheduled to reopen soon to tourism after three years of closure for restoration.

18 Ibid. pl. IV. Gardiner, ibid. p. 10, asked; 'Was it on account of the king's tender age that the actual appointment of Huy was deputed to an unnamed "overseer of the treasury"'?

19 Ibid. pl. XXII.

20 See Friederike Kampp-Seyfried, 'Die Verfemung des Names *P3-rn-nfr*,' in Heike Guksch and Daniel Polz, eds, *Stationen: Beiträge zur Kulturgeschichte Ägyptens Rainer Stadelmann gewidmet* (Mainz: von Zabern 1998), pp. 103–19.

21 Kampp and Seyfried, *Antike Welt* 26:5, pp. 340–1; figs. 31–2; cf. also Kampp, '4. Vorbericht . . .', *MDAIK* 50 (1994), pp. 175–88.

22 W. Raymond Johnson, 'Monuments and Monumental Art under Amenhotep III: Evolution and Meaning', in David O'Connor and Eric H. Cline, eds, *Amenhotep III: Perspectives on his Reign* (Ann Arbor: University of Michigan Press 1998), pp. 75–7, provides an informative overview of the site.

23 See now David O'Connor, 'The King's Palace at Malkata and the Purpose of the Royal Harem', in Zahi Hawass and Jennifer Houser Wegner, eds, *Millions of Jubilees: Studies in Honor of David P. Silverman* (Cairo: CSA 2010), p. 58.

24 Hayes, 'Inscriptions from the Palace of Amenhotep III', *JNES* 10 (1951), pp. 236–9, fig. 37 (upper right).

25 For an overview of the building activity of Tutankhamun (and Ay) at Karnak Temple, see now Elizabeth Blyth, *Karnak: Evolution of a Temple* (London and New York: Routledge 2006), pp. 117; 126–32; cf. also my article in *MDAIK* 44, pp. 1–11.

26 W. Hovestreydt, 'Secret Doors and Hidden Treasure . . .', in Jacobus van Dijk, ed., *Essays on Ancient Egypt in Honour of Herman te Velde* (Groningen: STYX 1997), p.192, would relate this scene to a series of later Ramesside reliefs showing a king presenting the Theban triad with the spoils of war. But, as he notes, here neither booty nor prisoners are shown. Another scene at Karnak including both which Hovestreydt, ibid., pp. 192–3, would attribute to Tutankhamun cannot have been sculpted during his reign because the walls it decorates stretch between the Ninth and Tenth Pylons. The reliefs will have been Horemhab's work, like those on the Tenth Pylon which he completed and decorated.

27 For a description and the associated texts, see Françoise Le Saout, 'Reconstitution des murs de la cour de la cachette', *Cahiers de Karnak* VII 1978–1981 (Paris 1982), pp. 244–5; pl. VIII (7a).

28 Cf. Beatrix Gessler-Löhr, *Die heiligen Seen ägyptischer Tempel: Ein Beitrag zur Deutung sakraler Baukunst* (Hildesheim: Gerstenberg 1983), pp. 161–4.

29 So Françoise Le Saout and Abd el-Hamid Ma'arouf, 'Un nouveau fragment de stèle de Toutânkhamon', *Cahiers de Karnak* VIII (1987), pp. 287–8; pls I–II; for the larger fragment, see Otto J. Schaden, 'A Tutankhamun Stela at Karnak', in the same issue of the periodical, pp. 279–84; pls I–II. Nozomu Kawai, *JEH* 3, pp. 288–9 n. 36, mentions his intention to publish another fragment of this stela which he located in a storage facility at Karnak.

30 Schaden, *Cahiers de Karnak* VIII, pl. II.2–3.

31 Le Saout and Ma'arouf, *Cahiers de Karnak* VIII, pl. II.

32 This technique is quite old, see ibid. pp. 285–6; its use is particularly common in corridors and at doorways. Kawai (see n. 29) has suggested in passing that Ankhesenamun may have followed her husband on this side of the stela.

33 Teeter, *The Presentation of Maat: Ritual and Legitimacy in Ancient Egypt* (Chicago: University of Chicago 1997), especially pp. 1–10.

34 Cf. Schaden, *Cahiers de Karnak* VIII, p. 282.

35 Jean-François Carlotti and Philippe Martinez, 'Nouvelles observations architecturales et épigraphiques sur la grande hypostyle du temple d'Amon-Rê à Karnak,' *Cahiers de Karnak* XIV (2013), pp. 231–77, and esp. p. 252 fig. 20 summarizing Tutankhamun's work here.

36 For the early history of the Mut Temple, see Betsy M. Bryan, 'The Temple of Mut: New Evidence on Hatshepsut's Building Activity', in Roehrig, ed., *Hatshepsut*, pp. 181–3.

37 Robert Vergnieux, *Recherches sur les monuments thébains d'Amenhotep IV* v. I, (Geneva: Société d'Égyptologie 1999), pp. 153–63.

38 See now Agnes Cabrol, *Les voies processionnelles de Thèbes* (Leuven: Peeters 2001), pp. 221–36.

39 Ibid. pp. 198–9; 410–11.

40 As Bill Murnane and I argued in our article, 'Tutankhamun, Ay, and the Avenue of Sphinxes between Pylon X and the Mut Precinct at Karnak', *BSEG* 15 (1991), pp. 31–5.

41 These reliefs have been recorded and published, with translations of the inscriptions and commentary, by the Epigraphic Survey, *Reliefs and Inscriptions at Luxor Temple* v. 1. *The Festival Procession of Opet in the Colonnade Hall* (Chicago: University of Chicago 1994).

42 So the conclusion of Wolfgang Waitkus, *Untersuchungen zu Kult und Funktion des Luxortempels* (Gladbeck: PeWe 2008).

43 The Epigraphic Survey, *Reliefs and Inscriptions at Luxor Temple* v. 2. *The Façade, Portals, Upper Register Scenes, Columns, Marginalia, and Statuary in the Colonnade Hall* (Chicago: University of Chicago 1998), pls 160–67.

44 Johnson, 'Honorific Figures of Amenhotep III in the Luxor Temple Colonnade Hall', in David P. Silverman, ed., *For His Ka: Essays Offered in Memory of Klaus Baer* (Chicago: University of Chicago 1994), pp. 133–44. As a proponent of a long co-regency between Amenhotep III and Akhenaten, Johnson suspects that Tutankhamun might be in fact the son of the former.

45 A. J. Spencer, *Excavations at el-Ashmunein* v. II. *The Temple Area* (London: British Museum 1989), pp. 15–16; 64–5.

46 Now in the British Museum, see for example EA 58469: M. L. Bierbrier, ed. *Hieroglyphic Texts from Egyptian Stelae . . . in the British Museum* v. X (London: British Museum 1982), p. 9; pl. 1: 1.

47 Fran Weatherhead and Elizabeth Shannon, 'Fragments of a painted royal figure with artist's grid from West Street 2/3', in Barry J. Kemp, ed., *Amarna Reports* v. IV (London: EES 1987), pp. 17–29; fig. 2.7 (reconstruction). Cf. the comments in my review, *BiOr* XLVI (1989), col. 605.

48 Susanne Binder, *The Gold of Honour in New Kingdom Egypt* (Oxford: Aris & Phillips 2008), pp. 85–7; 89.

49 Geoffrey Thorndike Martin, *The Memphite Tomb of Horemheb, Commander-in-chief of Tutankhamun* v. I. *The Reliefs, Inscriptions, and Commentary* (London: EES 1989), pp. 87–98; pls. 110a–112.

50 Two of the most remarkable are the tombs of Meryneith, 'Greatest of Seers of the Aten', and of Ptahemwia, 'Royal Butler, Clean of Hands', both discovered by the joint expedition of the Rijksmuseum and Leiden University, the successor of the EES–Rijksmuseum expedition; for updates on the mission's work and references to publications, see www.saqqara.nl.

51 Kunsthistorisches Museum 5816: Beatrix Gessler-Löhr, 'Bemerkungen zur Nekropole des Neuen Reiches von Saqqara vor der Amarna-Zeit II. Gräber der Bürgermeister von Memphis', *Oudheidkundige Medelingen uit het Rijksmuseum van Oudheden te Leiden* 77 (1997), pp. 57–8; pl. 10.

52 Hawass, *Discovering Tutankhamun*, pp. 31–2; 33 (illus.). Hawass's publication of these reliefs is in press in the Dorothea Arnold Fs.; a second article jointly authored with Ray Johnson is in preparation.

53 Eaton-Krauss and Graefe, *Small Golden Shrine*, pl. XV.

54 So ibid., pp. 26–6; 37–8.

55 As discussed at the conclusion of Chapter 3, pp. 48–9, the blocks with Tutankhamun's name found reused at Heliopolis may possibly derive from a construction project of the reign there.

56 Aidan Dodson, 'The Canopic Equipment from the Serapeum of Memphis', in Anthony Leahy and John Tait, eds, *Studies on Ancient Egypt in Honour of H. S. Smith* (London: EES 1999), p. 62; fig. 3.

57 Dodson (ibid.) describes the carving as 'especially exquisite', but the quality is 'high' only in comparison to the stoppers from the other nearly contemporaneous isolated burials.

58 See Bart R. Hellinckx, 'Tutankhamun's so-called Stole', *Orientalia Lovaniensia Periodica* 27 (1996), pp. 5–22.

59 For this institution, see Asraf Iskander Sadek, *Popular Religion during the New Kingdom* (Hildesheim: Gerstenberg 1987), pp. 29–36.

60 Ludwig Borchardt, *Das Grabmal des Königs Sa-hu-re* v. 1. *Der Bau* (Leipzig: Hinrichs 1910), fig. 165. On the basis of this mention, Sadek, *Popular Religion*, 30, attributes restoration of the goddess's cult here to Tutankhamun and/or Ay and Horemhab.

61 Ahmed Mahmoud Moussa, 'Two Blocks Bearing a Celebration of a Jubilee Festival and a Part of Cornice Inscribed with the Cartouches of Sety I from Memphis', *ASAE* 68 (1982), pp. 117–18; pl. IB. For the 'chapel' of Seti I, see now Brand, *Seti I*, pp. 147–9 (3.35 'Ptah Chapel of Seti I').

62 Tentatively proposed by Stephané Pasquali; see below, n. 64.

63 Moussa, *ASAE* 68, pp. 115–17, pl. IA.

64 Pasquali, *Topographie cultuelle de Memphis* v. 1a: *Corpus. Temples et principaux quartiers de la XVIIIe dynastie* (Montpellier: Université Paul Valéry 2011), pp. 66–8 (doc. A. 137–38). He cites style as the reason for attributing these reliefs to the end of Dynasty XVIII. I must admit to reservations on account of the poor quality of the photographs published in Moussa's article, but perhaps Pasquali has examined the originals?

65 Berlin 21840: Labib Habachi, 'Unknown or Little-known Monuments of Tutankhamen and of his Viziers', in John Ruffle et al., eds, *Glimpses of Ancient Egypt: Studies in Honour of H. W. Fairman* (Warminster: Aris & Phillips 1979), pp. 32–3; 41(notes); fig. I; pl. 1.

66 Egyptian Museum, Cairo, JE 88131: ibid. p. 35; fig. 2; pl. II; cf. now Pasquali, *Topographie* v. Ia, p. 50 (doc. A. 101).

67 Height. *c.* 50 cm, compared to *c.* 80 cm for the others.

68 In Chapter 3, p. 49, the possibility that Tutankhamun's reign witnessed construction, rather then restoration, in the delta was considered.

69 JE 57195: J. van Dijk and Eaton-Krauss, 'Tutankhamun at Memphis', *MDAIK* 42 (1986), pp. 39–41.

70 J. van Dijk, 'The Canaanite God Haroun and his Cult in Egypt', in Sylvia Schoske, ed., *Akten des Vierten Internationalen Ägyptologen Kongresses, München 1985 v. 4: Geschichte – Verwaltungs- und Wirtschaftsgeschichte – Rechtsgeschichte- Nachbarkulturen* (Hamburg: Buske 1991), pp. 247–56 and esp. 254–5.

71 Stéphane Pasquali, 'Les fouilles de S. Hassan à Giza en 1938 et le temple d'Osiris de Ro-Sétaou au Nouvel Empire', *GM* 216 (2008), pp. 77–8.

72 *Tutankhamun's Painted Box*, pl. III.

73 Desroches-Noblecourt, *Toutankhamon et son temps*, cat. 118–19.

Chapter 6

1 This chapter incorporates significant revision of some ideas expressed in my article 'The Burial of Tutankhamen, Part One', *Kmt* 20: 4 (Winter 2009–10), pp. 34–47.

2 As argued by Philippe Martinez, 'Un monument préamarnien ignore: Le Ramesseum', *Memnonia* 15 (2004), pp. 123–50.

3 Wolfgang Helck, 'Begräbnis Pharaos', in Ulrich Luft, ed., *The Intellectual Heritage of Egypt* (Fs. László Kákosy; Budapest: Univ. Eötvös Loránd 1992), pp. 267–76.

4 E.g., Kozloff, *Amenhotep III, passim*, who proposes that bubonic plague was responsible for numerous anomalies in the historical record, beginning in the reign of Amenhotep III; cf. Kemp, *City of Akhenaten and Nefertiti*, pp. 228–9 (with the caveat on p. 310 n. 46); idem et al., 'Life, death and beyond in Akhenaten's Egypt', *Antiquity* 87 (2013), pp. 64–78.

5 For this item of funerary equipment, see my monograph *The Sarcophagus in the Tomb of Tutankhamun* (Oxford: GI 1993).

6 For references and implications for the ownership of KV 42, see Eaton-Krauss, 'Who commissioned KV 42 and for whom?' *GM* 234 (2012), pp. 51–8.

7 I am very grateful to Ray Johnson for sharing with me this discovery which he is preparing for publication.

8 See the English summary of Nozomu Kawai, 'Objects from KV 22', in Sakuji Yoshimura, ed., *Research in the Western Valley of the Kings Egypt: The Tomb of Amenophis III (KV 22)* [in Japanese] (Tokyo: Waseda University 2008), pp. 262–3; pl. 30.2.

9 The granite lid itself was broken in two in antiquity, perhaps during transport to the Valley of the Kings.

10 Gabolde, *D'Akhenaton à Toutankhamon*, pp. 129–32; pl. XIV; ibid. pl. XV is his reconstruction of the lid incorporating a depiction of the radiant sun disk as on the sides of the basin.

11 Robins, 'Isis, Nephthys, Selket and Neith represented on the sarcophagus of Tutankhamun and in four free-standing statues found in KV 62', *GM* 72 (1984), pp. 21–4. Judging by the Burton photographs in my monograph (*Sarcophagus*, pls. II, V, and VIII), the figure of

Neith (which Robins does not comment upon) shows the same proportions as those of Nephthys and Selket.

12 Indeed, some Deir el-Medina craftsmen continued to paint figures according to the 'Amarna canon' down to the accession of Seti I – see Gay Robins, 'The proportions of figures in the decoration of the tombs of Tutankhamun (KV 62) and Ay (KV 23)', *GM* 72 (1984), pp. 27–32.

13 See my rejoinder, 'The Sarcophagus in the Tomb of Tutankhamun: A Clarification', *JEA* 84 (1998), pp. 210–11.

14 *Pace* Aly el-Khouly and Geoffrey T. Martin, *Excavations in the Royal Wadi at el-Amarna 1984* (Cairo: IFAO 1987), p. 16, suggesting that Tomb no. 27 with a sarcophagus slide could have been started for Tutankhaten.

15 Subsequent research on Dynasty XVIII tombs in the Valley (recently, for example, René Preys, 'Les tombes non-royales de la Vallée du Rois', *SAK* 40, 2011, pp. 315–38) has shown that dissenting opinions – see Sayed Tawfik, 'Tutanchamuns Grab – Provisorium oder kunstvolles Novum?' in Friedrich Junge, ed., *Studien zu Sprache und Religion Ägyptens* (Fs. Westendorf; Göttingen: F. Junge 1984), pp. 1131–40, and Claude Vandersleyen, 'Pour qui a été creusée de tombe de Toutankhamon?' in Jan Quaegebeur, ed., *Studia Paulo Naster Oblata* II. *Orientalia antiqua* (Leuven: Peeters1982), pp. 263–7 – are without foundation.

16 The traditional 90-degree change of axis was also planned – see Martin, *Royal Tomb* v. II, pp. 21; 27.

17 Jiro Kondo, 'The Reclearance of Tombs WV 22 and WV A in the Western Valley of the Kings', in Richard H. Wilkinson, ed., *Valley of the Sun Kings: New Explorations in the Tombs of the Pharaohs* (Tucson: University of Arizona Egyptian Expedition 1995), pp. 30–2.

18 The search for foundation deposits at KV 23's entrance and in the vicinity was unsuccessful though not exhaustive. However, the interpretation of foundation deposits found in the KV is straightforward in only a single case – cf. my comments in *GM* 234, p. 55.

19 Compare Nicholas Reeves, *Valley of the Kings: The Decline of a Royal Necropolis* (London and New York: Kegan Paul International 1990), pp. 40–2 and Reeves and Richard H. Wilkinson, *The Complete Valley of the Kings: Tombs and Treasures of Egypt's Greatest Pharaohs* (London: Thames & Hudson 1996), pp. 116–17 with my comments in reviews of those publications, *BiOr* 49 (1992), col. 710 and *BiOr* 56 (1999), col. 334, respectively.

20 Cf. Eaton-Krauss, 'Recent exhibition catalogues – some comments and corrections', *GM* 220 (2009), p. 122; eadem, 'Reprise: Akhenaten, Nefertiti, Amarna', *CdE* 88 (2013), pp. 75–6. The accession numbers of these colossi are, respectively: Cairo JE 59869; OI 14088; and Berlin ÄgM 1479/1.

21 Uvo Hölscher, *The Excavations of Medinet Habu* v. II. *The Temples of the Eighteenth Dynasty* (Chicago; University of Chicago Press 1939), p. 110 n. 2. Note that Luc and Marc Gabolde, 'Les Temples de Thoutmoses II et Toutânkhamon', *BIFAO* 89 (1989), p. 140, remind readers that Hölscher concluded there was no trace of a funerary temple of Tutankhamun at Medinet Habu.

22 Cf. Hölscher, *The Excavation of Medinet Habu* v. V. *Post Ramessid Remains* (Chicago: University of Chicago Press 1954), p. 6.

23 Viz. several small fragments discovered by excavations under the direction of Boyo G. Ockinga during the clearance of TT 148 (temp. Ramesses III/V). Until this writing only a few of them have been mentioned in print: see Ockinga, 'Use, Reuse, and Abuse of "Sacred Space": Observations from Dra Abu al-Naga', in Peter F. Dorman and Betsy M. Bryan, eds, *Sacred Space and Sacred Function in Ancient Thebes* (Chicago: Oriental Institute, University of Chicago 2007), p. 140 with figs. 9.10–13 and 9.21. I am grateful to Boyo for calling my attention to these fragments.

24 Prisse d'Avennes, *Monuments égyptiens: bas-reliefs, peintures, inscriptions . . .* (Paris: Didot 1847), pl. XI: 1; cf. the discussion of Wilhelm Spiegelberg, 'Zu den Jagdbilder des Tutenchamun', *OLZ* 28 (1925), cols. 569–71.

25 W. Raymond Johnson, 'Tutankhamen-Period Battle Narratives at Luxor', *Kmt* 20: 4 (Winter 2009–10), pp. 20–33, including in concise form results of his unpublished dissertation (University of Chicago 1992) 'An Asiatic Battle Scene of Tutankhamun from Thebes: A Late Amarna Antecedent of the Ramesside Battle-Narrative Tradition'. Shortly after completing it, Ray generously provided me with a copy.

26 Gabolde, 'Le père divin Äy. Corpus commenté des documents et état des questions', Université Louis Lumière Lyon 2, 1992. I am indebted to Marc for supplying a copy of it; like Ray's dissertation, it has proved invaluable in the preparation of the following remarks on the Mansion.

27 Following on the dismantling of the Mansion under Horemhab, not all the elements were immediately re-employed as fill in the construction of his pylons; for example, some lay unused until restoration work on the Treasury of Thutmose I at North Karnak was undertaken; see Jean Jacquet, *Karnak-Nord* v. V. *Le trésor de Thoutmosis Ier, etude architecturale* (Paris: IFAO 1983), pp. 32; 99.

28 Eaton-Krauss, *MDAIK* 44, p. 11; see now the thorough review of earlier studies on the building provided by Martina Ullmann, *König für die Ewigkeit: Die Häuser der Millionen von Jahren* (Wiesbaden: Harrassowitz 2002), pp. 189–93.

29 Cf. Donald B. Redford, *The Akhenaten Temple Project* v. 2: *Rwd-Mnw, foreigners and inscriptions* (Toronto: University of Toronto Press 1988), p. 20 n. 98.

30 As suggested 40 years ago by Ramadan Sa'ad, 'Fragments d'un monument de Toutânkhamon retrouvés dans le IXe pylône de Karnak', *Cahiers de Karnak* V (1975), p. 108.

31 Johnson, *Kmt* 20:4, p. 26.

32 Cf. Ullmann, *König für die Ewigkeit*, p. 195.

33 No advantage would have accrued to King Horemhab by ordering Ay's figure as a courtier to be altered to depict himself in a subservient role, incompatible with his exalted status as regent during Tutankhamun's reign, for which see van Dijk, 'The New Kingdom Necropolis of Memphis: Historical and Iconographical Studies' (Rijksuniversiteit dissertation, Groningen 1993), pp. 11–64.

34 Eaton-Krauss, *MDAIK* 44, p. 11 n. 74. Aidan Dodson, *Amarna Sunset*, p. 155 n. 65, objects to this suggestion of mine since it 'goes against normal New Kingdom practice' which, he asserts, was for a king to leave pre-accession depictions of himself untouched or, citing the case of Horemhab in particular, to have a uraeus added to his non-royal figures. Indeed, a uraeus was added to some – though not all – depictions of generalissimo Horemhab in the

reliefs of his non-royal tomb at Saqqara. But Dodson's analogy is false. The Saqqara tomb was not a *royal* monument, like the Mansion, nor is it known when the uraeus was added. Possibly that action was mandated only after King Horemhab's death, when the tomb was the site of a cult for his posthumous veneration.

35 Some suggest that it might have stood near the mortuary temple of Amenhotep III at Kom el-Heitan, because the Mansion of Tutankhamun is mentioned alongside Amenhotep's funerary temple in the titles of the owner of the small stele found at Deir el-Bahri cited above in Chapter 3, pp 46–7, 141 n. 57.

36 Ullmann, *König für die Ewigkeit*, p. 193. Ullmann (ibid., pp. 193–5) does not categorically exclude the possibility that a cult building of some kind existed on the west bank for Tutankhamun's benefit during Ay's reign. But the indications she cites for this entity are either hypothetical or misunderstood – for example, she describes the quartzite colossi usurped by Horemhab from Ay as originally intended to depict Tutankhamun (see p. 151 n. 20).

37 Johnson, 'Asiatic Battle Scene', pp. 30–1.

38 Teeter, *Presentation of Maat*, p. 101 (Doc. B4).

39 A. Egberts, *In Quest of Meaning: A Study of the Ancient Egyptian Rites of Consecrating the Meret-Chests and Driving the Calves* (Leiden: Nederlands Instituut voor het Nabije Oosten 1995), *passim*. The scene from the Mansion of Tutankhamun is Egbert's Doc. B.a-XVIII.13-Ka.1 (ibid. p. 222).

40 For blue painting of Amun's skin see Christian E. Loeben, 'Thebanische Tempelmalerei – Spuren religiöser Ikonographie', in Roland Tefnin, ed., *La peinture égyptienne ancienne* (Brussels: Fondation Egyptologique Reine Elisabeth 1997), pp. 118–20.

41 Egberts, *In Quest of Meaning*, p. 222 (Doc. B.a-XVIII.12.Kaw.1).

42 This series is the subject per se of Johnson's dissertation.

43 Martin, *Memphite Tomb of Horemheb* v. I, pls. 93 and 105. Martin (ibid. p. 162 n. 5) mentions the idea voiced earlier by others that reliefs depicting Horemheb's victories as king in the speos at Silsileh actually refer to his role in campaigns he led on behalf of Tutankhamun.

44 Johnson, 'Asiatic Battle Scene', p. 32; cf. idem, *Kmt* 20:4, p. 32.

45 Cf. Alfred Grimm, 'Ein Käfig für einen Gefangenen in einem Ritual zur Vernichtung von Feinden', *JEA* 73 (1987), pp. 202–6. Grimm believes he has identified evidence for annual ritual executions dating back to the time of Cheops.

46 For this practice and depictions of it, see Eaton-Krauss, *MDAIK* 44, p. 5.

47 Manfred Bietak, 'The Archaeology of the "gold of valour"', *Egyptian Archaeology* 40 (2012), pp. 32–3.

48 For this scene in particular, its antecedents and successors, see José M. Galán, 'Mutilation of Pharaoh's Enemies', in Eldamaty and Trad, eds, *Egyptian Museum Collections*, pp. 441–51; fig. 1; pl. 1.

49 As Johnson, *Kmt* 20:4, pp. 30–1 remarks; cf. Stephen P. Harvey's caveat in the review he provides of battle scenes prior to the New Kingdom in his dissertation, University of Pennsylvania, 'The Cults of King Ahmose at Abydos' (Ann Arbor: UMI 1998), pp. 303–6.

50 Compared in detail by Gabolde and Gabolde, *BIFAO* 89, pp. 146–75.

Chapter 7

1   Černy, *Hieratic Inscriptions from the Tomb of Tutankhamun* (Oxford: GI 1965), p. 4.

2   Tallet, 'Une jarre de l'an 31 et une jarre de l'an 10 dans le cave du Toutânkhamon', *BIFAO* 96 (1996), pp. 369–83.

3   So Rolf Krauss, 'Nochmals die Bestattung Tutanchamuns', *SAK* 23 (1996), pp. 227–49.

4   As argued (without specific reference to the burial of Tutankhamun) by Christoffer Thiess, 'Die Dauer eines altägyptischen Bestattungsrituals', *GM* 227 (2010), pp. 93–104. Thiess concludes that the figure of 70 days, while in general reasonable, may have been religiously motivated and did not reflect actual time.

5   See the review and commentary of Salima Ikram, 'Some Thoughts on the Mummification of King Tutankhamun', *Études et travaux* 26 (2013), pp. 291–301. For the possibility that unusual features of the mummy could be explained in terms of Osirian funerary beliefs (which Ikram describes at the outset of her discussion, ibid. p. 298, as speculation), see further below, p. 117.

6   The absence of the heart, which Ikram calls 'far more serious' than other anomalies, is perhaps not so problematic after all. Ikram herself (ibid. pp. 297–8; 300) takes due note of a scarab on the chest of the mummy (Obj. No. 256q) which though not inscribed with the appropriate spell of the Book of the Dead 'could have taken the place of the heart scarab' while the spell is found on another scarab (Obj. No. 269a (4)) among the king's funerary equipment.

7   Admitted by Ikram, ibid. pp. 293–4. Note that she has misunderstood Smith's comments about the mummy identified as Amenhotep III; the packing under the skin of the body was not inserted by Dynasty XXI restorers, but when the corpse was initially mummified in Dynasty XVIII. I am indebted to Renate Germer for discussing Ikram's article with me.

8   Cf. Strouhal, *Anthropologie* 48: 2, p. 98, who lists 'climatic conditions of the tomb' and time as other factors.

9   To account for the 'abnormal' position of the evisceration incision, Ikram, *Etudes et travaux* 26, p. 294 n. 21, mentions the possibility that a 'non-expert' did the embalming 'away from the Nile Valley' but thinks it 'rather unlikely'.

10   Darnell and Manassa, *Tutankhamun's Armies*, p. 211. Their study discusses 'Tutankhamun's wars' in Nubia and the Near East, but, as in earlier studies, they attribute the victories in the field to Horemhab as generalissimo.

11   The attempt at reconstructing the king's physical appearance, club foot and all, presented in a 'documentary' aired in Britain on BBC 1, 26 October 2014, was based on various medical diagnoses of what could have been wrong with him – none of which is undisputed. Cf. the illustrated notice of Dennis C. Forbes, 'New "Virtual Autopsy" Creates a Grotesque Tutankhamen', *Kmt* 25:4 (Winter 2014–15), pp. 24–5.

12   Delivered by his successor Ay or anyone else – see Jo Marchant, *The Shadow King: The Bizarre Afterlife of King Tut's Mummy* (Boston: Da Capo Press 2013), pp. 144–9.

13   Rühli and Ikram, 'Purported medical diagnoses of Pharaoh Tutankhamun, c. 1325 BC', *HOMO – Journal of Comparative Human Biology* 65 (2014), pp. 51–63. Salima kindly drew

my attention to this article and generously provided me with a preprint of it, for which I am indebted to her.

14 Ibid. p. 54.

15 Hawass et al., *JAMA* 303, p. 638.

16 See the comments of Rühli in the immediate aftermath of the press release: 'Akte Tut ungelöst', *SonntagsBlick Magazin* (Zürich) 11 (21 March 2010), pp. 26–8, as well as the letters to the editor of *JAMA* by James G. Gamble (Department of Orthopaedic Surgery, Stanford University Medical Center) and Christian Timmann (Department of Molecular Medicine, Bernhard Nocht Institute for Tropical Medicine, Hamburg) in *JAMA* 303, pp. 2472 and 2473, respectively.

17 I am reminded of being told that a chest X-ray in 1996 showed I had survived a 'bout' of tuberculosis, presumably as a child, without anyone in my family (nor I myself) having ever been aware of it.

18 Reeves, *Complete Tutankhamun*, pp. 178–9.

19 Ali Hassan, *Stöcke und Stäbe im pharaonischen Ägypten* (Munich: Deutscher Kunstverlag 1976). Inspired by the claims of the *JAMA* article, Dieter Kurth studied the inscribed staves from the tomb; he concludes that none of them supports the contention that the king needed a cane or crutches to get around: Kurth, in Beinlich, ed., *'Die Männer hinter dem König'*, pp. 67–86.

20 Renate Germer, *Die Pflanzenmaterialien aus dem Grab von Tutanchamun* (Hildesheim: Gerstenberg 1989).

21 Hawass et al., *JAMA* 303, p. 645.

22 Cf. Eaton-Krauss, *GM* 230, pp. 32–3; 35.

23 Rühli and Ikram, *HOMO* 65, p. 61.

24 Dodson has admitted to giving up his identification of traces of Smenkhkare's name in the texts of one coffinette – so Marc Gabolde, 'Under a Deep Blue Starry Sky', in Brand and Cooper, *Causing his Name to Live*, p.119 n. 86; see now James P. Allen, 'The Original Owner of Tutankhamun's Canopic Coffins', in Zahi Hawass and Jennifer Houser Wegner, eds, *Millions of Jubilees: Studies in Honor of David P. Silverman* (Cairo: CSA 2010), pp. 27–41.

25 Cf. Robins, *GM* 72, pp. 21–5.

26 Aidan Dodson, *The Canopic Equipment of the Kings of Egypt* (London and New York: Kegan Paul International 1994), p. 64, attributes the error to the poor lighting in the tomb.

27 As noted by Carter on his object cards for these pieces.

28 Dodson, *Canopic Equipment*, p. 62.

29 Edna R. Russmann, 'Vulture and Cobra at the King's Brow', in Elizabeth Goring et al., eds, *Egyptian Studies in Memory of Cyril Aldred* (London and New York: Kegan Paul International and National Museums of Scotland 1997), pp. 266–84.

30 The singular replacement of Nut in the texts on the lid of the sarcophagus with the solar deity Behdety was mentioned in Chapter 6, p. 88–9.

31 These are clearly recognizable on the enlarged photograph of the pectoral in T. G. H. James, *Tutankhamun: The Eternal Splendour of the Boy Pharaoh* (London and New York: Tauris Parke 2000), pp. 226–7.

32 For other pectorals that John R. Harris suspects were appropriated from a previous owner, see his 'Akhenaten and Neferneferuaten in the Tomb of Tutankhamun', in Reeves, ed., *After Tutankhamun*, pp. 61–2; 70–1 nn. 97–105

33 Abitz, *Statuetten in Schreinen als Grabbeigaben in den ägyptischen Königsgräbern der 18. und 19. Dynastie* (Wiesbaden: Harrassowitz 1979); see my review, *JARCE* 20 (1983), pp. 127–32.

34 Cf. Eaton-Krauss, *CdE* 56, pp. 262, 264.

35 Gay Robins, 'Two Statues from the Tomb of Tutankhamun', *GM* 71 (1984), pp. 47–50.

36 I consider it unlikely that they were 'previously wrapped' for Akhenaten's eventual use early on during his reign as implied by Harris, 'Akhenaten and Neferneferuaten in the Tomb of Tutankhamun', in Reeves, ed., *After Tutankhamun*, p. 58.

37 Horst Beinlich, 'Zwischen Tod und Grab: Tutanchamun und das Begräbnisritual', *SAK* 34 (2006), p. 25, disputes Abitz's idea that the position of the shrines was meaningful.

38 Kenneth A. Kitchen, *Ramesside Inscriptions, Translated and Annotated. Translations* v. 4. *Merenptah and the Late Nineteenth Dynasty* (Oxford: Blackwell 2003), pp. 116–17. I am indebted to Klaus Ohlhafer, Münster, who called my attention to this ostracon (oCG 25504) in the Egyptian Museum, Cairo.

39 A representative selection of the shabtis from KV 62 is illustrated in color in James, *Eternal Splendour*, pp. 110–27.

40 Martin, *The Royal Tomb at El-Amarna* v. I. *The Objects* (London: EES 1974), p. 41. Martin is one of three people currently working on the shabtis from KV 62.

41 It is not out of place here to recall that the different color of the gold in the gilding of one coffin of Queen Tiye's father Yuya (CG 51004) shows that its design had been altered. Robert B. Partridge, 'Tutankhamun's Gold Coffin: an ancient change in design?' *GM* 150 (1996), p. 98, remarked other such changes in a coffin's appearance – whether to change ownership which he implies was the reason, or to some other purpose.

42 Harris, 'Akhenaten and Neferneferuaten in the Tomb of Tutankhamun', in Reeves, ed., *After Tutankhamun*, pp. 61; 70 nn. 91–6. Harris also casts suspicion on the fourth, innermost shrine, ibid. p. 70 n. 96. Claude Vandersleyen, 'Royal Figures from Tutankhamun's Tomb: Their historical usefulness', in Reeves, ibid., p. 81 n. 43, also thinks it 'probable' that the third shrine was usurped, 'so neglected [*sic*] are the lay-out and engraving of the cartouches'.

43 I am indebted to Beatrix Gessler-Löhr for reminding me of the possibility that only some panels of the second shrine were made for a predecessor of Tutankhamun; cf. her comments on the use of the radiant sun hieroglyph in the texts of the second and third shrines, 'Pre-Amarna or post-Amarna? The Tomb of the God's Father Hatiay at Saqqara', in Linda Evans, ed., *Ancient Memphis: 'Enduring is the Perfection'* (Leuven: Peeters 2012), pp. 161–5.

44 So John Coleman Darnell, *The Enigmatic Netherworld Books of the Solar-Osirian Unity: Cryptographic Compositions in the Tombs of Tutankhamun, Ramesses VI and Ramesses IX* (Fribourg and Göttingen: Academic Press and Vandenbroeck & Ruprecht 2004), p. 469. Darnell, ibid. p. 161, is led to doubt the 'malevolent suppression of the Osirian element in Amarna religion' because he credits the false notion that the shrine had to have been made 'earlier' in Akhenaten's reign. For Osiris as a nocturnal manifestation of Re, see also the

hymn in the Memphite tomb of Horemhab translated by Jacobus van Dijk, 'An Early Hymn to Osiris as Nocturnal Manifestation of Re', in Martin, *Memphite Tomb* v. I, pp. 61–9.

45 Which was not the purpose of either of Alexandre Piankoff's books about the shrines: *Les chapelles de Tout-Ankh-Amon* (Cairo: IFAO 1952) and *Shrines of Tut-Ankh-Amon*.

46 A few of Vannini's photographs of the second shrine are reproduced at a very reduced scale in Hawass, *Discovering Tutankhamun*, pp. 92–3.

47 Vandersleyen, 'Royal Figures', in Reeves, ed. *After Tutankhamun*, pp. 74; 80 n. 18.

48 Harris, 'Akhenaten and Neferneferuaten in the Tomb of Tutankhamun', in Reeves, ed., *After Tutankhamun,* pp. 59–60, implies that the usurpation may have been so skillful as to defy discovery.

49 Initially in a lecture on 4 November 2009, at the symposium 'The Valley of the Kings after Howard Carter' in Luxor. Reeves's thesis is in press in the Dorothea Arnold *Festschrift*. In the interim a revised version of the lecture on the mask which he presented at the MMA on 5 April 2011 can be viewed on line at www.youtube.com/watch?v=bxN1hm1TmJO.

50 Horst Beinlich, 'Das Totenbuch bei Tutanchamun', *GM* 102 (1988), pp. 9–10.

51 Desroches-Noblecourt, *Life and Death*, p. 224.

52 Harris, 'Akhenaten and Neferneferuaten in the Tomb of Tutankhamun', in Reeves, ed., *After Tutankhamun*, p. 66 n. 47.

53 Ibid. p. 58.

54 Cf. Allen's comments, 'Two Altered Inscriptions of the Late Amarna Period', *JARCE* 25 (1988), p. 124 for the possibility of such a development in theology at that time.

55 For detailed discussion of the actual process, see my 'The Burial of Tutankhamen, Part Two', *Kmt* 21: 1 (Spring 2010), pp. 24–36. Cf. also the evidence observed by John Romer for the stocking of chambers opening off the burial chamber in KV 34 certainly before it was painted if not well in advance of Thutmose III's burial there: 'The Tomb of Tuthmosis III', *MDAIK* 31 (1975), pp. 329–31.

56 Loeben, 'La function funéraire des meubles égyptien', *EAO* 3 (1996), pp. 26–7.

57 This box and the other inscribed boxes from KV 62 are the subject of Loeben's unpublished master's thesis 'Die beschrifteten Truhen und Kästen des Tutanchamun' (Freie Universität Berlin, 1986); cf. his article, *EAO* 3 (1996), pp. 20–7.

58 Hawass's team could not obtain enough data from them to determine with certainly that they were Tutankhamun's daughters – see Hawass et al., *JAMA* 303, p. 641, caption to fig. 2: 'Fetus 1 and fetus 2 *can* [my italics] be daughters of Tutankhamun'.

59 Cf. William C. Hayes, *Royal Sarcophagi of the XVIII Dynasty* (Princeton: Princeton University Press 1935), pp. 16–17.

60 Beinlich, 'Zwischen Tod und Grab', *SAK* 34, pp. 17–31.

61 Robins, 'The Decorative Program in the Tomb of Tutankhamen (KV 62)', in Zahi Hawass and Janet Richards, eds, *The Archaeology and Art of Ancient Egypt: Essays in Honor of David O'Connor* v. 2 (Cairo: CSA 2007), pp. 321–42.

62 Easily recognizable with their characteristic high-riding kilts and the stiff cord around the neck for suspension of their seal of office, tucked down inside the upper edge of the kilt.

63 My statement that all the men pulling the sled have the Amarna foot (*Kmt* 21: 1, p. 34) is incorrect.

64 So most recently by Kawai, *JEH* 3, 271–3, countering the reservations of van Dijk, *The New Kingdom Necropolis of Memphis*, p. 57.

65 As has been noted countless times in the past, this vignette, like the scene of towing the bier, is unique in a royal tomb.

66 The elements bearing inscriptions for the lion-headed bier (Obj. No. 35) and the cow-headed one (Obj. No. 73) were confused; for the (mis)handling of them, see the comments of Carter and Mace, *Tut-ankh-Amen* v. I, p. 131. Of course this might be just another example of carelessness rather than indicative of any previous assembly.

67 For those found in the KV, see now the reappraisal of Konstantin Lakomy, ' "Embalming caches" im Tal der Könige', *GM* 228 (2011), pp. 21–32.

68 As proposed by Reeves, *Valley of the Kings*, pp. 67; 69; 84 nn. 64–5.

69 By Dorothea Arnold, in Herbert E. Winlock, *Tutankhamun's Funeral* (New York, New Haven, and London: MMA and Yale University Press 2010), pp. 12–15; 68 (note to p. 24); 72–3 (note to p. 44).

70 The top of the vertically projecting foot of the outer coffin was cut down when it was found to prevent the lid of the sarcophagus from resting tightly on the basin: Carter, *Tut.ankh.Amen* v. II, p. 90.

71 Reeves, *Complete Tutankhamun*, p. 70, citing Carter's unpublished notes now available online at www.griffith.ox.ac.uk/discoveringTut → detailed notes and drawings → Howard Carter's notes made in preparation of the complete publication of the tomb → tomb and tomb plan (TAAi.3.31).

72 Gay Robins, *GM* 72, 27–9; cf. Eaton-Krauss, *Kmt* 21:1, pp. 34–5.

73 On the cards for the 'magic bricks', Obj. Nos 257–60, Carter noted that the shade of yellow differed from that used for the background of the wall paintings as but one proof that the niches were closed only after the shrines were erected and the paintings executed.

74 Jané, 'The Meaning of Wine in Egyptian tombs: the three amphorae from Tutankhamun's burial chamber', *Antiquity* 85 (2011), p. 857.

75 I speculated tongue-in-cheek that the painters had drunk the wine: *Kmt* 21:1, pp. 34–5.

76 Jané, 'About the Orientation of the Magical Bricks in Tutankhamun's Burial Chamber', *JARCE* 28 (2012), pp. 111–18.

77 Wilkinson, 'Jewellery for a procession in the Bed-Chamber in the tomb of Tutankhamun', *BIFAO* 84 (1984), pp. 335–45; eadem, 'Evidence for Osirian Rituals in the Tomb of Tutankhamun', in Sarah Israelit-Groll, ed., *Pharaonic Egypt, the Bible and Christianity* (Jerusalem: Magus Press and Hebrew University of Jerusalem 1984), pp. 328–40.

78 Ikram, *Études et travaux* 26, p. 301.

79 Carter, *Tomb of Tut.ankh.Amen* v. III, p. 106.

80 The debris from funerary equipment found among the chips in the corridor could well have resulted from the haste, accompanied by the general carelessness observable elsewhere in the tomb.

81 For doubts about the idea that the items from KV 54, the 'embalming cache', were stored in the corridor, left open following an initial robbery, see p. 115 n. 69 above. The flared-leg stool Obj. Nos 142b+149 provides the only unambiguous evidence that KV 62 was robbed

in antiquity: Eaton-Krauss, *Thrones, Chairs, Stools and Footstools*, p. 122. If ancient Egyptian tomb robbers did enter KV 62, they penetrated neither the Burial Chamber nor the Treasury beyond; cf. Rolf Krauss, 'Zum archäologischen Befund im thebanischen Königsgrab Nr. 62' *Mitteilungen der Deutschen Orient-Gesellschaft* 118 (1986), pp. 165–81.

Epilogue

1 See, for example, Andrea Maria Gnirs, *Militär und Gesellschaft: Ein Beitrag zur Sozialgeschichte des Neuen Reiches* (Heidelberg: Heidelberger Orientverlag 1996), pp. 91–113, and most recently, Kawai, *JEH* 3, pp. 261–92. For the possibility that the affair of the Egyptian queen who requested a son of the Hittite king Shuppiluliuma was precipitated by Tutankhamun's death, see Chapter 2, p. 17.

2 He was not, however, depicted accompanying Tutankhamun in the lunette of the restoration stela as Gnirs, *Militär und Gesellschaft*, p. 98, supposes; see p. 137 n. 7 above. Dodson, *Amarna Sunrise*, p. 147, compares Ay's role to that of the 'chancellor' Bay for whom see idem, 'Fade to Grey: The Chancellor Bay, *éminence grise* of the Late Nineteenth Dynasty', in M. Collier and S. Snape, eds, *Ramesside Studies in Honour of K. A. Kitchen* (Bolton: Rutherford Press 2011), pp. 145–58.

3 Norman de Garis Davies, *The Rock Tombs of el-Amarna*. Part VI. *The Tombs of Parennefer, Tutu, and Ay* (London: EES 1908), pp. 15–24.

4 Davis et al., *Tombs of Harmhabi and Touatânkhamanou*, p. 133 (no. 15).

5 Černy, in his review of Wolfgang Helck, *Zur Verwaltung des Mittleren und Neuen Reiches*, *BiOr* 19 (1962), p. 142; see also Habachi, 'Unknown or Little Known Monuments', in Ruffle et al., eds, *Glimpses of Ancient Egypt*, pp. 35–6.

6 Rolf Krauss and Detlef Ulrich, 'Ein gläserner Doppelring aus Altägypten', *Jahrbuch Preußischer Kulturbesitz* XIX (1982), pp. 199–212.

7 Alexandre Piankoff, 'Le peintures dans la tombe du roi Aï', *MDAIK* 16 (1958) pl. XXI; cf. now the color photograph of these scenes in Otto Schaden, 'Paintings in the Tomb of King Ay (WV 23) and the Western Valley of the Kings Project', *Amarna Letters* 4 (Fall 2000), pp. 102–3.

8 Epigraphic Survey, *Reliefs and Inscriptions at Luxor Temple* v. 2, pp. xviii; 3; pls. 134–6.

9 Cf. Kawai, *JEH* 3, pp. 263–4, who rightly rejects this idea.

10 For example, restoring the name of Amenhotep III in the inscriptions on the colossal baboon statues at Ashmunein: Alan J. Spencer, *Excavations at el-Ashmunein* v. II. *The Temple Area* (London: British Museum Publications 1985), pp. 33; 63. Compare also the claims in the text of the rock-cut stela at Akhmim cited in Chapter 3, p. 37.

11 Cf. Martin, *Memphite Tomb* v. I, pp. 161–5; van Dijk, *New Kingdom Necropolis of Memphis*, pp. 12–24.

12 Van Dijk, ibid.

13 For Nakhtmin, see van Dijk, ibid., pp. 59–62.

14 Cf. Chapter 5, pp. 81, 149 n. 52.

15 Van Dijk, *New Kingdom Necropolis of Memphis*, pp. 30; 32, suggests these are intrusive; cf. now Hans D. Schneider, *The Memphite Tomb of Horemheb, Commander-in-Chief of Tutankhamun* v. II. *A catalogue of the finds* (London: EES 1996), pp. 18–19 (nos 61 and 65). Geoffrey T. Martin kindly informs me that in the second edition of *The Memphite Tomb of Horemheb* v. I (to be published shortly) he no longer tentatively reads Ay's *prenomen* in the seal impressions from Corridor E, Shaft IV of the tomb; rather the name is 'with little doubt' the *prenomen* of Tutankhamun.

16 Reeves, *Valley of the Kings,* pp. 71–2. My own opinion that this was the case is shared by Marc Gabolde (personal communication, September 2014). For speculation about the 'original' owner of KV 23, see Chapter 6, p. 93.

17 See Eaton-Krauss, *MDAIK* 44, p 11, with acknowledgment of Otto Schaden.

18 For Horemhab's continuing interest in his pre-royal tomb after his succession, see Maarten J. Raven et al., *The Memphite Tomb of Horemheb, Commander-in-Chief of Tutankhamun* v. V. *The Forecourt and Area South of the Tomb* (Turnhout: Brepols 2011), p. 27. The construction of the first pylon and forecourt in Phase 4 may even post-date his death. No clue has yet been found to aid in dating the addition of a uraeus to (some of) the figures of Horemhab or to determine if that action was simultaneous with the usurpation of Tutankhamun's cartouches in his favor.

Selected Bibliography

Bickel, Suzanne. *Untersuchungen im Totentempel des Merenptah in Theben.* v. 3. *Tore und andere wiederverwendete Bauteile.* Stuttgart: Steiner 1997.

Brand, Peter J. *The Monuments of Seti I: Epigraphic, Historical and Art Historical Analysis.* Leiden, Boston, and Cologne: Brill 2000.

Brand, Peter J. and Louise Cooper, eds. *Causing his Name to Live: Studies in Egyptian Epigraphy and History in Memory of William J. Murnane.* Leiden: Brill 2009.

Carter, Howard. *The Tomb of Tut.ankh.Amen* v. II; v. III. London: Cassell 1927; 1933.

Carter, Howard and A. C. Mace. *The Tomb of Tut.ankh.Amen* v. I. London: Cassell 1923.

Darnell, John Coleman and Coleen Manassa. *Tutankhamun's Armies: Battle and Conquest during Ancient Egypt's Late Eighteenth Dynasty.* Hoboken, NJ: John Wiley & Sons 2007.

Davis, Theodore M. *The Tombs of Harmhabi and Touatânkhamanou.* London: Constable 1912.

Desroches-Noblecourt, Christiane. *Tutankhamen: Life and Death of a Pharaoh.* New York: New York Graphic Society 1963.

Desroches-Noblecourt, Christiane. *Toutankhamon et son temps.* Exhibition catalogue. Paris: Réunion des Musées Nationaux 1967.

Dijk, Jacobus van. 'The New Kingdom Necropolis of Memphis: Historical and Iconographical Studies'. Rijksuniversiteit dissertation, Groningen 1993.

Dijk, Jacobus van, ed. *Essays on Ancient Egypt in Honour of Herman te Velde.* Groningen: STYX 1997.

Dijk, Jacobus van. 'A Cat, a Nurse, and a Standard-Bearer: Notes on Three Late Eighteenth Dynasty Statues', in Sue H. D'Auria, ed., *Offerings to the Discerning Eye: An Egyptological Medley in Honor of Jack A. Josephson.* Leiden and Boston: Brill 2010, pp. 321–32.

Dodson, Aidan. *Amarna Sunset: Nefertiti, Tutankhamun, Ay, Horemheb, and the Egyptian Counter-Reformation.* Cairo and New York: AUC Press 2009.

Dodson, Aidan. *Amarna Sunrise: Egypt from Golden Age to Age of Heresy.* Cairo and New York: AUC Press 2014.

Eaton-Krauss, Marianne. 'Miscellanea Amarnesia', *CdE* 56 (1981), pp. 245–64.

Eaton-Krauss, Marianne. 'Tutankhamun at Karnak', *MDAIK* 44 (1988), pp. 1–11.

Eaton-Krauss, Marianne. *The Thrones, Chairs, Stools, and Footstools from the Tomb of Tutankhamun.* Oxford: GI 2008.

Eaton-Krauss, Marianne. 'Mummies (and Daddies)', *GM* 230 (2011), pp. 29–35.

Eaton-Krauss, Marianne. 'Mut and Tutankhaten', *GM* 235 (2012), pp. 15–18.

Eaton-Krauss, Marianne and Erhart Graefe. *The Small Golden Shrine from the Tomb of Tutankhamun.* Oxford: GI 1985.

Edwards, I. E. S. *Treasures of Tutankhamun.* Exhibition catalogue. London: Trustees of the British Museum 1972.

Eldamaty, Mamdouh and Mai Trad, eds. *Egyptian Museum Collections around the World: Studies for the Centennial of the Egyptian Museum, Cairo*. Cairo: SCA 2002.

Epigraphic Survey. *Reliefs and Inscriptions at Luxor Temple* v. I. *The Festival Procession of Opet in the Colonnade Hall*. Chicago: University of Chicago Press 1994.

Epigraphic Survey. *Reliefs and Inscriptions at Luxor Temple* v. II. *The Façade, Portals, Upper Register Scenes, Columns, Marginalia, and Statuary in the Colonnade Hall*. Chicago: University of Chicago Press 1998.

Gabolde, Marc. *D'Akhenaton à Toutânkhamon*. Lyon: Boccard 1998.

Habachi, Labib, 'Unknown or Little Known Monuments of Tutankhamun and his Viziers', in John Ruffle et al., eds. *Glimpses of Ancient Egypt: Studies in Honour of F. W. Fairman*. Warminster: Aris & Phillips 1979, pp. 34–41.

Hawass, Zahi. *Discovering Tutankhamun: From Howard Carter to DNA*. Cairo and New York: AUC Press 2013.

Hawass, Zahi et al. 'Ancestry and Pathology in King Tutankhamun's Family', *Journal of the American Medical Association* 303: 7 (12 Feb. 2010), pp. 638–47 + eAppendix and other supplementary material, available online to subscribers only.

Karkowski, Janusz. *The Pharaonic Inscriptions from Faras*. Warsaw: Editions scientifique de Pologne 1981.

Kawai, Nozomu. 'Ay versus Horemheb: The political situation in the late Eighteenth Dynasty revisited', *JEH* 3 (2010), pp. 261–92.

Kemp, Barry. *The City of Akhenaten and Nefertiti: Amarna and its People*. London: Thames & Hudson 2012.

Kozloff, Arielle. *Amenhotep III: Egypt's Radiant Pharaoh*. Cambridge: Cambridge University Press 2012.

Kozloff, Arielle and Betsy M. Bryan. *Egypt's Dazzling Sun: Amenhotep III and his World*. Exhibition catalogue. Cleveland: Cleveland Museum of Art 1992.

Kurth, Dieter. 'Die Inschriften auf den Stöcken und Stäben des Tutanchamun', in Horst Beinlich, ed., *6th Symposium on Egyptian Royal Ideology: 'Die Männer hinter dem König'*. Wiesbaden: Harrassowitz 2012, pp. 67–88.

Martin, Geoffrey Thorndike. *The Memphite Tomb of Horemheb, Commander-in-Chief of Tutankhamun* v. I. *The Reliefs, Inscriptions, and Commentary*. London: EES 1989.

Martin, Geoffrey Thorndike. *The Royal Tomb at El-Amarna* v. II. *The Reliefs, Inscriptions, and Architecture*. London: EES 1989.

Murnane, William J. *Text from the Amarna Period in Egypt*. Atlanta: Scholars Press 1995.

Piankoff, Alexandre. *The Shrines of Tut-Ankh-Amon*. New York: Pantheon 1955.

Reeves, C. N. *Valley of the Kings: The Decline of a Royal Necropolis*. London and New York: Kegan Paul International 1990.

Reeves, C. N., ed. *After Tutankhamun: Research and Excavation in the Royal Necropolis at Thebes*. London and New York: Kegan Paul International 1992.

Reeves, C. N. and Richard H. Wilkinson. *The Complete Valley of the Kings: Tombs and Treasures of Egypt's Greatest Pharaohs*. London: Thames & Hudson 1996.

Robins, Gay. 'Isis, Nephthys, Selket and Neith represented on the sarcophagus of Tutankhamun and in four free-standing statues found in KV 62', *GM* 72 (1984), pp. 21–5.

Robins, Gay. 'The proportions of figures in the decoration of the tombs of Tutankhamun (KV 62) and Ay (KV 23)', *GM* 72 (1984), pp. 27–32.

Roehrig, Catherine H., ed. *Hatshepsut: From Queen to Pharaoh*. Exhibition catalogue. New York, New Haven, and London: MMA and Yale University Press 2005.

Russmann, Edna R. *Eternal Egypt: Masterworks of Ancient Egyptian Art from the British Museum*. Exhibition catalogue. London: British Museum Press 2001.

Schaden, Otto J. 'The God's Father Ay'. University of Minnesota dissertation. Ann Arbor, Michigan: University Microfilms 1977.

Schaden, Otto J. 'Tutankhamun – Ay Shrine at Karnak and the Western Valley of the Kings Project: Report on the 1985–1986 Season', *NARCE* 138 (1987), pp. 10–15.

Seidel, Matthias. *Die königlichen Statuengruppen* v. I. *Die Denkmäler vom Alten Reich bis zum Ende der 18. Dynastie*. Hildesheim: Gerstenberg 1996.

Smith, G. Elliot. *The Royal Mummies*. Cairo: IFAO 1912.

Strouhal, Eugen. 'Biological Age of Skeletonized Mummy from Tomb KV 55 at Thebes', *Anthropologie. International Journal of the Science of Man* (Prague) XLVIII/2 (2010), pp. 97–112.

Teeter, Emily. *The Presentation of Maat: Ritual and Legitimacy in Ancient Egypt*. Chicago: University of Chicago Press 1997.

Tutankhamun's Painted Box, reproduced in colour from the original in the Cairo Museum by Nina M. Davies with an explanatory text by Alan H. Gardiner. Oxford: GI 1962.

Van der Perre, Athena, 'The Year 16 graffito of Akhenaten in Dayr Abu Hinnis. A Contribution to the Study of the Later Years of Nefertiti', *JEH* 7 (2014), pp. 67–108.

Illustration Sources

Cover

Detail of CG 42097; Egyptian Museum, Cairo. Photograph: Forbes/KMT Communications.

Figures

1   The Hermopolis block; drawings by and courtesy of W. Raymond Johnson.
    a   Side A.
    b   Side A, reconstruction.
    c   Side B.

2   Painting fragment from the King's House at Tell el-Amarna. Drawing by and courtesy of Susanne Petschel after Lyla Pinch Brock, 'Tutankhamun in the "King's House" at Amarna? Cairo SR 111575/20647', *BACE* 9 (1998), p. 9, pl. 1.

3   Tutankhamun in his chariot; façade of the tutor's tomb at Akhmim. Adapted from Boyo Ockinga, *A Tomb from the Reign of Tutankhamun at Akhmim* (Warminster: Aris & Phillips 1997), pl. 36.

4   Lunette of a stela, provenance not known; Egyptian Museum, Cairo, JE 27076. Drawing by and courtesy of Nozomu Kawai.

5   Lunette of a stela, provenance not known; Egyptian Museum, Berlin, ÄgM 14197. Archive photograph; courtesy of Ägyptisches Museum, Staatliche Museen zu Berlin, Preußischer Kulturbesitz.

6   Back of the backrest of the gold throne from the tomb of Tutankhamun, Obj. No. 91; Egyptian Museum, Cairo, JE 62028. Photograph: Walter Segal; courtesy of the Griffith Institute. © Griffith Institute, University of Oxford.

7   Proper right side of the gold throne from the tomb of Tutankhamun, Obj. No. 91; Egyptian Museum, Cairo, JE 62028. Photograph: Walter Segal; courtesy of the Griffith Institute. © Griffith Institute, University of Oxford.

8   Inscription on a gilded scribe's palette from the tomb of Tutankhamun, Obj. No. 271e (2); Egyptian Museum, Cairo, JE 62094. Detail of a photograph by Harry Burton; courtesy of the Griffith Institute. © Griffith Institute, University of Oxford.

9   Cartouche shaped box from the tomb of Tutankhamun, Obj. No. 269; Egyptian Museum, Cairo, JE 61490. Photograph: Harry Burton; courtesy of the Griffith Institute. © Griffith Institute, University of Oxford.

10   The Restoration Stela from Karnak Temple; Egyptian Museum, Cairo, CG 34183.

11   Lunette of the Restoration Stela from Karnak Temple; Egyptian Museum, Cairo, CG 34183.

12   Amenhotep III (right) worshipping Amun (restored, at the left); relief from a granary;
     Karnak Temple, south blockyard.

13   Restored triad from the Karnak cachette depicting Amun seated between Thutmose I and
     Queen Ahmose; Egyptian Museum, Cairo, CG 42052. Photograph: Matthias Seidel.

14   a – b   Head of the quartzite colossus of Amun, Karnak Temple.
     c   Face of the quartzite colossus of Amunet, Karnak Temple.

15   Triad from the Karnak cachette depicting Amun, Mut, and Tutankhamun enthroned;
     Egyptian Museum, Cairo, CG 42097.

16   Head from a statue of Amun, excavated in the Monthu Temple; Luxor Museum of
     Egyptian Art, J. 67.

17   Colossal statue of Khonsu from the Khonsu Temple at Karnak; Egyptian Museum, Cairo,
     CG 38488. Adapted from Bodil Hornemann, *Types of Ancient Egyptian Statuary* v. 1
     (Copenhagen: Munksgaard 1951), no. 39.

18   a – b   Head of the Khonsu colossus from the Khonsu Temple at Karnak. After Georges
             Legrain, 'Trois monuments de la fin de la XVIIIᵉ dynastie', *Le Musée égyptien* v. II
             (Cairo: IFAO 1907), pls. I–II.

19   a   Statue of Tutankhamun praying as initially restored; Egyptian Museum, Cairo, CG
         42091. After Georges Legrain, *Statues et statuettes de rois et de particuliers* v. I
         (Cairo: IFAO 1906), pl. LVII.
     b   Statue of Amenemhet III praying; Egyptian Museum, Cairo, CG 42014. Adapted
         from Bodil Hornemann, *Types of Ancient Egyptian Statuary* v. 1 (Copenhagen:
         Munksgaard 1951), no. 168.

20   Tutankhamun's cartouches – Nebkheperure Tutankhamun, Ruler of Upper Egyptian
     Heliopolis – altered to read Djserkheperure, whom Re chose, Horemhab, beloved of
     Amun. Graphics: Christian J. Bayer.

21   Standard-bearing statue of Tutankhamun, provenance not known; British Museum,
     London, EA 37639. Adapted from H. R. Hall, 'Objects of Tutankhamun in the British
     Museum', *JEA* 14 (1928), pl. X (left).

22   Tutankhamun as an offering bearer, provenance not known; British Museum, London, EA
     75. Photograph courtesy of the Egyptian Dept., British Museum. © The Trustees of the
     British Museum.

23   a   Headless sphinx from the Processional Avenue between Pylon X, Karnak Temple,
         and the Mut Precinct.
     b – c   Sphinx with the head of Nefertiti, converted to a ram-headed sphinx with a statue
             of Tutankhamun added between the paws. Drawing: F. Laroche-Traunecker.

Adapted from Claude Traunecker, 'Aménophis IV et Néfertiti. Le couple royal d'après les talatates du XIe pylone de Karnak,' *BSFE* 107 (1986), p. 21 fig. 2.

24 'Stole' made of faience beads from the tomb of Tutankhamun, Obj. No. 2690; Egyptian Museum, Cairo, JE 61961. Photograph: Harry Burton; courtesy of the Griffith Institute. © Griffith Institute, University of Oxford.

25 Lintel from a structure of Tutankhamun: provenance not known; Egyptian Museum, Berlin, ÄgM 21840. Photograph: courtesy of Ägyptisches Museum, Staatliche Museen zu Berlin, Preußischer Kulturbesitz.

26 Detail; lintel from a structure of Tutankhamun, reused in the tomb of Prince Sheshonk at Mitrahineh; Egyptian Museum, Cairo, JE 88131. Adapted from Labib Habachi, 'Unknown or Little Known Monuments of Tutankhamun and his Viziers', in John Ruffle et al., eds, *Glimpses of Ancient Egypt: Studies in Honour of F. W. Fairman* (Warminster: Aris & Phillips 1979), p. 34 fig. 2.

27 South side and foot end of the sarcophagus in the tomb of Tutankhamun. Drawing by and courtesy of Helena Jaeschke.

28 Floor plan of KV 62, with the additions (Annexe, Burial Chamber, and Treasury) to the original, single chamber (Antechamber) indicated by broken lines. Adapted from the website of the Theban Mapping Project, www.thebanmappingproject.com.

29 Block from a hunting scene in the Mansion of Tutankhamun, Karnak. Present location not known. Drawing by Prisse d'Avennes. After Wilhelm Spiegelberg, 'Zu den Jagdbilder des Tutenchamun', *OLZ* 28 (1925), cols. 569–70.

30 Architrave from the Mansion of Tutankhamun showing the erasure of Ay's *prenomen* above Tutankhamun's; Karnak Temple, south blockyard.

31 a Segment of a pier from the Mansion of Tutankhamun showing the hacking of Tutankhamun's cartouches, save for the names of the gods Amun and Re; Karnak Temple, south blockyard.

  b Segment of a pier from the Mansion of Tutankhamun showing the hacking of a king's figure (Ay?); Karnak Temple, south blockyard.

32 Captive in a cage suspended above the deck of a ship; relief from the Mansion of Tutankhamun; Karnak Temple, south blockyard.

33 Drawing demonstrating that the statue of Selket from the canopic shrine in Tutankhamun's tomb (Obj. No. 266) was designed according to the Amarna canon. Drawing by and courtesy of Gay Robins.

34 Floor plan of KV 62's Burial Chamber showing the positions of the wine amphoras, Obj. Nos 180, 195, and 206, in relation to the niches for magic bricks, Obj. Nos 257–60. Drawing by and courtesy of Susanne Petschel, after Howard Carter, as illustrated in Nicholas Reeves and John H. Taylor, *Howard Carter Before Tutankhamun* (London: British Museum Press 1992), p. 153.

Plates

I   Lid of the coffin from KV 55; Egyptian Museum, Cairo, JE 39627. © Kenneth Garrett,
        Getty Images.

II   Tutankhamun on the lap of his wet-nurse Maia as depicted in her tomb at Saqqara.
        © De Agostini / S. Vannini, Getty Images.

III   a   Statue of a wet-nurse holding a royal child on her lap, from the Sacred Animal
            Complex at Saqqara; Egyptian Museum, Cairo, JE 91301.
        b   Detail; the boy's face and the scarab pendant on his chest.
        c   Detail; the boy's feet resting on a footstool decorated with figures of prostrate captives.

IV   a   Inlaid ebony throne from the tomb of Tutankhamun, Obj. No. 351; Egyptian
            Museum, Cairo, JE 62030. Photograph: Jürgen Liepe.
        b   Front of the backrest of the inlaid ebony throne. © De Agostini / W. Buss, Getty
            Images.

V   Scene on the front of the backrest of the gold throne from Tutankhamun's tomb,
        Obj. No. 91; Egyptian Museum, Cairo, JE 62028. © De Agostini / G. Dagli Orti,
        Getty Images.

VI   Detail, left side of the lunette of the Restoration Stela from Karnak Temple; Egyptian
        Museum, Cairo, CG 34183.

VII   Detail, relief on the east face of the north wing of Pylon III at Karnak Temple showing
        (above) the faint outline of the erased figure of Tutankhamun behind Amenhotep III
        and (below) five of the restored panels with Amenhotep III worshipping Amun.

VIII   Restored figure of Amun (in the center) holding Thutmose III by the hand with
        Tutankhamun's restoration inscription (usurped by Horemhab) behind the god.

IX   Re-erected quartzite colossi of Amun and Amunet in the alcove behind the Sixth
        Pylon, Karnak Temple.

X   Head of Tutankhamun from a limestone group depicting him standing in front of a
        life-sized seated male deity from Karnak Temple; Metropolitan Museum of Art, Acc.
        No. 50.6, Rogers Fund 1950. © The Print Collector / Alamy.

XI   a   Slightly under life-sized limestone statue of Amun with Tutankhamun's
            physiognomy from the Karnak cachette; Luxor Museum of Ancient Egyptian
            Art, J. 198.
        b   Back pillar of the statue.
        c   Head of the statue.

XII   The bust in Sydney (Nicholson Museum R40) joined to a cast of the head in Cairo,
        Egyptian Museum, CG 38888, with Mohamed Saleh. Photograph taken on the
        occasion of presenting the join in Sydney. Photograph courtesy of the Nicholson
        Museum, Sydney. © R. Workman.

XIII   (inset) Gold ring with Tutankhamun's *prenomen*; excavated at Tell el-Ajjul, Gaza; Jerusalem, Rockefeller Archaeological Museum, Inv. No. 33.708. Photograph: Clara Amit. © Israel Antiquities Authority.

XIV   Tutankhamun (usurped by Horemhab) presenting offerings to the Theban triad; relief on the outer face, east wall of Court I between the main temple and Pylon VII, Karnak Temple. Photograph by and courtesy of Christian E. Loeben.

XV   Tenth Pylon, Karnak Temple with the avenue of sphinxes flanking the processional avenue southwards to the Mut Precinct. Photograph by and courtesy of Christian J. Bayer.

XVI   Colonnade Hall of Luxor Temple from the south.

XVII   Tutankhamun censing and pouring a libation. Detail of the scene at the entrance to the Colonnade Hall, Luxor Temple. Photograph by and courtesy of Christian Bayer.

XVIII   The sarcophagus (Obj. No. 240) in the Burial Chamber of Tutankhamun's tomb. © J.D. Dallet, Getty Images.

XIX   Nephthys at the southwest corner of the sarcophagus (Obj. No. 240) in the Burial Chamber of Tutankhamun's tomb. © Robert Harding Picture Library Ltd / Alamy.

XX   Relief block from a scene of 'driving the calves'. Karnak Temple, south blockyard.

XXI   Detail of a hunting scene showing a wild steer beneath the hooves of the horses pulling the king's chariot.

XXII   Five of the gilded statuettes-in-shrines; figure of Sakhmet (Obj. No. 300a) in the foreground. Egyptian Museum, Cairo, JE 62704. © De Agostini / G. Dagli Orti, Getty Images.

XXIII   Two of Tutankhamun's larger gilded shabtis, Obj. Nos 330g (left) and 110 (right), with two smaller shabtis, now in the Luxor Museum of Ancient Egyptian Art. © The Art Archive / Alamy.

XXIV   Scene of towing the coffin on the east wall of KV 62's Burial Chamber. Photograph © Danita Delimont / Alamy.

In addition to those colleagues cited above, I would like to thank the following for helping me to obtain illustrations for this book: Richard B. Parkinson, Oriental Institute, University of Oxford; Ilona Regulski, Egyptian Department, British Museum; Alegre Savariego, Rockefeller Archaeological Museum, Jerusalem; Regine Schulz, Römer- und Pelizaeus-Museum, Hildesheim; Friederike Seyfried, Ägyptisches Museum, Staatliche Museen zu Berlin, Preußischer Kulturbesitz; Catharine Warsi, Griffith Institute, University of Oxford. Figures and plates not credited above are the property of the author.

Index

(TAA refers throughout to Tutankhamun/aten; italicized numbers denote pages with illustrations)